THE CONCISE COMMERCIAL DICTIONARY

Formerly THE COMMERCIAL DICTIONARY by A. G. P. PULLAN
and D. W. ALCOCK (adapted from THE AUSTRALIAN COMMERCIAL
DICTIONARY by R. KEITH YORSTON, B. COM., F.C.A. (Aust.))

AUSTRALIA
The Law Book Company Ltd.
Sydney : Melbourne : Brisbane

CANADA AND U.S.A.
The Carswell Company Ltd.
Toronto

INDIA
N. M. Tripathi Private Ltd.
Bombay

ISRAEL
Steimatzky's Agency Ltd.
Jerusalem : Tel Aviv : Haifa

NEW ZEALAND
Sweet & Maxwell (N.Z.) Ltd.
Wellington

PAKISTAN
Pakistan Law House
Karachi

THE CONCISE
COMMERCIAL
DICTIONARY

BY

P. G. OSBORN, LL.B. (Lond.),

of Gray's Inn, Barrister-at-Law

AND

S. T. GRANDAGE, A.C.A.

LONDON

SWEET & MAXWELL

1966

Published in 1966 by
Sweet & Maxwell Limited of
11 New Fetter Lane, London,
and printed in Great Britain
by The Eastern Press Limited
of London and Reading

OSBORN AND GRANDAGE

Part I

DICTIONARY OF
COMMERCIAL AND LEGAL TERMS

A

A1 At Lloyd's. A ship registered as of the highest class: 100 A1 is the highest possible class. See also LLOYD'S REGISTRY OF SHIPPING.

A and B lists. See CONTRIBUTORY.

a fortiori. [Much more; with stronger reason.]

a priori. [From the antecedent to the consequent; from the cause to the effect.]

ab initio. [From the beginning.]

abandonment of action. Where a party to legal proceedings ceases to contest it; discontinuance.

abandonment of cargo (or ship). In marine insurance, when there is a constructive total loss, the insured may relinquish all claim to the subject-matter insured to the insurer or underwriter by giving notice of abandonment to him within a reasonable time. Thereupon the insured is entitled to the insurance moneys, and the insurer or underwriter to the subject-matter insured. See also TOTAL LOSS.

abatement. (1) A proportionate decrease, deduction or allowance; *e.g.*, discount for prompt payment, or as follows:

(2) Abatement of legal proceedings; formerly the termination of proceedings for want of proper parties (*e.g.*, on death), but now, if the cause of action survives, the necessary change of parties will be effected.

(3) Abatement of debts—the proportionate reduction of payments where a fund is insufficient to meet all claims.

(4) Abatement of legacies—the receipt by legatees of part, or none, of their legacies owing to an insufficiency of assets. Legacies abate *pro rata*.

(5) Abatement of nuisance—the termination of a nuisance by the party aggrieved as an alternative to bringing an action. Notice may require to be given; *e.g.*, when an occupier cuts off branches of trees overhanging his land; when a road-user removes a fence unlawfully erected across a highway.

(6) Abatement of purchase-money—the reduction of the agreed purchase price by way of compensation, when a vendor has misdescribed property and is unable to convey it as described.

1

abduction of females. It is a misdemeanour, without lawful authority or excuse, to take out of the possession and against the will of any person having the lawful care of her, an unmarried girl under the age of sixteen (Sexual Offences Act, 1956).

abetting. See AIDING AND ABETTING.

able-bodied seaman. A seaman who has served at sea, normally for three years.

above par. At a price above nominal or face value; at a premium.

abrasion. Wearing or rubbing off, *e.g.*, loss of weight of coins caused by the ordinary wear and tear of circulation.

abridgment. A condensation or digest; as of the law of England.

abrogate. To repeal, annul or set aside.

absence for seven years. If a person has not been heard of for seven years, and the circumstances are such that, if alive, he would have been heard of, a presumption of death arises, but not as to the date of the death. A spouse remarrying after seven years in such circumstances does not commit bigamy, but the marriage will be invalid if the husband or wife was in fact alive at the time, unless a decree has been obtained of presumption of death and dissolution of marriage. See also DEATH, PRESUMPTION OF.

absenteeism. The practice of workers absenting themselves from work from time to time without adequate reason.

absolute. (1) A decree, rule or order of a court which is complete and becomes of full effect at once. (Contrast NISI.) (2) An estate which is not defeasible before its natural expiration.

abstract of title. A chronological statement of the instruments and events showing a person's title to land, commencing with the " root of title."

abuse of process. A frivolous or vexatious action; setting up a case which has already been decided by a competent court. The court may stay or dismiss such an action.

A person habitually prone to bringing such actions may be restrained by order of the court from instituting civil proceedings without leave.

abut. To border upon: *e.g.*, lands.

acceleration. Where an estate or interest in remainder or expectancy falls into possession sooner than it otherwise would, by reason of the particular estate or preceding interest being or becoming void.

acceptance credit. A method of settling local or international debts. A merchant bank (accepting house) opens credit facilities for a trader in whose credit-worthiness the bank trusts. The trader draws bills of exchange in favour of his customers on the bank up to the limit of his credit.

acceptance of bill of exchange. A written engagement to pay the bill when due; when the person on whom the bill is drawn writes his signature across the face of the bill with or without the word " accepted."

acceptance of goods. Where the buyer informs the seller that he has accepted them, or the buyer does any act to them which is inconsistent with the ownership of the seller; or after the lapse of a reasonable time.

acceptance of offer. The act of assenting to an offer. To create a contract the acceptance must be made while the offer subsists and by the offeree, who must know of the offer; the acceptance must conform with the offer and must either be communicated to the offeror or the requisite act must be done. See also ACCEPTANCE OF GOODS.

acceptance supra protest. Acceptance for honour of a bill of exchange.

When a bill of exchange is dishonoured by non-acceptance, or after acceptance it is dishonoured and is protested for better security (*e.g.*, where the acceptor becomes bankrupt), and is not overdue, anyone not already liable thereon may accept the bill for the honour of the drawer or any party liable thereon. See also PAYMENT FOR HONOUR.

acceptor. The person who accepts a bill of exchange drawn upon him. Until he accepts he is called the drawee.

accessory. A person concerned in a felony (*q.v.*) (*e.g.*, murder) other than as principal. He may be an accessory before the fact (*e.g.*, where he procures a gun for the murderer), or an accessory after the fact (*e.g.*, where he, knowing of the crime, shelters the murderer). See also AIDING AND ABETTING.

accident. (1) An unlooked-for mishap or an untoward event which is not expected or designed. Inevitable accident is, in general, a ground of exemption from liability in tort.

(2) *In equity*, accident is such an unforeseen event, misfortune, loss, act or omission as is not the result of any negligence or misconduct by the party applying for relief. If, *e.g.*, a deed or negotiable security is lost, equity will enforce the plaintiff's rights under the document on his giving, if necessary, a proper bond of indemnity to the defendant.

accident insurance. A contract of insurance to provide compensation for injuries sustained, or for loss of income incurred, through an accident. The National Insurance (Industrial Injuries) Act, 1946, instituted a system of insurance against personal injury caused by accident arising in connection with a person's employment.

accommodation bill. A bill of exchange which a person (the accommodation party) has signed as drawer, acceptor or indorser, without receiving value therefor and for the purpose of financing some other person by lending his, the accommodation party's, name.

accord and satisfaction. An agreement (the accord) between two parties that the debtor shall do or pay something in satisfaction of the cause of action and that the claimant shall accept the same. When the payment or performance is completed and satisfaction obtained, it is called " accord and satisfaction." A release by one party from his obligations in consideration of some payment or other consideration moving from him to the other party. Payment of £10 is not a discharge of a debt of

£15 but payment of £10 *before due date*, if the creditor agrees, would operate as accord and satisfaction and discharge the debt of £15.

account, action of. A claim for an account to be taken by the court may be made in an action by one party against another where there are mutual dealings, the results of which have not been agreed, or where moneys have been received by one party and they have not been accounted for to the other.

account, current. A running account between parties with items on both sides usually in chronological order; *e.g.*, a banking account. By the rule in *Clayton's Case*, in the absence of specific appropriation by the debtor or creditor, the sums first paid into a current account are deemed to be exhausted by the sums first paid out.

account day. Also called pay day or settling day. The fourth day of a Stock Exchange settlement: the day on which actual delivery of securities and payment take place.

account, deficiency. A statement prepared by or for a bankrupt showing how the deficiency, as revealed in the statement of affairs (*q.v.*), arose.

account, dividend. A bank account to the credit of which is placed, on declaration, the total amount of a dividend. The cheques, or warrants as they are often termed, are issued against this account.

account payee only. These words when written across the face of a cheque signify that the proceeds of the cheque are to be credited by the collecting banker to the account of the payee only. This is recognised in banking practice, and to disregard such instruction may amount to negligence.

account receivable. An amount owing by an ordinary trade debtor as distinct from a long term debt.

account sales. A statement of sales rendered by the consignee to the consignor, setting out the amount realised on sale of the goods and showing as deductions therefrom the allowable expenses incurred in selling and the amount for agent's agreed commission and sometimes showing, as a footnote, remittances on account (if any).

account, settled. A statement in writing of the accounts between two parties, one of whom is under a duty to account to the other, which both have agreed to and accepted as correct. A promise to pay the balance of the account is implied, and proceedings may be brought thereon.

account stated. (1) An admission of a sum of money being due from one person to another from which a promise to pay is implied in law. It differs from an account settled (*q.v.*) inasmuch as it applies to transactions with regard to which no person is under a duty to account to another, and with regard to which, therefore, the action for an account will not lie. The account may be stated either orally or in writing, and in any form. An account stated is not necessarily binding; it may be shown to have been given in mistake, or for a debt for which the consideration has failed or was illegal.

(2) An account which contains entries usually on debit and credit sides, and in which the parties have agreed that the items (if any) on one side should be set against the items upon the other side, and the balance should be paid.

account, Stock Exchange. The Stock Exchange year is divided into periods of two or three weeks, each period being called " the account." See ACCOUNT DAY.

accountant. A person skilled in accountancy and allied subjects. He may be a member of one, or more, of the bodies of professionally qualified accountants.

accountants' report. A report included in a prospectus, or similar document, by qualified accountants on the profits and assets of the company which is the subject of the prospectus, etc.

accounts, company. Every company must keep proper books of account with respect to (1) money received and expended, with particulars; (2) sales and purchases of goods; (3) assets and liabilities.

Every year at the annual general meeting the directors must lay before the members a profit and loss account and balance sheet (*q.v.*), the balance sheet being signed by two directors, or one director, if there is only one. See also AUDITORS.

accredit. To furnish an officially recognised agent with papers, called credentials or letters of credit, which certify his public character.

accretion. Where land abuts on tidal water its boundary is the mean high-water mark; with the variation of such mark the land may be added to gradually and imperceptibly by accretion or lessened in like manner by erosion. Land below the mark, as a rule, belongs to the Crown, subject to local variation.

accrue; accrual. A right is said to accrue when it vests in a person, especially when it does so gradually or without his active intervention, *e.g.*, by lapse of time, or by the determination of a preceding right. The fact of a right accruing is called its accrual. When a fund or other property is increased by additions which take place in the ordinary course of nature or by operation of law, the additions are said to accrue either to the original fund or property, or to the person entitled to it.

accrued. Vested, *e.g.*, an accrued right; accumulated to a stated date, *e.g.*, accrued rent, income, interest.

accumulated profits. Undistributed profits. Distribution to members of a company of accumulated profits will usually involve a liability to withholding tax (*q.v.*) on the amount of the distribution.

accumulation. The continual increase of principal by the re-investment of interest. If a direction to accumulate income is to be valid, it must be restricted to one of the six periods laid down by the Law of Property Act, 1925, ss. 164–166, as amended by the Perpetuities and Accumulations Act, 1964. But this rule does not apply to accumulations either for the payment of debts, for raising portions for issue, or in respect of the produce of timber or wood. See also PERPETUITIES, RULE AGAINST.

acid test. Measuring solvency by relating quick assets (*q.v.*) to short-term liabilities to determine whether the business should be able to meet its immediate liabilities as they fall due.

acknowledgment. The acceptance or admission of the truth, correctness, or existence of a state of things. Thus it may be the admission of a sum paid or debt due or owing; of the title to land or ownership of property, or the signature of a testator to a will.

The effect of a written acknowledgment of money due on an account where action has been barred by the Statute of Limitations is to set the time within which an action must be brought running afresh.

acquiescence. Assent to an infringement of rights, either expressed, or implied from conduct, by which the right to equitable relief is normally lost. See LACHES.

acquittance. A written acknowledgment of the payment of a sum of money or debt due; a discharge or receipt.

act of bankruptcy. An act of a debtor upon which a bankruptcy petition may be grounded, if committed within three months before presentation of the petition. These acts, broadly, are inconsistent with his continuing solvency. There are nine acts of bankruptcy under the Bankruptcy Act, 1914. All of them stem from an inability to pay debts as they fall due.

act of God. An accident or event which happens independently of human intervention and due to natural causes such as a storm, earthquake, etc. When the law creates a duty, and the party bound to perform it is prevented from so doing by the act of God, he is not liable for its non-performance if he was under no duty to foresee or provide against its happening.

act of indemnity. An Act passed to legalise transactions which, when they took place, were illegal, or to exempt particular persons from pecuniary penalties or punishments for acts done in the public service, as in time of war, or by inadvertence, which were breaches of the law.

act of parliament. See STATUTE.

act of state. An act done by the sovereign power of a country or its agent, within the limit of the power vested in it. Such an act cannot be questioned or made the subject of legal proceedings in any court of law.

actio personalis moritur cum persona. (A personal action dies with the person.) Formerly a right of action in tort was destroyed by the death of the injured or injuring party. Now, since the Law Reform (Miscellaneous Provisions) Act, 1934, the general rule is that on the death of a person all causes of action subsisting against or vested in him survive against, or for the benefit of, his estate.

action. The right of suing in a court of justice for that which is due; the form prescribed by law for the recovery of one's due, or the lawful demand of one's right. An action now means any proceeding in the High Court commenced by writ or in such other manner as may be prescribed by rules of court.

active accounts (machine accounting). Those which have been operated upon in a prescribed period, *e.g.*, a month.

active market. The term used by the press and stock exchange to describe a quoted stock in which frequent dealings occur.

active partner. One who takes a working part in the management of the business of the firm. See PARTNERSHIP.

active trust. A trust calling for actual duties by the trustee. See BARE TRUSTEE; TRUST.

actual military service. Soldiers (including officers) on actual military service, and mariners and seamen at sea, may make a valid disposition of property by an informal will, even if under 21 years of age. See WILL.

actual total loss. An expression of marine insurance applied to goods which have become a total loss, for whatever reason.

actuary. A mathematician who compiles statistics, *e.g.*, tables of mortality, and makes assumptions therefrom; *e.g.*, of the average expectation of life, mainly for insurance purposes. He calculates insurance premiums, present value of reversions, surrender value of life insurance policies, building societies' tables, etc.

ad colligenda bona defuncti. A limited or temporary grant of letters of administration of the estate of a deceased where goods are of a perishable nature and where a general grant would be delayed.

ad valorem. In proportion to value; of taxes and stamp duty. Applied to duties which are graduated according to the value of the subject-matter taxed.

addendum. Something to be added.

adding machine. One whose function is to add, subtract and total figures on a list or visually. The process may be mechanical or electronic.

address for service. An address, within the jurisdiction, where writs, notices, summonses, orders, etc., may be served. An address for service as regards the plaintiff must be stated in the endorsement upon the writ (R.S.C., Ord. 6, r. 5); and as regards the defendant, in the memorandum of appearance (Ord. 12, r. 3).

addressing machine. By the use of stencils in the form of metal plates re-curring names and addresses (*e.g.*, for dividends) can be listed or applied to envelopes by machine.

adjudication order. An order of Court declaring a debtor bankrupt and placing his property under the control of a Trustee in Bankruptcy.

adjustment. (1) In marine insurance the operation of settling and ascertaining the amount which the insured is entitled to receive under a policy, and of fixing the proportion which each underwriter is liable to pay.

(2) An amendment to a written record, price, contract, etc.

administration, letters of. Where a person possessed of property, whether real or personal, dies intestate, or without an executor, the Probate, Divorce and Admiralty Division will grant to a proper person an authority under the seal of the court, called letters of administration, by which the grantee, the administrator, becomes clothed with powers and duties similar to those of an executor. In addition to the oaths taken by the administrator, he enters into a bond (Judicature Act, 1925, s. 167).

If the deceased has made a will, but failed to appoint executors, the court will grant letters of administration with the will annexed (*cum testamento annexo*) to a person interested in the estate; *e.g.*, a devisee, legatee, or the trustees of a settlement of land made previously to the death (*ibid.*, s. 166). Since 1925, probate or administration may not be granted to more than four persons in respect of the same property, and if there is a minority, or a life interest arises, administration is to be granted either to a trust corporation (*e.g.*, the Public Trustee) with or without an individual, or to not less than two individuals (*ibid.*, s. 160). A trust corporation may be granted probate or administration, and either solely or jointly with any other person (*ibid.*, s. 161).

Where the deceased dies wholly intestate, administration is, except in special circumstances, *e.g.*, insolvency, granted to persons interested in the residuary estate, on application made by them, or to trustees of the settlement in respect of the settled land (*ibid.*, s. 162).

Administration may be granted *pendente lite* (*q.v.*) to an administrator subject to the control of the court, and who has not the power of distributing residue (*ibid.*, s. 163). If a personal representative to whom a grant has been made resides abroad for twelve months after the death, special administration may be granted to a creditor or other person interested (*ibid.*, s. 164). Where an infant is sole executor, administration with the will annexed is to be granted to his guardian or other person until majority (*ibid.*, s. 165). Probate and letters of administration are capable of transferring a legal estate to personal representatives (Law of Property Act, 1925, s. 11 (2)).

Admiralty Court. The Admiralty Court had exclusive jurisdiction in salvage, life salvage, bottomry, possession of ships, etc. Admiralty jurisdiction is now vested in the Probate, Divorce and Admiralty Division of the High Court of Justice, including the jurisdiction of a Prize Court.

admission. A statement, oral, written or inferred from conduct, made by or on behalf of a party to a suit, and admissible in evidence, if relevant, as against his interest. Admissions are either formal or informal.

(1) Formal admissions for the purpose of the trial may be made on pleadings, as, *e.g.*, where a contract and its breach are admitted, but infancy or fraud is alleged in defence, or as a result of a notice to admit.

(2) Informal admissions may be made before or during the proceedings. See also CONFESSION.

adopt. Voluntarily to make one's own, as follows:

(1) A contract—to accept it as binding notwithstanding some defect entitling the party to repudiate it.

(2) A child—to assume, in accordance with the Adoption Acts 1958 to 1964, the responsibilities and privileges of the natural parents of a child in relation to " the future custody, maintenance and education " of the child.

(3) A transaction—a person who, having received goods on approval, pledges them, thereby does an act adopting the transaction, with the result that the property in the goods passes to him, and the original owner cannot recover them from the pledgee receiving them in good faith.

adulteration. The mixing with any substance intended to be sold of any ingredient which is dangerous to health or which makes the substance something other than that which is sold or intended to be sold. It is an offence under the Food and Drugs Act, 1955.

advance. In banking, a loan to a customer against securities, or otherwise. In business, money paid on account by a purchaser before delivery, or by a consignee before sale.

advancement. Benefiting. (1) The application by a trustee, as permitted by the Trustee Act, 1925, of a portion of the capital money subject to the trust for the benefit of the person entitled to the capital of the trust property. The portion which may be so applied is limited to one-half of the presumptive or vested share of that person in the trust property.

(2) In equity it is presumed, if a purchase or investment is made by a father, or person *in loco parentis*, in the name of a child (or by any person under an equitable obligation to support or make provision for another), that such provision is intended as an advancement of the child, so as to rebut the ordinary presumption in such cases of a resulting trust in favour of the person who paid the money. The presumption of advancement may be rebutted or corroborated.

adventure. An enterprise or speculation; the sending of goods abroad in a ship under the charge of a super-cargo or other agent to sell or dispose of them to advantage. An adventure in the nature of trade is a trade for income tax purposes.

adverse possession. Occupation of land inconsistent with the right of the true owner.

advertisements. Public notices or announcements. The display of advertisements is controlled under the Town and Country Planning Acts.

advertising. All methods, other than variations in quality or price, by which a business enterprise attempts to increase the demand for its products.

advice, letter of. A letter from one merchant or banker to another, giving information of business transactions. Thus a banker will send a letter of advice to his correspondent, or agent, to inform him of the drafts or bills drawn upon him, and giving particulars of the dates, amounts, and payees.

advice note. A document given to a purchaser of goods to inform him that the goods have been dispatched to him.

9

advice of receipt. An advice of delivery of a registered postal packet which a sender may obtain from the post office by payment of a small fee.

advowson. The right of presentation to a church or ecclesiastical benefice (*i.e.*, of appointing the parson).

affidavit. A written statement voluntarily signed and sworn before a person competent to administer an oath, *e.g.*, a justice of the peace, usually made in connection with legal proceedings.

affiliated companies. Companies which are associated because of common ownership; the subsidiaries of a holding company and the holding company.

affinity. Relationship by marriage.

affirm. (1) Where a contract is voidable, if the party at whose option it is voidable elects to waive his right and to carry out the contract as if it had been valid, he is said to affirm it.

(2) A court of appeal is said to affirm the judgment of a court below if it upholds that judgment.

(3) A person is said to affirm who declares that taking an oath is contrary to his religious belief, or that he has no religious belief and who makes an affirmation (*q.v.*).

affirmation. A solemn declaration by a person who affirms, in lieu of making a statement on oath. See AFFIRM.

affreightment. A contract made either by charterparty or by bill of lading, by which a shipowner agrees to carry goods in his ship for reward.

after date. The wording of a bill of exchange fixing the date of payment, thus: " Three months after date, pay . . . "

after sight. Used similarly to the words " after date "; the time must be specified and commences only from the date of acceptance by the drawee.

age admitted. Policies of life assurance are so indorsed when the assured has submitted satisfactory proof of his age.

age error arrears. If, after issue of a policy of life assurance it is discovered that the age of the assured was understated in error, the premium is amended and the amount of underpaid premiums, with interest to date, is chargeable.

agenda. A schedule or list of the items of business to be dealt with at a meeting.

agent. A person employed to act on behalf of another. The fundamental object or purpose of an agent is to establish contractual relations between his principal and third parties. When this is effected the agent normally drops out. An act of an agent, done within the scope of his authority (actual or implied) binds his principal. The authority may be given by writing, words or conduct. If a person purports to contract as principal, though with the intention and expectation that another will take it over, that other person, even if willing to do so, cannot ratify the contract; *i.e.*, he cannot gain any rights or undergo liabilities in respect of it. If, however, a person contracts as agent, even without authority, his principal may ratify the contract. If a person purports to contract as principal, but in fact is acting on behalf of an undisclosed principal, that principal may be made liable on the contract when his existence is discovered, and similarly he may enforce the contract. A person who signs as agent, but has no principal, is personally liable on the contract.

General agents are those appointed to act in all transactions, such as those under a general power of attorney (*q.v.*) or in transactions of a certain class, as a banker or a solicitor. The scope of authority of such agent is the authority usually possessed by such agents, unless notice is given to third parties of some limitation.

Special agents are those appointed for one particular purpose. The agent's scope of authority is the actual authority given him.

An agent who misappropriates property of his principal is guilty of larceny or fraudulent conversion.

agent of necessity. One who is deemed in urgent circumstances to have authority to act on behalf of another, as follows: (1) those accepting bills of exchange for the honour of the payee, (2) masters of ships, whose authority arises from emergencies of the voyage, (3) carriers by land in similar circumstances, as regards perishable goods and livestock, (4) a deserted wife or a separated wife, if there is no agreement as to maintenance, who may pledge her husband's credit for necessaries for herself and her children. See also HUSBAND AND WIFE.

agent's commission. To be entitled to commission, the services of the agent must have been the effective cause of bringing about the required transaction; as, *e.g.*, an estate agent in selling a house. In that case it is commonly understood that the agent's commission will be paid to him by the vendor out of the purchase price received by him on the sale.

aggregation. The gathering together of different parcels of estate into one total for the purpose of assessment to estate duty.

agio. Money-changing: The percentage charged for changing paper money into cash, or an inferior for a more valuable currency; the excess value of one currency over another.

agistment. The taking in and feeding or depasturing of horses, cattle, or similar animals by a person upon his land for reward. An agister is, therefore, a bailee for reward, and is liable for damage to the cattle if he uses less than ordinary diligence.

agnate. Relative on the father's side of the family. See COGNATE.

agreement. In its ordinary sense, agreement is the consensus of two or more minds in anything done or to be done; *e.g.*, in making a social engagement. In its legal sense, agreement is the concurrence of two or more persons in expressing a common intention with the view of altering their rights and duties. An enforceable agreement is a contract (*q.v.*).

agreement, preliminary. An agreement, usually for purposes of discussion, preparatory to a more formal agreement.

aiding and abetting. The criminal offence of helping or counselling a criminal in, or procuring, the commission of a criminal offence. It renders the aider and abettor liable to the same prosecution and punishment as a principal offender. See also ACCESSORY.

air, carriage by. The Carriage by Air Act, 1932, applied to all international carriage by aircraft of persons, luggage and goods, and made the carrier liable for loss unless he established that he was not in default. The liability of the carrier was, however, limited in amount: by the Carriage by Air Act, 1961, the maximum liability of the carrier for each passenger is 250,000 francs. See also the Carriage by Air (Supplementary Provisions) Act, 1962.

alias. [*alias dictus*, otherwise called.] If a person, having the proper name of A B causes or allows himself to be known as C D, he may properly be described as A B *alias* C D. See also NAME, CHANGE OF.

alibi. [Elsewhere.] A defence whereby an accused alleges that, at the time when the offence with which he is charged was committed, he was elsewhere. Corroboration (*q.v.*) is usually expected.

alien. A person who is not a British subject, a British protected person or a citizen of the Commonwealth countries or the Republic of Ireland. An alien is unable to hold shares in a British ship or vote at elections but has full capacity to contract. He is liable to deportation (*q.v.*). See NATIONALITY.

alien ami (or friend). The subject of a foreign state with which this country is at peace.

alienation. The transference of ownership of real or personal property. Alienation may be voluntary, *e.g.*, by conveyance or will; or involuntary, *e.g.*, seizure under a judgment order for debt.

alien enemy. A person who is a subject of a state at war with Her Majesty. The test, however, is not his nationality, but the place in which he resides or carries on business. Thus alien enemy includes a British subject or subject of a neutral country voluntarily resident or carrying on business in a state at war with Her Majesty, and citizens of a state in effective enemy occupation.

An enemy alien cannot contract with a British subject or enforce a contract made with a British subject prior to a war, but he may be sued in England and defend the action. If resident in England with licence of the Crown he has full legal capacity.

alimony. Alimony is of two kinds: (1) Alimony pending suit is a sum paid by the husband to the wife as a means of support pending the hearing of a suit for nullity, divorce, judicial separation or restitution of conjugal rights.

(2) Permanent alimony is the provision ordered by the court to be paid by the husband to the wife after a decree of judical separation; payment by the wife to the husband may be ordered where the latter is insane. See also MAINTENANCE.

allegation. A statement or assertion of fact made in any proceeding, as, for instance, in a pleading; particularly a statement or charge which is, as yet, unproved. See also AVERMENT.

alleged. Charges, etc., made in the course of legal proceedings, but as yet unproved.

allegiance. The natural, lawful and faithful obedience which every subject owes to the Crown. It is either natural and perpetual where a person is born a subject, or has been naturalised; or local and temporary, where a person is merely a resident in the British dominions, or retains a British passport on leaving.

allegiance, oath of. The express declaration of allegiance made by high officers of state, judges and others, on appointment, and by persons obtaining naturalisation.

allied companies. See HOLDING COMPANY.

allocatur. [It is allowed.] The certificate of the taxing officer as to the amount of costs allowed. It may be indorsed on the bill or be a separate document.

allonge. A slip of paper annexed to a bill of exchange for indorsements when there is no room for them on the bill.

allotment. (1) The allocation or appropriation of property to a specific person (or persons) called the allottee.

(2) The appropriation to an applicant by a resolution of the directors of a company of a certain amount of share or loan capital in the company, in response to an application.

In general, no allotment can be made until the third day after the first issue of the prospectus—the time of the opening of the subscription lists. See also MINIMUM SUBSCRIPTION.

allotment, letter of. The letter of allotment which is sent by the secretary of a company to the allottees of share or loan capital, where a letter of application has been received, and the applicant has been successful. Otherwise a letter of regret may be sent to him.

The letter of application and the letter of allotment together constitute the contract as to the taking up of share or loan capital. See also LETTER OF RENUNCIATION.

allotment, return of. A return filed with the Registrar of Companies showing details of allotments of shares to members.

allottee. The person to whom share or loan capital in a company has been allotted in response to an application.

allowance. (1) A deduction made from the price charged for articles on account of shortages, delayed delivery or other defects; or as a customary allowance, e.g., tare and tret.

(2) Deductions provided for in taxation.

(3) The admission that charges, costs, claims, etc., have been duly incurred, and are in order for payment.

alloy. A baser metal mixed with a finer metal, especially with gold or silver for coinage; the object being to make the coins harder and more durable.

alteration. An erasure or addition. A material alteration of an instrument (*e.g.*, an alteration of the date of a bill of exchange whereby payment would be accelerated) invalidates the instrument unless all parties agree thereto. Agreed alterations to a document should be signed or initialled by the makers or parties to it. Alterations to a bill of exchange which are not apparent on ordinary inspection may be disregarded by a holder in due course. It is presumed that alterations in deeds are made before execution, unless the contrary is proved.

alternate director. A substitute director to represent a director who is prevented, by absence abroad or illness, from acting.

alternative cost. The cost of producing one commodity expressed in terms of another.

amalgamation. The merger of two or more companies or their undertakings. In some cases the operation is effected by the registration of a new company, which takes over the several undertakings of the existing companies; in other cases one of the companies absorbs the other company or companies.

ambassador. A diplomatic agent residing in a foreign country as representative of the state by whom he is despatched. He is recognised as such on presentation to the sovereign of the foreign state of his credentials. See also CONSUL.

ambiguity. A double meaning. A *patent* ambiguity is one which is apparent on the face of the instrument, as where a blank is left. A *latent* ambiguity is one not apparent on the face of the instrument, as where a testator bequeaths property to his niece Jane, and it is proved that he has two nieces so named. Parol evidence is admissible to explain a latent, but not (in general) a patent, ambiguity.

amendment. The correction of some error, or omission, or the curing of some defect:
(1) in a motion already before a meeting, by another motion. It is usually by way of adding, deleting or substituting words to, from or in the original motion;
(2) in a statute, by the passing of an amending statute;
(3) in judicial proceedings, by filing documents correcting the error with the consent of the other party or parties, or by order on application to the court.

amends, tender of. An offer to pay a sum of money by way of satisfaction for a wrong alleged to have been committed.

American law. In the United States, the State of New York adopted as its law the law of England as it existed on April 19, 1775, thereby adopting both the common law and the statutes in forces in England on that day. All the other original states and the states subsequently admitted to the Union did substantially the same thing, except the State of Louisiana, the law of which is based on the Code Napoléon. The law so adopted is to this day the law of the various states, except in so far as it has been modified by legislation or judicial decisions. American decisions are not binding on our courts, but may have persuasive authority.

amicus curiae. [A friend of the court.] One who calls the attention of the court to some point of law or fact which would appear to have been over-looked; counsel who undertake to assist the court in a matter in which they are not engaged professionally.

amortisation. (1) The gradual reduction of a liability, by paying it off by instalments, usually through the operation of a sinking fund.

(2) The gradual charging against revenue of expenditure, the benefit from which will be derived over a long period at the end of which the object of the expenditure will have no residual value, *e.g.*, the periodical writing off over the term of occupancy of a premium paid for a lease, or of the cost of a patent over its term.

(3) Redemption of bonds and shares by means of annual drawings from a sinking fund, or the complete extinguishment of a loan by a single payment out of some special fund set aside for that purpose.

analogue computer. A computer in which representation is by a physical quantity (*e.g.*, angular position) which is made proportional to the thing being represented. *Cf.* DIGITAL COMPUTER.

ancillary. Auxiliary or subservient. A work is ancillary to a trade or business, when it is not necessary thereto, or a primary part thereof. The objects clause of a company's Memorandum of Association (*q.v.*) is usually of sufficient generality to enable several ancillary trades to be legally undertaken.

and reduced. The court in approving of a reduction of the capital of a company *may* order, in certain cases, the company to add to its name as the last words thereof the words " and reduced."

annotation. A note that describes, explains, comments on, or sets out additional information or details.

annual accounts. The financial statements presented to the proprietors of a business annually. In company practice the minimum legal requirement is the balance sheet, profit and loss account and reports by directors and auditors.

annual general meeting. See GENERAL MEETING.

annual return. Limited companies must by law file a return each year with the Registrar of Companies after the Annual General Meeting has been held. The information supplied includes details of the share capital and secured indebtedness, an up-to-date list of members and a copy of the annual accounts.

annual value. The gross annual value of premises for rating purposes is the rent which the landlord would secure in the open market, he being responsible for necessary repairs and the tenant being responsible for rates.

The net annual value, upon which rates are payable, is determined by deducting the statutory allowances from the gross annual value.

annuitant. One who receives an annuity.

annuity. A yearly payment of a certain sum of money for a term of years or during the life of an individual. Annuities given by will are pecuniary legacies payable by instalments, and, where the will directs the purchase of an annuity for A for life, A is entitled to take the purchase-money instead. Purchased annuities are only liable to personal tax to the extent of the interest element.

annulment. To annul is to cancel or to deprive of legal effectiveness or operation, either *ab initio* (*i.e.*, retrospectively), as in nullity of marriage; or from the date of the annulment, as in the case of annulment of an adjudication in bankruptcy.

ante. [Before.]

ante nuptial. [Before marriage.]

antedate. To back-date or affix a date earlier than the true date.

In general, an instrument, although antedated, operates only from the date it is made, and antedating may amount to fraud if the instrument is proferred as having been made on the date it bears. A post-dated (or after-dated) instrument, however, only operates from the date inserted; *e.g.*, a post-dated cheque.

anticipation. The act of assigning, charging or otherwise dealing with income before it becomes due. The former restraints on anticipation of married women were abolished by the Married Women's (Restraint upon Anticipation) Act, 1949.

appeal. The judicial review by a higher court of the decision of an inferior court; usually at the instance of the party aggrieved by that decision. In civil cases, any order may be made by the Court of Appeal which could have been made by the lower court, or a new trial may be ordered.

appearance. Entering an appearance is a formal step taken by a defendant to an action after he has been served with the writ of summons; its object is to intimate to the plaintiff that the defendant intends to contest his claim; or, in a friendly action, to take part in the proceedings.

application. An application for shares or debentures of a company in pursuance of a prospectus issued generally, is irrevocable until after the expiration of the third day after the time of the opening of the subscription lists. See ALLOTMENT.

applied economics. That branch of economics which is concerned with the study of practical economic problems, using the principles of pure economics (*q.v.*).

appreciation. (1) An increase in the value of something and in this sense the opposite of depreciation (*q.v.*). In general an appreciation in value of investments or business assets is subject to tax in the U.K.

(2) The process of setting a value on something.

apprenticeship. Those who wish to join a skilled occupation, *e.g.*, printing, frequently serve for a specified period under the tutelage of skilled operatives. *Cf.* ARTICLED CLERK.

appropriation. (1) To make a thing the property of a person. To appropriate goods to a contract means to identify and set aside goods in fulfilment of the contract. Where there is a contract for the sale of unascertained or future goods by description, when suitable goods are appropriated to the contract, the property in the goods thereupon passes to the buyer.

(2) The setting aside by a personal representative of property, real or personal, to satisfy a gift; *e.g.*, of a fund to provide for an annuity. See also APPROPRIATION OF PAYMENTS.

appropriation account or statement. An account or statement of a business which shows the profits available for distribution or appropriation and how they are dealt with.

appropriation of payments. The right of saying in reduction of which of several debts due by a debtor to a creditor, a payment made by the debtor shall go. The debtor has this right in the first instance; it vests in the creditor only in the event of the debtor not specifying the account or debt to which the payment is to be applied. If no appropriation be made by debtor or creditor the law appropriates the payment, in the case of current accounts, to the earliest debt. (The rule in *Clayton's Case.*) In the case of debts bearing interest; *e.g.*, debentures or mortgages, the general rule is that payments are appropriated to interest, in the first place.

approval, sale on. The sale of a chattel with a right to the buyer to return the article if not satisfied therewith. If he does not return it in the time specified or otherwise adopts the contract; or, if no time is specified, then within a reasonable time, the sale is complete.

approved ports. (1) Places approved by the Commissioners of Customs and Excise for the landing or shipment of goods. (2) Seaports and airports approved for purposes of the Aliens Order.

arbitrage. Profiting from the difference in price the same thing may have in different markets at the same time, achieved by buying in the cheaper and selling in the other almost simultaneously. Generally applied to dealings in foreign exchange; *e.g.*, dealers buy and sell currencies, taking advantage of disparities in the quoted rates of foreign exchange in different countries; also to the business of buying a security on one market and selling it on another.

arbitration. As an alternative to litigation, parties to a dispute may by written agreement refer present and future differences to arbitration, and if in contravention of the agreement legal proceedings are instituted, they may be stayed by the court on the application of the defendant. One or more persons may be appointed to be arbitrator; if two, there is usually an umpire. The decision of an arbitrator or arbitrators is called an award (*q.v.*) and is binding in the same manner as a decision of a court (Arbitration Act, 1950).

The advantages of referring a dispute to arbitration are as follows:

(1) Avoidance of delay; convenience and simplicity of procedure; reduction of expense; and avoidance of publicity.

(2) Should the matter be of a technical nature a person having the required technical qualifications may be appointed arbitrator; for example, to arbitrate on the suitability of any electronic computer.

(3) In general, the finality of decision.

Arbitration is likely to be of advantage in disputes involving issues of fact; *e.g.*, whether goods are up to sample, or the assessment of damages or compensation. But if the matter is very complicated, or if intricate questions of law are likely to arise, legal proceedings may be the better course. It is not unusual, also, for arbitration to be more expensive than litigation.

Matters may have to be referred to arbitration under statute; *e.g.*, under the Agricultural Holdings Act, 1948, or by order of court. See REFERENCE.

arbitration, industrial. Under the Industrial Courts Act, 1919, provision is made for the Minister to refer matters in dispute, with the consent of both parties, to one or more arbitrators with a view to a settlement. Their award is not binding. The Industrial Disputes Tribunal was set up in 1957 to arbitrate on industrial disputes. It replaced the National Arbitration Tribunal. See CONCILIATION; ARBITRATION.

arbitrator. A person to whose decision matters in dispute are referred, and who conducts an arbitration (*q.v.*).

arrangement. An agreement between a debtor and some or all of his creditors whereby arrangements are made for the payment of his debts by way of composition or instalments as an alternative to the bankruptcy of the debtor. Two types of arrangement are provided for: (1) Scheme of composition; (2) Deed of arrangement. (Bankruptcy Act, 1914; Deeds of Arrangement Act, 1914.)

A scheme of arrangement arrived at and agreed upon between a company and its creditors may be sanctioned by the High Court.

arrest. To arrest anyone is to restrain him and deprive him of his liberty by seizure of his person. Arrests may be made by a peace officer (*q.v.*), and by private persons in case of felonies. The remedy of a person wrongfully arrested is an action for false imprisonment (*q.v.*). See also ATTACHMENT.

arrest for debt. A judgment debtor who has the means to pay, but refuses to pay the debt, may be arrested under the Debtors Act, 1869.

articled clerk. Some professions, *e.g.*, chartered accountants and solicitors, require that entrants shall first have served a practising member of the profession under written articles of agreement. The period of service may be reduced for those who have attained levels of education higher than the minimum standard.

articles. Clauses of an agreement; or the document itself, *e.g.*, articles of clerkship, partnership, etc.

articles of association. See ASSOCIATION, ARTICLES OF.

artificial person. A corporation or a company which is vested with legal powers and liabilities and subject to rights and duties, so far as possible, as though it were a natural person.

assay. In mining, the testing of samples of ore to ascertain how much metal they contain; the testing of coins, etc., to ascertain how much gold or silver they contain.

assembly line. A method of production which has been extensively developed in the assembly of machinery, *e.g.*, the motor car. A line conveys the article under construction between operatives who complete successive stages of assembly.

assent. The agreement, express or implied, of an executor to handing over to a legatee the thing bequeathed; the assent of the personal representative of the deceased to the vesting of real estate in the person entitled to receive it (Administration of Estates Act, 1925).

A vesting assent is the means whereby settled land is conveyed to a new tenant for life or statutory owner on a change of ownership of the settled land. (Settled Land Act, 1925.)

assented. Shares and stock are so described in a stock exchange, when the holder has agreed to a change in the conditions of issue, or to accept an offer to purchase his holding.

assessment. The ascertainment of the amount of a person's liability, *e.g.*, for taxation, rates, damages, etc.; or the formal evidence of such ascertainment; *i.e.*, the entry made in the appropriate book with all due formality; *e.g.*, an income tax assessment.

assessor. (1) A person called in to assist a court in trying a question requiring technical or scientific knowledge, *e.g.*, in Admiralty proceedings involving questions of navigation or seamanship. He has no voice in the decision of the court.

(2) A person called in by insurance companies, in the event of a loss, *e.g.*, by fire, for the purpose of examining the facts, and of advising whether the claim is a genuine one, and in that event the amount of the loss.

assets. Assets are those things which a business owns, or on which it has spent money, provided that the expenditure was not incurred as part of revenue expenditure. Assets represent an embodiment of invested resources. They are classified into several categories, *e.g.*, fixed, current, tangible, intangible.

assets, company in liquidation. In a winding up the assets of a company are applied as follows: (1) The costs and expenses of the winding up; (2) preferential debts., *i.e.*, one year's rates and taxes, wages and salaries for the last 4 months, not exceeding £200; (3) unsecured debts.

Debts (2) and (3) rank and abate equally among themselves. A secured creditor realises his security and ranks as unsecured for any balance remaining.

assets, marshalling of. See MARSHALLING.

assign. To transfer property.

assignee. A person to whom an assignment is made. The assignee of a debt takes " subject to equities "; *i.e.*, subject to any existing claims or defences open to the debtor against the assignor.

assignee, official. See OFFICIAL RECEIVERS.

assignment. Generally, a transfer of property, *e.g.*, of a lease, mortgage, or patent rights. Assignment is by operation of law on death or bankruptcy.

The transfer by a debtor of the whole or portion of his property to a trustee for the benefit of his creditors generally is an act of bankruptcy.

assignment of choses in action. Formerly choses in action (*q.v.*) were not assignable at common law, but choses in action, both legal and equitable, were assignable in equity. If the chose in action were legal, the assignee could only sue in the name of the assignor, but if equitable he could sue in his own name Now, any debt or other legal chose in action may be assigned so as to vest in the assignee the legal right to such debt or other legal chose in action with all the remedies for it and the power to give a good discharge.

The conditions of a legal assignment are: (1) it must be in writing and signed by the assignor; (2) be absolute and not by way of charge only; (3) notice in writing of the assignment must be given to the debtor; equitable assignments remain valid and effective.

assignment of contract. Liabilities under a contract cannot be assigned without the consent of the other party to the contract. They can only be assigned by novation (*q.v.*). Rights under a contract can be assigned by novation (*q.v.*); legal assignment; equitable assignments (*q.v.*) or operation of law.

Contracts involving personal credit, ability or qualifications cannot be assigned; *e.g.*, to marry; contracts of service.

assignor. One who assigns, or transfers to another.

assigns. Persons to whom assignments are made.

associate director. One who acts as a director but who is not formally appointed a director. He is in effect a consultant of the directors, selected and appointed by the directors and responsible to them. The scope of his duties, powers and remuneration are determined by the directors and not by law or by the shareholders.

associated companies. Companies with common interests or associations which may arise from the following:
  (1) Control of two or more companies by the same individuals.
  (2) Mutual shareholdings insufficient to constitute one company a subsidiary of another.

(3) Mutual trade associations.

(4) some directors who are members of two or more boards to enable the companies to pursue common policies.

The term is so general that the meaning depends on the context.

See also SUBSIDIARY COMPANY.

association. A combination of persons (whether incorporated or not) for a specific purpose. See ASSOCIATIONS NOT FOR PROFIT; PARTNERSHIP; SYNDICATE; TRADE ASSOCIATION.

association, articles of. The regulations for the management and internal arrangement of a company and being the terms and conditions on which the shareholders agree, amongst themselves, as to how the business of the company shall be carried on. Table A (*q.v.*) of the First Schedule to the Companies Act, 1948, consists of a specimen set of articles applicable in the case of a company limited by shares. Tables B–E give specimens applicable to other types of company. Companies may adopt the appropriate Table of the Companies Act in whole or in part.

association clause. The concluding clause of a company's memorandum which recites the desire of the subscribers (*i.e.*, signatories) to the memorandum to be formed into a company. They must write opposite their signatures the number of shares to be taken by each of them.

association, memorandum of. Seven or more persons (or, for a private company, two or more persons) may, by subscribing their names to a memorandum of association and otherwise complying with the statutory requirements as to registration, form an incorporated company with or without limited liability. The memorandum must state, *inter alia*, (a) the name of the company, with " limited " as the last word in the case of a company limited by shares or by guarantee; (b) whether the registered office is to be situate in England or in Scotland; (c) the objects of the company.

The memorandum can be altered by a special resolution, or on application to the court, as provided in the Companies Act, 1948.

associations not for profit. An association formed for promoting commerce, art, science, religion, charity, etc., on the footing that its profits or income shall be applied to its objects only, and that no dividend shall be paid to its members. The Board of Trade may grant a licence authorising registration of the association with limited liability, but without the addition of the word " limited " to its name.

assurance. Contracts in which indemnity does not form the basis of the agreement, owing to the certainty of the happening of the event upon which the assurance is effected; *i.e.*, life assurance. (*q.v.*). Assurance and insurance are often used interchangeably. See also INSURANCE; PROPOSAL FOR INSURANCE.

at call. Money deposited with bankers and others the repayment of which may be demanded without notice.

21

at discretion. Instructions given by a client to his broker to buy or sell a stock or commodity at the broker's discretion as to price.

at limit. Instructions given by a client to his broker placing a limit upon the price at which securities or commodities may be purchased or sold, as the case may be.

at sight. Bills of exchange drawn " at sight," are payable on demand, no days of grace (*q.v.*) being allowed.

attachment. (1) The arrest of a person under a writ of attachment is employed in ordinary cases of disobedience to an order, judgment, etc., or other contempt of court. The writ is issued by leave of the court or a judge on notice to the person concerned, and directs his arrest. The person remains in prison until he has cleared his contempt or is discharged.

(2) The attachment of debts is a proceeding employed where a judgment for the payment of money has been obtained against a person to whom a debt is owed by another person. See also GARNISHEE ORDER.

(3) Foreign attachment is a process whereby the plaintiff in an action of contract against a defendant who is absent from the jurisdiction is enabled to have property of, or debts due, to the defendant within the jurisdiction applied to satisfy the plaintiff's claim. The claim must arise within the jurisdiction.

attest. To bear witness to any act or event; *e.g.*, to sign as witness to the signature or execution of a deed or will.

attestation. The formal act of witnessing a signature; *e.g.*, of a will.

attestation clause. The statement in a deed or will, etc., that such deed or will has been duly executed in the presence of witnesses.

attested copy. A copy of a document which has been examined and certified correct by a qualified person who has examined it.

attorney. One appointed to act for another; the donee of a power of attorney (*q.v.*). The term attorney-at-law was formerly applied to persons admitted to practise in the superior courts of common law. See now SOLICITOR.

Attorney-General. The principal law officer of the Crown.

attorney, power of. See POWER OF ATTORNEY.

attornment. (1) The acknowledgment of a person that he holds goods on another's behalf; (2) the agreement of the owner of land to become the tenant of another person.

au fait. To be well instructed in; thoroughly conversant with.

auction, sale by. The sale of each separate lot is complete on the fall of the auctioneer's hammer. Until then any bidder may retract his bid. The seller or his employee cannot bid unless notice is given beforehand; otherwise the sale is fraudulent. The sale may also be announced to be subject to a reserve price being reached. Printed conditions are usually contained in the sale catalogue.

auctioneer. An agent to sell goods or property at a public auction. He is deemed the agent of both parties, and can sign the necessary memorandum of the sale of real estate on their behalf. He is remunerated by commission on the amount realised.

audit. The examination of the books, records, financial documents and statements of a business with a view to determining their accuracy during and at the end of the period covered by the audit. At the end of the examination the auditor reports that he is satisfied with the accuracy of the records and that the summary financial statements (usually the annual accounts (*q.v.*)) present a fair view of the financial history of the business during the period under review. If he is not satisfied the auditor reports on the aspect of the financial statements which he considers to be inaccurate or misleading.

audit, internal. An audit (*q.v.*) conducted by staff of a business organisation on behalf of management. The scope and nature of the audit is determined by management and not by statute. However, the duties of the internal auditor are likely to overlap with those of the statutory auditor to a certain extent.

auditor. One who conducts an audit (*q.v.*). The auditors of certain businesses, *e.g.*, public companies, must be members of a body of accountants recognised as being professionally competent.

auditor's report. The opinion of the auditor on the financial statements whose accuracy he has been examining. Under the Companies Act the auditor must report on certain specific aspects of a company's financial records and statements.

authorised capital. The total amount of share capital, of all classes, which a company is authorised, by its memorandum of association, to issue. Alternative adjectives to authorised are nominal and registered.

authorised clerk. A clerk authorised to enter a stock exchange and deal on behalf of a member of the exchange.

authorised investments. Securities in which a trustee is permitted to invest the funds of a trust, either by authority of the trust instrument or the relevant Trustee Act.

automatic data processing. Data processing (*q.v.*) largely performed by automatic means.

automation. The co-ordinated automatic control of machine systems and the automatic transport, testing and treatment of materials and products throughout a sequence of operations. The term embraces automatic data processing systems used to control machine systems.

average. The apportionment of loss incurred in mercantile transactions, such as contracts of affreightment or insurance, between the person suffering the loss and other persons concerned or interested; the contribution payable by such others to the person so suffering the loss (sometimes the term is applied to the loss or damage itself).

A general average loss is one caused by or directly consequential on a general average act. There is a general average act where any extraordinary sacrifice or expenditure is deliberately and voluntarily made or incurred in time of peril to preserve the property imperilled in the common adventure. When such an act has taken place the loss must be shared by all interests which stood to lose by the danger. Thus if goods are thrown overboard in a moment of distress to preserve the ship and cargo and the ship is thereby saved, or if harbour dues and charges are incurred by a ship putting into port to shelter from a storm, the ship and cargo must stand their proportion of the loss or expenditure.

A particular average loss is a partial loss to goods in transit, caused by a peril insured against, which falls exclusively on the owner or underwriter of the insurable property, and in respect of which he has no right to recover a contribution from other persons interested in the same voyage. A particular average loss occurs where the goods or any part of them reach their destination accidentally damaged, *e.g.*, damage caused by sea water, heat from engines, failure of refrigeration plant, etc.

average cost. The product of the total cost of production incurred during a period divided by the number of units of output.

averaging. The operation of buying or selling further stock when the price of the stock has moved against the operator, to reduce the average loss upon the original bargain.

averment. An allegation in pleading. See ALLEGATION.

award. The finding or decision of an arbitrator in an arbitration. It must follow the terms of the agreement (*q.v.*), be certain, final, reasonable, legal, possible, and dispose of all the differences submitted to arbitration.

An award is final because the same questions cannot be litigated again, and if proceedings should be commenced in respect of the same dispute, the award can be pleaded as an estoppel (*q.v.*). No appeal can be made from an award to the courts as in the case of a judgment. The powers of the court in respect of an award are limited to remitting the award to the arbitrator or umpire who made it, or setting it aside altogether; there is no power to vary an award.

The award can be set aside if the procedure at the arbitration was so defective as to make the award a nullity, as where the arbitrator or umpire was unfit to conduct the proceedings; or the court may remit the award for reconsideration where some error appears which can be corrected.

A valid award can be enforced as though it were a judgment.

award, industrial. An award made in a trade dispute (*q.v.*) by the members of an industrial court, to whom the matter has been referred by the Minister of Labour under the Industrial Courts Act, 1919, as amended.

ayes. The affirmative votes: those who vote in the affirmative.

B

back dating. See ANTEDATE.

back duty. The income tax which is found to be due for past years from a taxpayer, as the result of an investigation by inspectors of taxes into his affairs, owing to there not having been full disclosure by the taxpayer of his income year by year.

back-freight. Freight for the carriage of goods returned undischarged from the port to which consigned.

backing. The underlying support for a country's note issue; which may be gold or securities. The fiduciary issue is that part of a note issue which is not backed by gold.

backwardation. A percentage paid by a seller of stock deliverable upon account day of a stock exchange, for the privilege of delaying delivery until the next account day. *Cf.* CONTANGO.

bailee. A person to whom the possession of goods is entrusted by the owner but not with the intention of transferring the ownership.

Any person is a bailee, who, otherwise than as a servant, either receives possession of a thing for another, or holds possession of a thing for another, upon an undertaking with that other, to keep and return or deliver to him the specific thing according to his directions.

A bailee has a special property or qualified ownership in the goods bailed, and may recover from a person who wrongly injures the goods the amount of the injury as damages, which (to the extent they exceed his own interest) are held by the bailee on account of the bailor.

The bailment is determined, and the right to possess the goods reverts to the bailor, if the bailee does an act entirely inconsistent with the terms of the bailment. Loss caused by an act not authorised by the terms of the bailment, though not otherwise negligent, will fall on the bailee, unless inevitable in any case. A bailee is bound to take care of the goods bailed and is liable for negligence, in general, as follows:

(1) Where the bailment is entirely for the benefit of the bailor; *e.g.*, a gratuitous deposit, the bailee is only liable for gross negligence; *i.e.*, culpable default, as in failing to take care to avoid a foreseen risk.

(2) Where the bailment is solely for the benefit of the bailee; *e.g.*, a gratuitous loan of chattels, the bailee is liable even for slight negligence, *i.e.*, the omission of the care a vigilant person takes of his own goods.

(3) Where the bailment is for the common benefit of both bailor and bailee; *e.g.*, pawn, or warehousing for hire, the bailee is bound to use ordinary care, and is liable for ordinary negligence, *i.e.*, failure to take the care which an ordinary prudent man takes of his own goods.

A bailee whose original possession was innocent, could not be convicted of larceny at common law unless and until he committed a trespass by breaking bulk. Now, by the Larceny Act, 1916, s. 1 (1), a bailee who fraudulently converts to his own use, or to the use of any person other than the owner, anything capable of being stolen which he possesses as bailee, is guilty of a felony. See BAILMENT.

bailiff. An officer of a court. His duties consist of serving and executing the process of the court. In trials by jury, he is placed in charge of the jury.

bailment. A delivery of goods on a condition, expressed or implied, that they shall be restored by the bailee to the bailor, or according to his directions, as soon as the purpose for which they are bailed shall be answered; *e.g.*, transport of goods by a carrier. See BAILEE.

bailor. One who entrusts goods to a bailee (*q.v.*). The bailor has the general property in, or ownership of, the goods bailed.

balance of payments. A country's international receipts and payments account, it shows the difference between the total payments to other countries and the total receipts from them. On it principally depends the level of a country's central reserves of gold and foreign currencies.

balance of trade. The difference between the value of imports and exports of a country with another or with all others. A " favourable " balance occurs when the value of exports exceeds that of imports. Only visible goods are involved; therefore invisible trade, such as insurance and banking, is excluded.

balance sheet. A financial statement showing, at a certain date, the sources from which an enterprise has derived its funds (liabilities) and the various ways in which those funds have been invested or applied (assets).

bale. A large package of goods, usually bound with wire or iron.

ballast. Heavy material, *e.g.*, lead, stone, etc., placed in the hold of a ship to steady it when not carrying sufficient cargo.

ballot. Voting in secret; a selection made by the drawing of lots.

Baltic Exchange. The Baltic Exchange in London is a world market for the chartering, sale and purchase of ships, and of various bulk commodities, primarily grain. There is also an air market for the chartering of aircraft.
     The Baltic Exchange originated as a coffee house, membership is by election and much of the business done is transacted by word of mouth.

banging a market. Openly offering securities at decreasing prices, with a view to lowering the prices.

bank. See BANKER; BANKING.

bank certificate. A certificate issued by a bank certifying to the balance of a particular account at a specified date.

bank charges. A charge for services rendered by a bank to the customer, and debited to his account.

bank draft. See BANKER'S DRAFT.

Bank holidays. Public holidays on which banks as well as other business establishments are closed. These are at present Easter Monday, Whit Monday, the last Monday in August and Boxing Day. In Scotland New Year's Day is a Bank holiday instead of Boxing Day, and the first Monday in May is substituted for Easter Monday. Ireland has a Bank holiday on St. Patrick's Day (March 17), and Northern Ireland on Orangeman's Day (July 12).

bank note. A bank note is a promissory note issued by a bank payable to bearer on demand. It is a negotiable instrument; it may be reissued after payment; in effect it is current money.

Bank notes for England and Wales are issued only by the Bank of England, and are legal tender for £1 and ten shillings only in Northern Ireland and Scotland.

The Bank of England has virtually the monopoly of note issue in Great Britain, but certain Scottish and Irish banks still have the power to issue notes.

Bank of England. The central bank and banker to the Government. It is a corporation established in 1694 by Royal Charter. It is the only Bank in the country whose notes are legal tender. It was nationalised in 1946 and its directors are now appointed by the Government, under whose direction it acts.

bank pass book or statement. Loose sheets issued by a bank to its customers, containing a copy of the customer's account in the bank's ledger.

bank rate. The minimum rate of interest at which the Bank of England, acting in its capacity of lender of last resort, will discount first-class bills of exchange. A change in the bank rate is usually reflected by an immediate corresponding change in all short-term rates.

banker. A person or body of persons, whether incorporated or not, which carries on the business of banking. The relationship between banker and customer is that of debtor and creditor, with a superadded obligation on the part of the banker to honour the customer's cheques if the account is in credit.

The business of banking includes receiving money on current account or on deposit; accepting bills of exchange; making, discounting, buying, selling, collecting or dealing in bills of exchange, promissory notes and drafts whether negotiable or not; buying, selling or collecting coupons; buying or selling foreign exchange by cable transfer or otherwise; issuing for subscription or purchase or underwriting the issue of loans, shares or securities; making or negotiating loans for commercial or industrial objects; or granting and issuing letters of credit and circular notes.

bankers' clearing house. See CLEARING HOUSES.

bankers' commercial credits. A method of financing international trade, whereby in short, a buyer's bank opens a credit, irrevocable for a certain time, in favour of the seller which he can draw on by presenting shipping documents.

banker's draft. A draft, payable on demand, drawn by or on behalf of a bank upon itself. It is the equivalent of a cheque, but as good as cash, as it is unthinkable that it will not be met.

banking. The business of banking in the United Kingdom has grown from deposit banking with private banks, through the formation of joint stock banks and extensive amalgamations, until today a few large commercial banks with many branches provide a wide range of services for their customers, some of which are listed under BANKER (*q.v.*). Specialist banking, *e.g.*, merchant banking and investment banking, exists alongside commercial banking to undertake business which a commercial bank does not do, *e.g.*, the provision of long-term or risk capital for industry, and to specialise in aspects of banking which the commercial banks provide as part of their overall services, *e.g.*, discounting bills of exchange.

bankrupt. A person in respect of whose estate a receiving order (*q.v.*) has been made and who is subsequently adjudicated bankrupt (Bankruptcy Act, 1914).

bankruptcy. Proceedings having for their main object the realisation of an insolvent debtor's property and its distribution among his creditors *pro rata* (Bankruptcy Act, 1914). See ACT OF BANKRUPTCY, and *infra*.

Bankruptcy Court. The courts having jurisdiction in bankruptcy are the High Court (Chancery Division) and the county courts. If a debtor has resided or carried on business for the greater part of six months preceding the petition in the London Bankruptcy District (City of London or districts comprised within the Metropolitan county courts) or for a longer time during that six months than in any other district, the petition must be presented to the High Court.

bankruptcy notice. A notice served upon a debtor by a person who has obtained against him in any court a final judgment or final order for any amount, requiring the debtor to pay the debt or to secure or compound it to the satisfaction of the creditor or the Bankruptcy Court. Noncompliance with the order within seven days if the notice is served in England, or such time as is prescribed after service if service is effected elsewhere, constitutes an act of bankruptcy. (Bankruptcy Act, 1914.)

Bar Council. The representative body of the English Bar, it has certain disciplinary powers and acts in an advisory capacity on matters affecting the profession.

bare trustee. One who holds property on trust for another, whose instructions he must obey as to the disposing of it. See CUSTODIAN TRUSTEE.

bargain. (1) An agreement between two parties settling the terms of a transaction between them. (2) A purchase or sale of stocks, shares or securities on a Stock Exchange.

bargain and sale. A contract for the sale of any estate or interest in land or chattels, followed by payment of the purchase price.

barratry. Every wrongful act wilfully committed by the master or crew of a ship to the prejudice of the owner or charterer without his knowledge or connivance, *e.g.*, sinking the ship or stealing the cargo. Barratry is one of the perils of the sea generally insured against in policies of marine insurance.

barrister. One learned in law who has been called to the Bar by a Society of one of the four Inns of Court (*q.v.*), following the passing of the required examinations. A barrister has the exclusive right of audience in the superior courts, but he may not sue for his fees, which are an *honorarium*.

barter. Exchange of one commodity for another, without the use of money or claims to money (such as credit).

base fee. A qualified or partial estate in land which ceases when the qualification ends; *e.g.*, where a tenant in tail, *i.e.*, the owner of an entailed estate, executes a disentailing deed barring his own issue from succeeding him; the base fee comes into existence, but lasts only so long as there are issue, in accordance with the entail. The base fee will be enlarged into a fee simple when the base fee and the remainder or reversion come into the same ownership. It can now only exist in equity, but in personal as well as real property.

base stock. A method of valuing stock-in-trade, which recognizes that a business must hold a certain minimum amount of stock (its base stock). The base stock is regarded virtually as a fixed asset and is valued at its original cost. It is not accepted by the Inland Revenue as a valid method of stock valuation for taxation purposes.

basic wage. The minimum wage fixed by agreement, tribunal or statute, payable to a worker by the employer for the work done, exclusive of allowances, overtime pay, etc.

basis period. The accounting period of a business ending in the year preceding the year of assessment, the profits of which are taken as the profits of the year of assessment for income tax purposes.

bear. A speculator who expects prices to fall and sells securities he does not possess, hoping that he will make a profit by subsequently re-purchasing at a lower price. See SHORT TERM GAINS.

bear account. Where there is an excess of bear sales over bull purchases on the Stock Exchange.

bearer. The person in possession of a bill of exchange or promissory note payable to bearer.

bearer debenture or bonds. Securities payable to bearer and transferable by delivery.

below par. At a price less than nominal or face value; at a discount. See ABOVE PAR.

beneficial interest. The interest of a person entitled to the advantages or benefit derived from property as contrasted with the interest of a nominal or legal owner; the interest of a person in whose favour a trust is created; *i.e.*, an equitable interest.

beneficial owner. The person who enjoys or who is entitled to the benefit of property; a beneficiary (*q.v.*).

beneficial ownership. The equitable right of ownership of property which is vested in trustees on behalf of the beneficiaries under the trust.

beneficiary. The beneficial owner of property; the person for whose benefit property is held by trustees.

bequest. A gift of personal property by will. A residuary bequest is a gift of the residue of the testator's personal estate. A specific bequest is a bequest of a particular item of personal property, *e.g.*, a Bentley car.

berth. (1) A place for sleeping on board a ship, train or aircraft. (2) A place where a vessel loads or unloads cargo.

betterment. Improvement to real property, or the increase in value of real property, owing to local public works.

betting. A form of wager under which money is payable on the result of some uncertain event; *e.g.*, a horse race; bets are laid or staked at odds by one party and taken by the other.

The provision of betting facilities on dog racing tracks is dealt with in the Dog Racing (Betting Days) Act, 1963.

betting shops. Licensed premises to which persons may resort for the purpose of betting with the holder of the licence, or his agent or servant. Licences may be granted by the local justices to holders of bookmakers' permits (Betting, Gaming and Lotteries Act, 1963).

bi-annual. Half-yearly.

bid. An offer to buy at a given or stated price a thing which is being sold by auction (*q.v.*).

biennial. Taking place once every two years.

bilateral monopoly. The market situation in which a single seller confronts a single buyer, *e.g.*, an employers' association dealing with a trade union.

bill. Primarily a letter or writing; *e.g.*, a bill of exchange (*q.v.*): an account for payment.

bill broker. A person who is engaged in the purchase and sale of bills of exchange; he operates in discount business on the London money market.

bill discounted. A bill of exchange, upon which a banker or other person has advanced money for a percentage called discount. The person for whom the bill is discounted remains liable until the bill is paid, though the discounter looks of course to the acceptor or maker in the first instance.

bill of costs. A statement or account delivered by a solicitor to his client setting out in detail the work done on behalf of the client, and showing the amount charged for each item, including disbursements. See also TAXATION OF COSTS.

bill of entry. An account of the goods entered at the Customs House, both inwards and outwards, showing the name of the importer or exporter, the quantity and prices of merchandise and whither or whence transported.

bill of exchange. An unconditional order in writing, addressed by one person to another, signed by the person giving it, requiring the person to whom it is addressed to pay on demand or at a fixed or determinable future time, a sum certain in money, to, or to the order of, a specified person, or to bearer. A bill of exchange is a negotiable instrument.

A bill is given by the drawer, and addressed to the drawee, who becomes the acceptor by writing his name across the face of the bill. The bill is payable to the payee, who must be named or indicated with reasonable certainty. If the payee is a fictitious or non-existent person the bill may be treated as payable to bearer. The law was codified in the Bills of Exchange Act, 1882. See also BILL PAYABLE, BILL RECEIVABLE.

bill of health. A document given to the master of a ship inward bound describing the sanitary state of the port and vicinity from which he comes, including every overseas port of call on the voyage, and of the vessel, passengers and crew while at the port.

An outward bill of health is issued on application by the master or owner or agents of any vessel visiting the port, by a quarantine or other authorised officer. See QUARANTINE.

bill of lading. A document signed and delivered by the master (or his agent) of a ship to the shipper of goods being shipped. It specifies the name of the master, the port and destination of the ship, the goods, the consignee, and the rate of freight. One copy of the bill of lading is usually sent to the merchant's agent or to the person to whom the goods are to be delivered, another goes with the goods and another is kept by the merchant. The bill must be produced to the ship's agent before the delivery of the goods can be obtained. In the case of a draft or cash against documents, when the goods would be consigned to the order of the shipper's agent (usually a bank), the consignee will not be able to obtain the bill of lading until the draft is accepted or cash paid. A person consigning goods to his own order would indorse the bills of lading before posting them to his agent. A bill of lading is not a negotiable instrument, but it does possess a certain similarity to a negotiable instrument in so far as if it is drawn "to the order" or "to assigns" of the person named: it may be indorsed and transferred by delivery. A bona fide transfer will defeat the right of stoppage *in transitu* of an unpaid seller.

bill of sale. In general, an instrument whereby personal chattels are conditionally assigned by one person (the mortgagor or grantor) to another (the mortgagee or grantee) as security for a loan made by the latter to the former, or for money owing by the former to the latter. A bill of sale in this sense usually provides that upon the payment of the amount outstanding and the observance by the debtor of all conditions and covenants contained in such instrument, the property in the goods will be re-transferred to the original owner.

Bills of sale include assignments, transfers, declarations of trust without transfer, inventories of goods with receipt attached thereto or receipts for purchase money of goods and other assurances of personal chattels and also powers of attorney and authorities to take possession of personal chattels as security for a debt (Bills of Sale Act, 1878, s. 4).

bill of sale, absolute. A document whereby the property in personal chattels is absolutely and unconditionally assigned to the creditor.

bill of sale (shipping). A sale of a ship or share therein is effected by a bill of sale in the prescribed form, which must contain a description of the ship sufficient to identify her.

bill of sight. The customs entry made by an importer who is unaware of the particulars of the goods, which are ascertained by the customs officer, thus enabling the importer to make a perfect customs entry of them.

bill payable. A bill of exchange drawn on a drawee and accepted by him.

bill rate. The rate of discount on bills of exchange; it varies with the current short-term borrowing rate of interest and the quality of the bill being discounted.

bill receivable. A bill of exchange remitted to a trader in payment for value received, or drawn by a trader upon his customer. In the accounts of a bank, " Bills receivable and other Advances," means bills discounted for customers and other advances to customers.

bi-metallism. A system of currency based upon a double standard (*e.g.*, gold and silver) as distinguished from a system based upon a single standard (mono-metallism).

binary number. The representation of a number in binary notation, *i.e.*, 0 or 1. This representation is widely used in digital computers, its advantage being that numbers can be expressed in terms of only two alternative choices or conditions.

binding over. (1) Requiring a person to enter into a recognisance to perform some necessary act; *e.g.*, to prosecute, or to give evidence.

(2) The making of an order by the court discharging an offender conditionally on his entering into a recognisance to be of good behaviour and to appear for sentence when called upon. See RECOGNISANCE.

black, declare. To boycott. See BOYCOTTING.

black list. A list of names of persons or concerns with whom business dealings are undesirable, or not to be had.

black marketing. Dealing (buying or selling) in goods or services at a greater price than that fixed by regulation, or unauthorised dealing in prohibited or rationed goods.

blank, acceptance in. An acceptance written before a bill is completed. Where delivered by the acceptor, it is an authority to fill up the paper as a complete bill for any amount which the stamp duty thereon will cover.

blank cheque. A cheque which the drawer has signed but on which the amount has been left blank.

blank, indorsement. An indorsement in blank specifies no indorsee, and a bill so indorsed becomes payable to bearer. When a bill has been indorsed in blank, any holder may convert the blank indorsement into special indorsement, by writing above the indorser's signature a direction to pay the bill to the order of himself or some other person.

blank transfer. A transfer of shares which is executed without the name of the transferee being filled in. Such a transfer, with the certificate of the shares, is frequently lodged as security for money, the intention being that the purchaser or mortgagee may later on fill in the blank and perfect his security by getting himself registered, if necessary.

The circulation of blank transfers is prohibited by the Finance Act, 1963.

blasphemy. The offence of publishing by speech or in writing any contemptuous or irreverent words vilifying or ridiculing God, Jesus Christ, the Holy Ghost, the Testaments or Christianity, with intent to shock or insult believers, or to pervert or mislead the ignorant and unwary. If, however, the decencies of controversy are observed, one may attack the fundamentals of any religion.

blending. A mixing or combining together of certain quantities and grades of a product (such as tea or whisky) in order to obtain a product of a specified quality.

blockade. An act of war carried out by a belligerent detailing warships and/or aircraft to prevent access to or departure from a defined part of the enemy's coast.

In modern times, blockade is maintained at a distance by the searching of all ships for contraband destined for the enemy.

block offer. The offer for sale over a short period of a large number (block) of units by a unit trust. It is used to launch units for the first time and to draw the public's attention to units which are already on offer.

blue chip. An industrial share of the highest class. The term, however, is too uncertain for the courts to give effect to it.

board. A body of persons to whom collectively powers of control or government are committed or delegated; e.g., the directors of a company; the Board of Inland Revenue. See COMMISSIONERS OF INLAND REVENUE.

board meeting. A meeting of the directors of a company as prescribed by the articles of association of a company.

board of referees. A body of persons to whom a dispute is referred for decision, e.g., the Board of Referees appointed by the Treasury for, inter alia, hearing appeals against surtax directions made by the Special Commissioners against companies.

board of trade. The department of Government whose responsibility is matters concerning the internal and external trade and commerce of Britain.

bona fide. In good faith, honestly, without fraud, collusion or participation in wrong-doing; hence genuine.

bona vacantia. Goods without an apparent owner in which no one claims a property, such as lost property, shipwrecks, treasure trove, or the personal property of an intestate without next-of-kin.

The finder of lost property is *prima facie* entitled to it, but, in general, *bona vacantia* belongs to the Crown in right of its prerogative.

33

The property of a dissolved company is, subject to an order of the court, to be deemed *bona vacantia*, subject to the power of the Crown to disclaim.

bond. A promise under seal to pay a sum of money with a condition added that if the person who binds himself does or forbears from doing some act the obligation shall be void, *e.g.*, a bond to be of good behaviour; a bond properly to administer a deceased's estate.

bond warrant. A document issued by the proprietor of a bonded store entitling the holder upon giving up the warrant to receive the goods specified therein.

bond washing. A colloquialism for the activity of selling securities, usually carrying a fixed rate of interest, cum-dividend and re-purchasing them ex-dividend in order to secure a tax advantage. Taxation legislation has been introduced, which is aimed at eliminating this form of tax avoidance.

bonded goods. Dutiable goods in respect of which a bond for the payment of the duty has been given to the Customs. Duty is payable on the clearance of goods in bond for home consumption, but the goods may be re-exported to another country from bond without the payment of duty.

bonded warehouse. A secure place approved by the Customs and Excise Commissioners for the deposit of dutiable goods upon which duty has not been paid. See BONDED GOODS.

bonus. A gift above that which is due; *e.g.*, a sum paid to employees of a business in respect of a profitable year's working.

In Life Assurance, it refers to the amount of the company's profits added to the policy after an actuarial valuation of the whole of the policies in force. It may be a " cash bonus," payable immediately, or a " reversionary bonus," which is added to the value of the policy, and payable at maturity of the policy or death of the life assured.

bonus shares or debentures. The shares or debentures which are issued by a company pursuant to a capitalisation of reserves.

book debts. Amounts showing in a trader's books as due to him.

book value. Items in a balance sheet are usually included at the value at which they originally came into the books (book value), instead of at their realisable or replacement cost.

bookkeeping. The process of recording in books or other suitable medium (*e.g.*, cards), the financial transactions of an accounting entity.

bookmaker. One who carries on the business of receiving or negotiating bets. A person acting as bookmaker on his own account must hold a bookmakers' permit. See BETTING; BETTING SHOPS.

books of account. Any bookkeeping (*q.v.*) record constituting part of an accounting system.

boom. See TRADE CYCLE.

34

boom market. A market in which buying demand greatly exceeds selling pressure. In these circumstances prices rise.

borrowing powers. A trading company has implied powers to borrow, but not before the company is entitled to commence business. Normally the directors exercise the company's borrowing powers and issue debentures in the name of the company accordingly. The extent of the borrowing powers is usually laid down in a company's Articles of Association.

bottomry bond. A bond entered into by the owner of a ship or his agent, whereby, in consideration of a sum of money advanced for the purposes of the ship, the borrower undertakes to repay the same with interest if the ship terminates her voyage successfully, the debt being lost in case of the non-arrival of the ship. It binds or hypothecates either the ship, the freight or the cargo, or all of them. See HYPOTHECATION.

bought and sold notes. Documents delivered by brokers to their principals on the conclusion of a contract of sale and purchase, the bought note being delivered to the buyer, and the sold note to the seller. The notes should contain the names of both the contracting parties, the quantity of the article bought and sold, and the price if agreed upon. They constitute the contract between the parties.

bounty. A subsidy paid by a government on exports, imports, or products with a view to establishing some new industry or fostering some particular trade.

boycotting. The concerted refusal of a number of persons to have any dealings with another person. It frequently takes the form of a refusal to supply a particular class of goods or services to the person boycotted. See BLACK LIST.

brand. A distinctive sign (*e.g.*, a letter, numeral or diagram) made upon property such as stock, cases, casks or other goods to indicate ownership and/or the quantity or quality of the contents.

breach of contract. The breaking of the obligation which a contract imposes. A total breach is the total failure of one party to comply with the obligations imposed by the contract. The injured party may have the right to treat the contract as discharged and refuse to perform his part. He may sue for damages, or for an amount equivalent to the value of labour performed or goods supplied, or in certain cases, specific performance (*q.v.*), or an injunction (*q.v.*) may be decreed.

The breach of part of the contract may permit the injured party to rescind the whole contract, or merely afford him the right of bringing an action for damages. The failure to perform may go right to the root of the contract (breach of condition) or may only affect a less important term of the contract (breach of warranty). Where there is a breach of condition the injured party may exercise any of the remedies available in a total breach; where there is a breach of warranty, the injured party may sue for damages.

breach of the peace. An offence against public order such as riots, unlawful assemblies. See BINDING OVER.

breach of trust. An improper act, neglect or default on the part of a trustee in regard to his trust, either in disregard of the terms of the trust, or the rules of equity. The measure of the trustee's liability is the loss caused thereby to the trust estate.

break-even point. That level of output at which total revenue is equal to total costs, *i.e.*, at which neither profit nor loss on operations results. See SELLING COSTS.

breaking bulk. The taking by a bailee of things from a package entrusted to him, or otherwise separating some part of the goods from the rest; *e.g.*, if a carrier broached a cask and drank part of its contents.

break-up value. The value of an asset at its price when sold as scrap, *e.g.*, an out-of-date machine may be sold for the value as scrap metal of its component parts.

The break-up value of a business is the value realised by selling off its assets *in specie*, as opposed to selling the business as a going concern, including its goodwill.

brief. A document containing a statement of facts, copies of pleadings, affidavits, correspondence, etc., furnished by an instructing solicitor to a barrister to enable him to represent the client in legal proceedings. It constitutes the authority to the barrister to appear.

British Commonwealth of Nations. The Commonwealth is a free association of sovereign independent states. It has no written constitution but its members are bound together by a community of ideas and interests which spring from a common historical background and political heritage. For the most part they have certain constitutional features in common, as parliamentary democracies. At the head of the Commonwealth countries, except the Republics, and Malaysia, is the Queen who is locally represented by a Governor-General. The Republics with Presidents at their head, and Malaysia, do not owe allegiance to the Crown, but look to the Queen as the symbol of the free association of the member nations of the Commonwealth.

British Institute of Management. A body formed to promote education in management studies in Great Britain.

British ship. A ship owned by natural-born or naturalised British subjects or by corporations incorporated under British laws. See also SHIP.

British Standards Institution was founded in 1901, and incorporated by Royal Charter in 1929. It is the recognised organisation for preparing and publishing voluntary national standards for industrial and consumer products, and also for activities such as indexing.

British subject. A person of British nationality. Every person who is a citizen of the United Kingdom or colonies, or a citizen of one of the Commonwealth countries has the status of " British subject." The expression " British subject " and " Commonwealth citizen " have the same meaning. Provision, however, is made for persons who are British subjects without citizenship, and for British subjects who become naturalised in a foreign state. The latter do not automatically cease to be British subjects. (British Nationality Acts, 1948, 1958.) See also NATIONALITY.

British Transport Commission. The authority which was formed to administer the transport system of the country which was brought under state control on January 1, 1948. Nationalised undertakings included the railways, railway owned canals and docks and certain other waterway systems, and long distance road haulage concerns.

Under the Transport Act, 1962, the Commission ceased to exist and was replaced by the British Railways Board, London Transport Board, British Transport Docks Board, British Waterways Board, and the Transport Holding Company.

broker. A mercantile agent who buys and sells goods for his principal, without being entrusted either with the possession or control of the goods or of their documents of title. He has no property in the goods which he buys or sells, and therefore no lien. He brings the parties together, and when a contract is concluded, he takes his commission and drops out of the transaction. A broker is not in general personally liable on a contract in the absence of custom or usage to the contrary, unless he signs a written memorandum in his own name; nor can he sue in his own name on the contract. See also AGENT; INSURANCE BROKER; STOCKBROKER.

brokerage. The commission charged by a broker to his client for the negotiation of a transaction.

bucket shop. The business of providing means for speculation in stock, shares, etc., carried on by an " outside broker," *i.e.*, a broker who is not a member of a recognised stock exchange, etc., and who is not therefore subject to the rules and regulations of such a body.

budget. A forecast of future revenue and expenditure over a defined period. Budgets are used by business and government as a basis for economic and financial decision. They are also used as a measure of performance, by comparing budgeted with actual results. This latter process is known as budgetary control.

building lease. A lease of land for a term at a ground rent, with a covenant by the lessee to erect buildings thereon.

building society. A society established for the purpose of raising deposits at interest from the public, which it uses to make advances at interest on mortgage of property. To the depositor building societies represent a safe medium for the investment of savings at a fixed rate of interest; to those who obtain advances (mortgagors) they represent the most important source of credit for those who wish to buy their own houses. Various Building Society Acts regulate the formation and activities of such societies, which are controlled by the Registrar of Building Societies.

bulk buying. Buying goods in large quantities.

bull. A Stock Exchange term for a speculator who buys securities with a view to a quick resale at a higher price.

bullion. Bulk gold or silver as opposed to relatively small value coin. Gold bullion in the U.K. takes the form of 400-oz. bars. The reserves backing a country's currency are held partly in bullion.

business. A wider term than trade. It includes a trade profession or employment and any activity carried on by a body of persons, whether corporate or unincorporate, *e.g.*, farming, which is not usually classified as a trade.

business cycle. An American term for the trade cycle (*q.v.*).

business day. In general all days are business days except for Sundays, bank and religious holidays.

business name. See FIRM NAME.

by-product. A product made from the residue of the material remaining after a manufacturing process.

C

C.I.F., or C.F.I. (Cost, insurance, freight.) A C.I.F. contract is a contract for the sale of goods where the seller's duties are:
(1) to ship at the port of shipment, within the time named in the contract, goods of the contract description;
(2) to procure on shipment a contract of affreightment under which the goods will be delivered at the destination contemplated by the contract;
(3) to effect, upon the terms current in the trade, an insurance of the goods which will be available for the benefit of the buyer;
(4) to make out an invoice of the goods;
(5) to tender to the buyer the bill of lading, the invoice and the policy of insurance.
It is the duty of the buyer to take up these documents and pay for the goods. See F.O.B.

calculating machine. A general description of machines which can complete the basic arithmetical functions of multiplication and division, plus usually, addition and subtraction. The process may be mechanical or electronic.

calendar month. A period of time consisting of 30 days in April, June, September and November, and of 31 days in the remaining months except February, which consists of 28 (and in leap-year) 29 days. See also MONTH.

call. A demand upon the holder of partly paid-up shares in a company for payment of the balance, or an instalment of it. Calls are rarely used, but payment by fixed instalments of the issue price of share or loan capital occurs frequently.

38

call option. A Stock Exchange term for the right to buy a certain security during a specified period at the price ruling at the time the bargain is struck. *Cf.* PUT OPTION.

capacity. The maximum output that a business or industry is capable of producing at a given time within its existing framework.

capital. In a general sense, capital is accumulated wealth used in producing more. One of the factors of production in economics; it is the accumulation, for either a person, a firm or the community, of income-producing commodities, equipment, buildings and the like.

In regard to companies, capital is of the following descriptions:

(1) Authorised, nominal or registered capital. The capital as stated in the memorandum of association; it is the total amount that may be offered for subscription.

(2) Issued capital. The nominal value of the shares of the company which have been actually allotted. It usually includes both the shares issued other than for cash and shares issued for cash. Shares are issued otherwise than for cash mostly as consideration for the acquisition of assets or for services rendered.

(3) Uncalled capital. That portion of the nominal value of the shares actually issued which has not yet been called up.

(4) Called-up capital. That portion of the issued capital which has been called up, or, in the case of shares issued for a consideration other than cash, deemed to have been called up.

(5) Paid-up capital. The amount of money that has been paid or deemed to have been paid on shares actually allotted. See also CAPITAL RESERVE; CAPITAL, WORKING.

capital allowances. Tax allowances granted against business profits on certain capital assets in order to give relief for depreciation on those assets.

capital assets. See ASSETS.

capital expenditure. Expenditure from which benefits may be expected over a relatively long period; expenditure on capital or fixed assets. Contrast " revenue " expenditure in which the benefits are expected to be derived within a relatively short period, usually within the same accounting period.

capital gain. Upon the sale of an asset at a price higher than that paid for it a capital gain is realised. Upon realisation of a capital gain, tax is usually payable by either an individual or a company, but there are certain important exceptions. (Finance Act, 1965).

Capital Issues Committee. A Committee set up to advise the Treasury on applications for new capital issues, under the Borrowing (Control and Guarantees) Act, 1946. Most controls ended in 1958.

capital reserve. Any reserve which is not free for distribution through the Profit and Loss account.

capital, working. Excess of current assets over current liabilities (*q.v.*).

capitalised value. The capital value of an asset based on its current earning power in relation to the expected rate of return from that type of asset. Thus the capital value of an asset earning £300 on which the expected return is 10% would be £3,000.

carat. (1) The twenty-fourth part of pure gold. So many " carats " means that so many parts out of twenty-four are pure gold and the rest alloy, *e.g.*, 9 carat.

(2) A measure of weight used for diamonds.

cargo. Goods shipped for carriage.

carrier. One who has received goods for the purpose of carrying them from one place to another for hire, either under a special contract, *i.e.*, as a bailee for reward, or as a common carrier.

carrier, common. One who undertakes to transport from place to place for hire the goods of such persons as may choose to employ him. Such transport undertakings are obliged to carry the goods (except dangerous articles) of any person who offers to pay his hire.

carrying over. An arrangement by which the parties to a Stock Exchange bargain continue the transaction into the next account. The process involves such charges as contango and backwardation.

cartel. (1) A cartel consists of a number of private independent entrepreneurs who voluntarily agree to co-ordinate their policy in order to affect the market of a commodity to a significant extent.

(2) An agreement between States as to the exchange of prisoners during war.

cash. Strictly currency, although frequently the term is used to include cheques.

cash against documents. Amount invoiced to be paid on presentation of bill of lading.

cash basis of accounting. A method of accounting by which revenue in terms of actual cash received is matched against expenditure in terms of actual cash payments, no account being taken of amounts collectable or payable at the beginning and end of the accounting period. It is a crude and inaccurate method of preparing financial accounts. It is not widely used and will not be accepted by the Inland Revenue as a valid method of preparing the accounts of new businesses, except in special circumstances.

cash book. A book of prime entry for cash transactions. It usually records transactions which pass through the bank account(s), pure cash (currency) transactions being recorded in a separate petty cash book.

cash discount. See DISCOUNT.

cash on delivery; C.O.D. A sale C.O.D. is one upon condition that cash shall be paid on delivery of the goods.

cash order. An order issued by a concern enabling the holder to obtain goods from a retailer. The concern issuing the order agrees to pay the retailer on demand for goods so purchased and the holder to make payment to the issuer by instalments.

cash ratio. The relation between a bank's reserve of cash and its total deposits. The English commercial banks maintain a cash ratio of approximately 8% at the present time.

casting vote. The extra and deciding vote which a chairman may be empowered to give when there is an equality of votes, if the articles, rules or regulations, so provide.

cause of action. The fact (or combination of facts) which gives rise to a right of action.

caveat. [A warning.] A notice given by the party interested (caveator) to the proper officer of a court of justice to prevent the taking of a certain step without warning. It may be entered in connection with dealings in land registered in the Land Registry, with the grant of marriage licences, to stay the probate of a will or letters of administration, etc.

caveat emptor. [Let the buyer beware.] There is no duty on a seller to disclose to the buyer material facts which he knows will influence him in coming to a decision. Even if he knows that the buyer is ignorant of, or under some misapprehension as to an important fact, he is under no duty to enlighten him. In general there is no implied warranty or condition as to the quality or fitness for any particular purpose of goods under a contract of sale. But this rule has been greatly modified by the Sale of Goods Act, 1893. See SALE OF GOODS.

caveator. A person who enters a caveat.

cede. To yield, hence to assign or to transfer.

ceiling prices. The maximum price at which specified goods, shares, etc., and other items may be bought or sold.

census. An official counting, especially of population, from which various statistics are prepared.

census of production. The Board of Trade is required to make a survey of industrial production each year and returns are required from persons carrying on undertakings within the field of this survey. (Statistics of Trade Act, 1947.)

central bank. The banker to the government and the other banks. In general, it does not enter into competition with the other banks. It is usually in a position to affect the rate of interest and the volume of credit, which are the principal methods of control for the government's monetary policy, for the administration of which the central bank is usually responsible. See BANK OF ENGLAND.

central processor. That part of a computer system which incorporates the units of control, calculation and main storage.

certificate of incorporation. The certificate issued by the Registrar of Companies showing that a company is duly incorporated. See also CERTIFICATE, TRADING.

certificate of origin. Certificates vouching for the country of origin of goods imported from abroad.

certificate of shares. A certificate under the common seal of a company specifying the shares or stock held by a member of the company. It is prima facie evidence of his title. See also SHARE CERTIFICATE.

certificate, trading. A public company, after incorporation, cannot commence its business operations or exercise any borrowing powers until there has been issued to it a certificate entitling it to commence business. Before this certificate can be issued, the prospectus or statement in lieu thereof must be filed with the Registrar, and a statutory declaration must be filed.

certified copy. A copy of a document, signed and certified as a true copy of the original by authorised persons who have examined it with such original.

certiorari. [To be more fully informed of.] The order directed by a superior court to an inferior judicial tribunal whereby proceedings are removed into the superior court so that justice may be done.

cesser. Determination or ending of; *e.g.*, a term, annuity, etc.

cestui que trust. A beneficiary (*q.v.*).

chain stores. A group of retail stores engaged in the same type of business, and in common ownership.

chairman. The person who presides at a meeting. A lady is referred to as " Madam Chairman."

chamber of commerce. An organisation of business men formed generally to promote and protect internal and external trade, commerce and shipping, to undertake settlement by arbitration of trade disputes and promote commercial education.

champerty. The rendering by a third person (including a solicitor) of assistance to a litigant who has agreed to share with him the profit of such litigation. See MAINTENANCE.

Change. Formerly a place where merchants met to transact business, now replaced by Exchange.

change of voyage. See DEVIATION.

charge. In property law, a charge is a form of security, for the payment of a debt or performance of an obligation, consisting of the right of a creditor to receive payment out of some specific fund or out of the proceeds of the realisation of specific property. The fund or property is said to be charged with the debt thus payable out of it. Similarly, a testator may indicate that a certain part of his estate is to provide for a particular gift. That part of the estate is then said to be charged with the gift; *e.g.*, an annuity.

In criminal law, a charge is an accusation of the commission of an offence or crime.

In bookkeeping, an account which is debited is said to be charged.

charging order. An order made in favour of a judgment creditor that stock or shares in a public company or bank deposit standing in the name of the judgment debtor or held in trust for him shall stand charged with the payment of the judgment debt. It prevents the transfer of the stock, etc., and entitles the judgment creditor to all the remedies to which he would have been entitled as if the judgment debtor had made such a charge in his favour.

charity. The word in its legal sense comprises four principal divisions: trusts for the relief of poverty; trusts for the advancement of education; trusts for the advancement of religion and trusts for other purposes beneficial to the community not falling under any of the preceding heads. Charities are given certain privileges; *e.g.*, exemption from income tax; exemption from payment of death duties on gifts by will; the rule against perpetuities does not operate where property is to pass from one charity to another, etc.

The Charities Act, 1960, provides for the registration of charities—and an institution is presumed to be a charity while on the register.

Charity Commissioners. These Commissioners exercise powers of management and control over charities, so as best to promote and make effective their work (Charities Act, 1960).

charter. A grant from the Crown to a corporation or society conferring special privileges, powers, etc.; *e.g.*, The Institute of Chartered Accountants in England and Wales.

chartered company. A company incorporated by the Crown by Royal Charter, which prescribes its powers.

charterer. A person who hires or charters a ship for a voyage or a certain period.

charterparty. A written agreement by which a shipowner lets an entire ship, or a part of it, to the charterer for the conveyance of goods, binding himself to transport them to a particular place for a sum of money which the charterer undertakes to pay as freight for their carriage. The principal stipulations refer to the places of loading and delivery, the mode and time of paying the freight, the number of laying days (that is, the time allowed for loading and unloading), and the rate of demurrage (*q.v.*).

The charterparty may operate as a demise or lease of the ship itself with or without the services of the master and crew. The charterer then becomes for the time the owner of the vessel, and the master and crew become his agents or servants. The test is: Has the owner parted for the time with the whole possession and control of the ship?

chattels. Any property other than freehold land. Leasehold and other interests in land less than freehold are termed " chattels real," as they savour of realty. Chattels personal are movable, tangible articles of property.

cheap money. When money can be borrowed at a low rate of interest in the money market. Bank rate and other rates of interest must be low for a cheap money policy to be practicable.

cheque. A bill of exchange (*q.v.*) drawn on a banker, payable on demand. It is a mandate by a customer to his banker to pay the amount of the cheque according to its tenor. The person making the cheque is called the drawer, and the person to whom it is payable is called the payee.

A cheque drawn to bearer is payable to the person holding it. The wording " or Bearer " after the name of the payee is sufficient.

A cheque having the words " or Order " printed or written upon its face formerly had always to be indorsed by the named payee before payment could be obtained. The Cheques Act, 1957, however, abolished the necessity of indorsing a cheque if the customer pays it in to his own account. But indorsement is still necessary if it is desired to negotiate the cheque.

The duty and authority of a banker to pay a cheque drawn on him by his customer are ended by:

(1) the receipt of a countermand of payment; (2) notice of the customer's death, bankruptcy or lunacy; (3) notice of liquidation where the customer is a company; or on receipt of instructions by a receiver; (4) receipt of a garnishee order covering the customer's account. See CROSSED CHEQUE.

choses in action. Proprietary rights in personalty enforceable by action (as opposed to choses in possession). Such as a right of action for detention of a particular object, a debt, a claim for damages for tort or for breach of contract. In the broader sense the term is sometimes used to embrace all forms of personal property of a non-tangible nature, *e.g.*, shares, patents. See ASSIGNMENT.

cipher. A secret writing; anything so written.

circa. [About]. Prefixed to a date to indicate approximation.

circuits. Divisions of England and Wales, appointed for the judges to go to administer justice in the several counties comprised in the respective circuits. At present they are the Northern Circuit; the North Eastern Circuit; the Midland Circuit; the South Eastern or Home Circuit; the Oxford Circuit; the Western Circuit; and the Wales and Chester Circuit.

circular notes. See LETTER OF CREDIT—CIRCULAR.

circulating assets. See ASSETS.

citation. (1) Quotation of law cases or statutes as authority for a proposition used in argument.

(2) The operation of calling upon a person who, usually, is a party to an action or proceeding to appear before a court in that action or proceeding, including a divorce petition.

civil servant. A servant of the Crown; a member of the staff of a Government Department, paid out of moneys voted by Parliament, and under the control of the Treasury; as contrasted with members of the armed forces.

class gift. A gift in a will to a number of persons collectively under a general description; *e.g.*, " to such of my children as survive me."

44

class resolution. A resolution passed by a special class of shareholders in accordance with their rights under the articles of association, *e.g.* preference shareholders.

classical economists. The English writers on political economy of the end of the eighteenth and early nineteenth centuries: *viz.*, Adam Smith, Malthus, Ricardo and others.

clear. (1) To pass a cheque through the clearing house (*q.v.*).
(2) To free goods from the control of the Customs, by entering them at the Customs, and paying Customs duties.

clear days. Where anything is to be done, *e.g.*, three clear days before a certain date, it means that three complete days are to elapse between the doing of the thing and the date named; whereas, if a thing is to be done three days before a certain date only two complete days need elapse between the doing of the thing and that date. But where an order directs anything to be done within ten clear days, it means that such thing is to be done at latest on the tenth of the ten complete days after the order is made.

clearance. A certificate issued by the Customs to the effect that a ship has complied with Customs requirements and is at liberty to put to sea.

clearing houses. Institutions maintained by the commercial banks, in London and the provinces, for the purpose of facilitating the settlement between themselves of cheques, bills or notes. The settlement of the balances is by cheques drawn on the Bank of England.
The clearing banks are Barclays, Coutts & Co., District, Glyn Mills & Co., Lloyds, Martins, Midland, National, National Provincial, Westminster, Williams Deacon's.

clerical error. A mistake in writing made inadvertently. Executed documents and wills containing them may be rectified by the Court.

clerical work. Writing, book-keeping, sorting papers, filing, typing, duplicating, machine calculating, drawing and the editorial preparation of matter for publication. See also EMPLOYMENT.

client. In general, the customer of a professional man; in particular, any person who retains or employs a solicitor.

clientele. The body of clients or customers.

close company. A term introduced into legal and commercial usage in the U.K. by the Finance Act, 1965. It is used of a company, the majority of the shares of which are held by a small group of people, such as a family. A large majority of private companies come within the definition.

closed shop. Works or offices where only members of the appropriate union(s) are permitted to work. The employers agree not to employ non-union labour.

closure. The closure is a motion (*q.v.*) employed at a meeting to terminate debate and bring a matter to the vote. Its object is to prevent undue obstruction.

club. An association of persons for social, literary, sporting or gambling purposes. It is not a legal entity. Its internal affairs are regulated by its rules on the basis of which its members contract with one another. The club as such cannot be made legally responsible to strangers, but its members may be, if so provided. Normally it is the officers or committee who incur liability.

code. (1) A system of letters, figures or word-groups with arbitrary meanings. Used in telegrams, cables, etc., to ensure secrecy and economy in business transactions. See also CODIFICATION.

(2) In computer usage code is a machine language on the basis of which the machine works and into which instructions and data have to be translated.

codicil. An instrument executed by a testator (*q.v.*) for adding to, altering, explaining or confirming a will previously made by him. It becomes part of the will, and must be executed with the same formalities as a will. The effect of a codicil is to bring the will down to the date of the codicil, and thereby to make the same disposition of the testator's estate as if the testator had at that date made a new will, with the original dispositions as altered by the codicil.

codification. The process of converting the law of a country, or a portion of it, into a code, whether that law consists of statutes or case-law or customs or all three. In English law codification has been applied only to particular branches of law, *e.g.*, Bills of Exchange Act, 1882. See also CONSOLIDATION.

coding. Under the P.A.Y.E. system of collecting income tax from individuals code numbers are given to employees by the tax authorities based on the tax allowances available to that person. An employee's coding determines the amount of tax to be deducted from pay.

cognate. Of the same nature; derived from the same ancestor.

coin. Pieces of metal issued by the authority of a government to serve as a medium of exchange; currency.

coinage standards. Standards of weight of each coin of the realm are maintained by the Board of Trade. (Weights and Measures Act, 1963).

collateral consanguinity. The relationship between persons (collateral relations) who are descended from the same ancestor (*e.g.*, brothers, cousins, etc.); as opposed to lineal consanguinity, which exists between persons of whom one is descended from the other (father and son, grandfather and grandson, etc.). The latter persons are referred to as lineal ancestors or lineal descendants as the case may be.

collateral security. Security which is given in addition to the principal security. Thus a person who borrows money on mortgage (the principal security) may deposit shares with the lender as collateral security. See SECONDARY SECURITY.

collective bargaining. A method of fixing the terms and conditions of employment by means of bargaining between representatives of an organised body of employees and an association of employers.

collusion. The agreement between persons, apparently in a hostile position or having conflicting interests, to do some act in conjunction, in order to injure another or deceive a court; especially, in the latter case, in divorce proceedings: but see the Matrimonial Causes Act, 1965.

Command papers. A series of papers presented to Parliament from time to time by command of the Crown.

commencement of business. See CERTIFICATE, TRADING.

commerce. Fundamentally, the exchange of goods for money or other goods, *i.e.*, trade, and all services which assist the carrying on of trade; trading, whether home or foreign. See also LAW MERCHANT; MERCANTILE LAW.

commercial causes. Causes (or cases) arising out of the transactions of merchants and traders; amongst others those relating to the construction of mercantile documents, export or import of merchandise, affreightment, insurance, banking and mercantile agency and mercantile usages.

commercial court. The court of the Queen's Bench Division presided over by a single judge for the hearing of commercial causes (*q.v.*).

commission. (1) An order or authority conferred on a person or body of persons to do an act or exercise powers; *e.g.*, an officer in the armed forces.

(2) The body charged with a commission from the Crown; *e.g.*, the National Parks Commission.

(3) The usual remuneration of an agent.

(4) An authority, being an order issued by a court, to examine parties or witnesses, who, owing to absence abroad, or to illness, cannot be present at the hearing.

Commissioners of Customs and Excise. The persons collectively appointed by Letters Patent charged with the duty of managing the revenue of customs and excise, and also purchase tax and protective duties.

Commissioners of Inland Revenue. The heads of the Inland Revenue Department, one of whom is chairman, responsible for the care and management of income tax, surtax, etc. They act as a Board.

committee. (1) A person or persons to whom has been committed or delegated a particular duty; (2) a body of persons selected to perform certain duties.

committee of inspection. A committee appointed by the creditors of a bankrupt from among themselves to superintend the administration of the bankrupt's property. A committee of inspection may also be appointed in the winding up of a company from among the creditors and contributories.

commodatum. A species of bailment, being a gratuitous loan.

common carrier. See CARRIER, COMMON.

common employment. The common law rule that a master is not liable to his servant for injuries resulting from the negligence of a fellow servant in the course of their common employment. The rule was abolished by the Law Reform (Personal Injuries) Act, 1948.

common law. That part of the law of England formulated, developed and administered by the common law courts based on the common customs of the country and unwritten. The common law has been preserved and expanded by judicial decision, and has been altered by legislation. It is opposed to equity (the body of rules administered by the Court of Chancery); to Statute law (the law laid down in Acts of Parliament); to special law (the law administered in special courts, such as ecclesiastical law, and the law merchant); and to the civil law (the law of Rome). See also EQUITY.

Common Market, The. The European Economic Community.

common seal. Every corporation must have a seal, which must be used to authenticate the more important documents executed on its behalf.

Commonwealth citizen. A British subject (*q.v.*).

Commonwealth of Nations, British. See BRITISH COMMONWEALTH OF NATIONS.

Commonwealth preference. Reduction or exemption from duties payable under the Customs Tariff on imported goods of Commonwealth origin.

commorientes. Persons dying together. Where two or more persons have died and it is uncertain which of them survived it is presumed that they died in order of seniority; *i.e.*, the younger survived the elder.

Companies Act, 1948, is the main Act relating to companies.

companies' contracts. Companies incorporated under, or defined by, the Companies Act, 1948, can, by their agents, enter into contracts in writing or by parol in cases where private persons can do so.

companies limited by guarantee. May be either of two kinds, namely, those having a share capital, and those not having a share capital. They must state in the memorandum that each member undertakes to contribute to the assets of the company in the event of its being wound up while he is a member, or within one year after he ceases to be a member, for payment of the debts and liabilities of the company contracted before he ceases to be a member, and of the costs, etc., of the winding up, and for adjustment of the rights of the contributories among themselves, such amount as may be required not exceeding a specified amount. They are formed mainly for non-profit making purposes.

Companies Liquidation Account. An account kept by the Board of Trade with the Bank of England into which is paid all moneys received in connection with the winding up of companies in England.

company. An association of persons formed for the purpose of some business or undertaking, each member having the right of assigning his shares to any other person, subject to the regulations of the company.

An incorporated company is a corporation (*q.v.*) formed by registration under the Companies Acts, or in special cases by Act of Parliament or by Charter. Companies are limited or unlimited. In the case of a limited company the liability of members is limited to the amount unpaid on their shares, or by the amount they have guaranteed to contribute in the case of a company limited by guarantee. In the case of an unlimited company each shareholder is liable to contribute to the debts of the company to the full extent of his property. Joint stock companies are those having a joint stock or capital which is divided into numerous transferable shares.

A private company is one which (a) restricts the right to transfer its shares; (b) limits the number of its members to 50; and (c) prohibits any invitation to the public to subscribe for any shares or debentures of the company. Any two or more persons may form or carry on a private company, whereas it takes seven to form or carry on a public company.

An exempt private company is one in which (a) no body corporate is the holder of shares or debentures; (b) no person other than the holder has any interest in its shares or debentures; (c) The number of members holding debentures is not more than 50; (d) No body corporate is a director of the company and neither the company nor any director is privy to any arrangement whereby the policy of the company is capable of being determined by persons other than directors, members, debenture holders or trustees for the debenture holders.

An " overseas " company is one incorporated outside Great Britain, but having a place of business within the United Kingdom. They have to deliver certain particulars to the Registrar, and are regarded for the purpose of winding up as unregistered companies.

company director. An individual elected by the shareholders to manage a company in conjunction with the other directors. A director has certain powers and duties under a company's articles of association and under the Companies Act.

comparative statement. A balance sheet, profit and loss or revenue account or statistical statement which shows in convenient form (usually by means of tabulation) the corresponding figures for some prior dates or periods for the purpose of comparison.

compensation. Pecuniary recompense for some loss or damage incurred. See COMPULSORY PURCHASE; DAMAGES.

compensation for loss of office. A lump sum payable to directors who have to give up office owing to unexpected changes; *e.g.*, on an amalgamation (*q.v.*); or a payment by an employer in consideration of the employee releasing him from his obligations under a service agreement. See GOLDEN HANDSHAKE.

competition. The environment in which commerce is carried on in the economy. The extremes are perfect competition and monopoly.

competitive market. A market where there are a number of keen buyers on the one hand, and a number of anxious sellers on the other.

completed audit. See AUDIT.

composition. An arrangement between a debtor and his creditors whereby the creditors agree to accept, in full discharge of their debts, something other than prompt payment of the full amount owed. A debtor who has not been made bankrupt may enter into a composition with his creditors; or, after bankruptcy, the creditors may agree to a composition and if the court approves of the composition, it may annul the adjudication order.

compos mentis. [Sound in mind.]

compound. (1) To compound for a debt is to accept in satisfaction thereof a lesser amount or something other than the sum owed. See ACCORD AND SATISFACTION.

(2) In the case of certain more serious criminal offences, where the offence is known to have been committed, compounding the offence is an agreement not to prosecute, which is itself an offence.

compound interest. Interest upon interest; *i.e.*, where the interest on a loan is not paid at the due date the amount of the interest is added to the principal, and thereafter interest accrues on the increased amount and so on from time to time.

compounded spirits. Plain spirits to which essences have been added.

compromise. The settlement of a dispute as a result of agreement between the parties.

compulsory purchase. The compulsory acquisition of land or property belonging to private persons for public purposes; either under the prerogative of the Crown, or more commonly under statutory powers; *e.g.*, under the Town and Country Planning Acts. Compensation is agreed, or else determined by the Lands Tribunal (*q.v.*).

computer. Any machine capable of automatically accepting data, applying a sequence of processes to the data, and supplying the results of these processes. A feature of a computer is the high speed with which it processes data.

concealment. Non-disclosure of a fact by a party to a contract. If active, and therefore fraudulent, it is a ground for rescission, but not otherwise, except in contracts *uberrimae fidei*, *e.g.*, in a policy of insurance.

concession. A grant by a government or other authority of a right or privilege; *e.g.*, to prospect for minerals.

conciliation. Conciliation boards are constituted under the Conciliation Act, 1896, for the purpose of settling disputes between employers and workmen.

In industrial disputes the first step is to obtain an amicable settlement if possible, and the second to refer the matter to arbitration (*q.v.*).

condition. A provision, *e.g.*, in a contract or a will, which makes the existence of a right dependent on the happening of an event; the right is then conditional, as opposed to an absolute right. A true condition is where the event on which the existence of the right depends is future and uncertain. An apparent condition is where the event is merely unascertained, or is not in its nature uncertain.

An express condition is one set out as a term in a contract or deed. An implied condition is one founded by the law on the presumed intention of the parties, with the object of giving such efficacy to the transaction as the parties must have intended it should have.

A condition precedent is one which delays the vesting of a right until the happening of an event; a condition is concurrent where the parties to a contract have reciprocally to perform certain acts at the same time; a condition subsequent is one which destroys or divests an existing right upon the happening of an event.

A condition in a contract is a stipulation going to the root of the contract, the breach of which gives rise to a right to treat the contract as repudiated. See also WARRANTY.

conditions of sale. The conditions under which a purchaser takes property sold to him. In the case of auction sales, a copy of the conditions may be advertised prior to the day of sale, posted in a conspicuous place in the sale room on the day of sale, printed with the particulars or catalogue of the property to be sold or copies may be distributed amongst the intending bidders. Where real property is the subject of sale the conditions contain (*inter alia*) provisions as to title to be accepted by the purchaser and how it is to be proved and amount of deposit. When the sale is concluded the purchaser signs a memorandum endorsed on the conditions, the whole becoming the contract of sale. Conditions of sale are frequently attached to goods specifying (*inter alia*) what warranties attach or do not attach and, generally, the purchaser will be deemed to have notice of such conditions and the sale will be affected by them accordingly.

condonation. Forgiveness of a matrimonial offence and the restoration of an offending spouse to the same position as formerly. Condonation is not necessarily to be presumed from the continuance or resumption of marital intercourse (Matrimonial Causes Act, 1965).

conduct money. Money given to a witness to defray his expenses of coming to, staying at, and returning from the place of trial.

confederation. A form of union among independent states for their mutual benefit, but in which the central authority has no powers over the individual citizens of the member States.

confession. An admission of guilt made to another by a person charged with a crime. It is admissible only if free and voluntary; *i.e.*, if it is not forthcoming because of any inducement, or threat, held out by a person in authority. It must not be made under hope of reward (other than spiritual) or fear of punishment in relation to the proceedings. Admissions may be obtained from a person by questions fairly and properly put to him by a police officer.

The Judges' Rules govern the practice in regard to police questioning a suspected person with a view to obtaining a confession.

conflict of law. See PRIVATE INTERNATIONAL LAW.

consanguinity. Relationship by blood.

consecutive computer. One which performs its computation in sequence, rather than concurrently. *Cf.* SIMULTANEOUS COMPUTER.

consensus ad idem. [Agreement as to the same thing.] The exact similarity between offer and acceptance necessary for a binding contract.

consideration. A valuable consideration in the sense of the law may consist either in some right, interest, profit or benefit accruing to one party, or some forbearance, detriment, loss or responsibility given, suffered or undertaken by the other.

Valuable consideration is essential to the validity of every simple contract; it is not necessary in the case of a contract under seal. In order to support a contract the consideration must be legal, of value though not necessarily adequate, and it may be present or future but not past.

consignee. The person to whom goods are sent.

consignment. The sending of goods to another person; or the goods so sent. In a special sense, consignment is the sending of goods by the owner to an agent to dispose of on the owner's behalf.

consignor. The person who sends goods.

consolidated accounts. The combined annual accounts (*q.v.*) of a holding company and its subsidiaries. They consist of a consolidated balance sheet and profit and loss account which embody the financial position and profit or loss as a whole of a group of companies.

consolidated fund. The fund into which all revenue of the United Kingdom is paid and from which the payments approved by Parliament are made. The Exchequer account represents the amount of the fund with the Bank of England.

consolidation. A statute, which for convenience, repeals all previous enactments relating to a particular subject and reproduces the same matter in the one statute.

consols. An abbreviation denoting consolidated funds or consolidated stock.

conspiracy. The agreement of two or more persons to do an unlawful act, or to do a lawful act by unlawful means, whether the act is committed or not. This is a criminal offence. Conspiracy is also a tort for which a person injured has an action for damages.

constitution. The form in which a State is organised. The system or body of fundamental principles and rules in accordance with which a State is governed.

A constitution may be (1) unwritten, resting mainly on custom and convention, *e.g.*, the British Constitution, or (2) written, drawn up in legal form, *e.g.*, the Commonwealth of Australia Constitution which establishes a Parliament, Executive and Judiciary, and defines the respective spheres of government of the Commonwealth and states.

construction. The process of ascertaining the meaning of a written document, statute, etc.

constructive. A right, liability or status created by the law without reference to the intention of the parties, *e.g.*, a constructive trust (*q.v.*) or constructive notice.

constructive notice. See NOTICE.

constructive total loss. See TOTAL LOSS.

constructive trust. A trust which is raised by construction of equity in order to satisfy the demands of justice and good conscience without reference to any presumed intention of the parties. Such trusts arise in the following cases:

    (1) vendor's lien for unpaid purchase-money;

    (2) purchaser's lien for prematurely paid purchase-money;

    (3) where a person makes a profit in a fiduciary position or out of a trust property;

    (4) where a stranger intermeddles in a trust;

    (5) where a morgagee sells under his power of sale, he is a trustee of any surplus realised.

constructive trustee. The person deemed to be a trustee in the case of a constructive trust (*q.v.*).

consul. An official appointed by a government to reside in a foreign country to facilitate and extend commerce between the subjects of the country which appoints him and those of the country to which he is accredited, and generally to look after the interests of the nationals of the country which has appointed him. A consul is not entitled to diplomatic privileges or immunities unless, *e.g.*, he is recognised as a member of the staff of an embassy. Also see AMBASSADOR.

consular invoice. An invoice that has to be certified to by the consul or other consular officer of the country to which goods are being exported.

consulate. The office or official residence of a consul.

contango. A percentage paid by a buyer of stock of which delivery is to be taken on a certain date, for being allowed to delay taking delivery until some later date. See BACKWARDATION.

contango day (making-up day). First day of Stock Exchange settlement days.

contempt of court. (1) Failure to comply with an order of a superior court, and in certain cases (where specific statutory provision is made), with an order of an inferior court.

    (2) Any act or resistance of, or insult to, or disrespect of the authority or dignity of a court, which (i) in case of a superior, committed anywhere, or (ii) in case of an inferior court, committed in the face of the court.

    (3) Conduct likely to prejudice the fair trial of an accused person.

    Punishment for contempt may be by fine, imprisonment or merely expulsion from the court.

contingent. Conditional; an interest in property which awaits or depends on the happening of a future event which may or may not happen, as opposed to a vested interest; *e.g.*, a gift by will to A for life and then to B but if B predecease A then to C: C's interest is contingent. See EXECUTORY INTEREST; REMAINDER; VESTED.

contingent liability. A liability which will only arise upon the happening of an uncertain event, *e.g.*, on the insolvency of a principal debtor, a guarantor or surety will become liable. In preparing a balance sheet of a company the aggregate or estimated amount of contingent liabilities must be shown in a note to the balance sheet, unless otherwise provided for.

continuation. A sale with an agreement to re-purchase, on the Stock Exchange.

continuing guarantee. A guarantee given to cover a series of transactions over a period of time.

contra. [Against.] Contra accounts arise between two persons having mutual dealings, where the amounts are usually set off one against another, so that only the balance is receivable or payable.

contraband. Goods prohibited to be imported or exported; whether in peace or war.

contract. An agreement enforceable at law; an agreement entered into by two or more persons, whereby a person or persons promise to another or others, to do or to refrain from doing some specified act or acts.

For a contract to be valid and legally enforceable there must be—

(1) the intention of the parties to create legal relationship;

(2) an offer by one party and its acceptance by the other, resulting in a definite agreement between the parties. See CONSENSUS AD IDEM;

(3) form, *i.e.*, by deed or consideration (*q.v.*);

(4) legal capacity of the parties to contract;

(5) legality of the objects of the agreement.

There are the following kinds of contract:—

(1) Of record, entered into through the machinery of a court of justice, *e.g.*, a judgment or a recognisance.

(2) Speciality, by deed; *i.e.*, by writing, sealed and delivered.

(3) Simple or parol; *i.e.*, by writing other than a deed, or oral.

(4) Quasi (*q.v.*).

A contract may be void (*q.v.*), voidable (*q.v.*), or unenforceable (*q.v.*). The following contracts to be valid are required to be in writing:

(1) Bills of exchange, cheques and promissory notes.

(2) Assignments of copyright (Copyright Act, 1956).

(3) Contracts of marine insurance (Marine Insurance Act, 1906).

(4) An acknowledgment of a debt barred by the Statute of Limitation.

(5) For the repayment of money under the Moneylenders Act, 1927.

(6) For the hire-purchase of goods under the Hire Purchase Act, 1965.

The following contracts are required to be evidenced in writing:

(1) Contracts of guarantee or suretyship, but not contracts of indemnity.

(2) Contracts for the sale or other disposition of land, or any interest in land.

The following contracts are required to be by deed:

(1) A gratuitous promise, *i.e.*, a promise for which the promisor receives no consideration to support his promise.

(2) Appointment of an agent where he is given authority to contract by deed (called a POWER OF ATTORNEY).

(3) A transfer of a British ship or of a share therein.

(4) A lease of land for a period exceeding three years.

(5) Transfers of shares in a company governed by the Companies Clauses Consolidation Act, 1908.

See also COMPANIES' CONTRACTS; CORPORATION.

contract note. A note issued by a broker, setting out full particulars of the contract made by the broker on behalf of his principal.

contractual relations. That relation which exists between two parties who have made an agreement affecting their future legal relations, whereby one party becomes entitled to acts or forbearances on the part of the other, or each party becomes so entitled.

contribution. The payment of a proportionate share of a liability which has been borne by one or some only of a number equally liable. By the Law Reform (Married Women and Tortfeasors) Act, 1935, it was provided that any tortfeasor may recover contribution from any other tortfeasor liable in respect of the same damage.

contributory. A person liable to contribute to the assets of a company in the event of its being wound up, and includes any person alleged to be a contributory until the list of contributories has been definitely settled. It also includes a person who continues to be a shareholder until the winding up.

There are two classes of contributories: present members and past members (those who have ceased to hold shares within the 12 months immediately preceding the liquidation). Registered members of the company at the commencement of the liquidation have their names entered on the " A " list of contributories. The names of members who have been registered holders of shares at any time during the 12 months immediately preceding the commencement of the winding up, and who at the time of the liquidation do not hold those shares, are recorded on the " B " list of contributories, including the names of shareholders whose shares had been forfeited, or surrendered, within 12 months of the liquidation.

The members entered on the " A " list are primarily liable to contribute to the assets of the company. A past member is not liable to contribute in respect of shares for which he has been entered on the " B " list, unless it appears to the court that the existing members are unable to satisfy the contributions required to be made by them, for the purpose of payment of the debts and liabilities of the company, the cost and expenses of the winding up and the adjustment of the contributories among themselves. The liability in respect of shares shown in the " B " list is the amount remaining unpaid on such shares taking into consideration the amount paid to the company by both the past and present members. The liability is further restricted to an amount sufficient to pay the debts contracted before the " B " contributory ceased to be a member in relation to such shares.

A present shareholder who holds fully paid shares may be entered on the " A " list in order that he may participate in any surplus after creditors have been paid.

contributory negligence. A defence in an action of negligence (*q.v.*) whereby the defendant alleges that the plaintiff's own negligence was the actual cause of the damage, or that the plaintiff could have avoided the damage by the use of reasonable care. Formerly a plaintiff guilty of such contributory negligence could not recover against the defendant, but by the Law Reform (Contributory Negligence) Act, 1945, loss is apportioned according to the degree of default of the plaintiff and defendant respectively.

control unit. Part of the central processor (*q.v.*) of a computer, it transmits the programme (*q.v.*) instructions to operating units and controls central and peripheral units in certain functions.

controlling interest. A holding, or several holdings which vote together, of shares carrying more than 50% of the voting rights in a company constitutes a controlling interest.

conversion rights. Loan capital which gives the holder the right to convert his holding into shares of the company at specified prices during a specified period is said to carry conversion rights.

co-operative society. A voluntary association of persons (usually small producers or consumers) who have come together to achieve some common object (such as the purchase of raw materials or the sale of necessities) through a collective economic enterprise. The members, each of whom has equal voting rights in matters of management, subscribe the capital, maximum holding of which is £500, and profits are distributed to them in proportion to their dealings with the society. The Industrial Provident Societies Acts regulate the formation and activities of such societies.

co-partnership. Partnership (*q.v.*).

copyright. The sole right to produce or reproduce any original literary, dramatic, musical or artistic work or any substantial part thereof in any material form; to perform, or in the case of a lecture to deliver, an original literary, dramatic or musical work, or any substantial part thereof in public; if the work is unpublished, to publish the work or any substantial part thereof. It includes the sole right:

    (a) to produce, reproduce, perform, or publish any translation of of the work;

    (b) in the case of a dramatic work, to convert it into a novel or other non-dramatic work;

(c) in the case of a novel or other non-dramatic work, or of an artistic work, to convert it into a dramatic work, by way of performance in public or otherwise;

(d) in the case of literary, dramatic, or musical work, to make any record, perforated roll, cinematograph film, or other contrivance by means of which the work may be mechanically performed or delivered.

The object of copyright is to afford protection not to ideas but to the particular form of expression by which an author conveys his ideas to the world. In this it is distinguished from a patent or design.

Copyright exists, except where otherwise expressly provided by statute, for the life of the author and for fifty years after his death. In the case of joint authorship, copyright subsists during the life of the author who dies first, and fifty years after his death, or during the life of the author who dies last, whichever period is the longer.

Copyright is assignable by writing, or by will, and a licence may be granted in consideration of royalties or otherwise. (The Copyright Act, 1956). See also INDUSTRIAL DESIGN.

co-respondent. A person called upon to answer a petition jointly with another; as in divorce proceedings.

corner. To obtain such control of available supplies of a commodity as to be able to raise prices and obtain high profits on sale.

coroner. An officer of the Crown whose main duty is to hold inquests upon bodies of persons who have died from other than natural causes; on treasure trove; and, in the City of London, into the causes of fires.

corporation. A succession or body of persons having, in the eyes of the law, an existence and rights and duties distinct from the persons constituting it. It has a name, a common seal, and perpetual succession. A corporation sole consists of only one member at a time, who is invariably the holder of an office; *e.g.*, the Sovereign, or a bishop, or the Treasury Solicitor. A corporation aggregate is a corporation with a number of members; *e.g.*, incorporated companies, or municipal corporations. Corporations are created by royal charter, by a special Act of Parliament, or by a general Act; *e.g.*, the Companies Act, 1948. The powers of a chartered corporation are the same as those of an individual; other corporations are restricted to the objects and powers conferred on them on incorporation.

A corporation can be held liable for a wrong done by it through its agents or servants, and can be punished by fine for an offence or crime.

The contracts of corporations may be entered into with no more formality than is required of an individual (Corporate Bodies Contracts Act, 1960).

corporation tax. The tax on the profits of companies which was introduced by the Finance Act, 1965 to replace income tax and profits tax. Corporation tax is combined with withholding tax (*q.v.*) payable on dividends paid by companies.

corporeal. Tangible. See also INCORPOREAL PROPERTY.

corpus. [The body.] The capital of a fund as contrasted with its income.

corpus delicti. The body of essential facts constituting a criminal offence; *e.g.*, a murder.

corroboration. Independent evidence confirming other evidence; it is obligatory in some cases, *e.g.*, in breach of promise actions and paternity proceedings, but in practice it is expected in a number of other cases; *e.g.*, of the evidence of an accomplice.

cost. Is the measurement of the different expenditures involved in achieving a certain result or output of production. It is a term which is also applied to expenditure itself and has many meanings according to context, *e.g.*, total cost, marginal cost, opportunity cost, fixed cost, variable cost, etc.

cost accounting. That branch of accounting which involves special consideration of the problems arising out of the recording and analysis of income and expenditures and the interpretation and managerial use of cost data.

costs. See BILL OF COSTS.

counsel. A barrister in his professional capacity.

counterclaim. A claim made against the plaintiff by a defendant in the same action. It need not relate to the same subject-matter and could be the ground of a separate action against the plaintiff by the defendant.

counterfoil. The complementary part of a cheque, receipt, dividend, etc., which is retained by the drawer, giver or recipient respectively.

county court. An inferior court exercising jurisdiction in civil matters within prescribed limits of the value of the subject-matter at stake, and in a defined district or area of the country. County Courts may entertain actions for breach of contract or tort, but unless there is agreement between the parties, there is no jurisdiction in actions for libel, slander, seduction or breach of promise of marriage. They have full powers in bankruptcy, and may be given Admiralty jurisdiction. There is a limited jurisdiction in equity, *e.g.*, on a trust, mortgage, etc., and in probate matters. (County Courts Act, 1959.)

County Courts have jurisdiction in actions for the recovery of or relating to land up to the value of £400, and in certain matters arising under the Landlord and Tenant Acts, where the rateable value of the holding does not exceed £2,000 (County Courts (Jurisdiction) Act, 1963).

coupon. A detachable slip, *e.g.*, the coupons attached to a bond to enable the holder to collect interest. The coupons are numbered and dated and marked with amount of interest payable on their surrender.

court. A place where law is administered; the judge or judges who sit in a court. " Court " may include chambers.

Courts are of two principal classes: of record and not of record. The acts and judicial proceedings of a court of record are enrolled for a perpetual memory and testimony, and it has authority to fine and imprison for contempt of its authority.

Courts are also divided into superior and inferior courts. Superior courts are those which are not subject to the control of any other court except by way of appeal (*e.g.*, the High Court), while inferior courts (*e.g.*, courts of petty sessions) are subject to the control of the High Court by orders.

Bodies exercising powers judicially, but not being courts, are often described as tribunals.

court of petty sessions or **petty sessional court.** A court of summary jurisdiction consisting of two or more justices, now known as the magistrates' court. (Magistrates' Courts Act, 1952.)

court of quarter sessions. The sittings of the justices of any county or division of a county assembled in general or quarter session, and of the recorder in a borough having a separate court of quarter sessions.

Proceedings at quarter sessions consist of the trial of criminal indictments, and of an appellate jurisdiction in appeals from petty sessions and courts of summary jurisdiction.

court of record. See COURT.

court of summary jurisdiction. A court having jurisdiction to give judgment or make an order forthwith; *e.g.*, to convict an offender. (Magistrates' Courts Act, 1952.)

court-martial. A tribunal, consisting of military, naval or air-force officers, convened to try offences committed by soldiers, sailors or airmen respectively. The Court-Martial Appeal Court was established by the Courts-Martial (Appeals) Act, 1951.

covenant. A clause in a deed whereby a person engages in terms or in effect that a certain thing is true or has or has not been done, or shall or shall not be done; it generally connotes a personal covenant which can be sued on at law.

Covenants for title are those entered into by the vendor of land in a conveyance as to his title. They are indicated by the use of appropriate words; *e.g.*, " as beneficial owner."

cover. (1) Any form of security given to cover a liability, *e.g.*, security or cash lodged by a client with his broker when the client buys securities without making payment in full.

(2) For the dividend of a company. The relationship between the earnings of a company and the amount distributed by way of dividend out of those earnings. Distribution in full means that the dividend is covered once. The term is also used of assets cover for a loan or debenture stock.

covering. The buying back of stock sold " short." See BEAR.

covernote. A document given to an insured by an insurance company to cover the risk, until a policy is issued.

coverture. The status or condition of being a married woman.

credit. (1) An entry on the right-hand side of an account, in book-keeping, it represents value given by the person or account credited.

(2) Extension of the period of payment of a debt; *e.g.*, a sale on " thirty days' credit " indicates that the due date for payment is at the end of the month following that in which the purchase was made.

(3) Claims to cash effected through banks in favour of their clients and created either by advances by the banks or deposits by the clients.

In general, credit is the belief in a person's trustworthiness: confidence in his integrity. A witness can be cross-examined to credit: *i.e.*, as to his credibility. Obtaining credit for money by false pretences, or by an undischarged bankrupt, are offences.

credit (banker's). See BANKER'S COMMERCIAL CREDITS.

credit card. Customers of finance companies may present credit cards to hotels, retailers, etc. The supplier notes the details on the card and invoices the finance house for payment. The finance house collects the customer's bills together and invoices him collectively at regular intervals. It is a means of obtaining credit which is of most use to those travelling away from their home or normal place of business.

credit foncier. Loan made on the security of real property.

credit note. A note issued by a trader, setting out that the person to whom it is directed is entitled to be credited by the issuer with a certain amount; *e.g.*, for goods which the other person has returned.

credit rating. An assessment or estimate of the credit-worthiness of persons mainly for the use and guidance of hire-purchase concerns and traders.

credit-sale agreement. An agreement for the sale of goods, under which the purchase price is payable by five or more instalments. When the total purchase price exceeds £5, the seller must state in writing the cash price. There must also be a memorandum in writing as in hire-purchase (*q.v.*) agreements. The conditions and warranties in the Sale of Goods Act, 1893, apply, unless varied or excluded.

credit squeeze. A colloquialism for a policy of credit restriction throughout the economy by the monetary authorities.

credit transfers. A method of payment through banks without cheques. The creditor having agreed, the debtor prepares a standard form of credit voucher showing the amount due, the name of the creditor and his branch bank. The debtor hands the voucher to his bank who charge his account with the payment. Alternatively, a debtor may hand the prepared credit voucher to any bank with cash to cover the payment plus 6d.

The vouchers are cleared through to the creditor's bank and credited to his account.

creditor. A person to whom a debt is owing by another person, called the debtor. See also SECURED CREDITOR.

crime. A public wrong, being a wrong against the welfare of the community, forbidden by law on pain of punishment inflicted at the suit of the Crown, as opposed to a tort or civil wrong, being a wrong against an individual in respect of which he is entitled to bring a civil action for redress. Some acts may amount to both a tort and a crime. Crimes may be indictable offences: *i.e.*, tried on indictment by a jury; or offences dealt with summarily by a magistrate or justices of the peace.

crop lien. A lien given over a growing crop or agricultural or horticultural produce as security for an advance. If duly registered it is not affected by the bankruptcy of the lienor.

cross-action. An action allowed to be brought by a defendant against a plaintiff, in certain circumstances, in respect of the same subject matter as that of the plaintiff's action against the defendant. See COUNTERCLAIM.

crossed cheque. Cheques may be crossed or uncrossed (open cheques). A crossed cheque cannot be paid over the counter but must be collected through a banker, *i.e.*, it must be paid into some banking account. If the banker on whom the cheque is drawn pays it in a manner contrary to the crossing, he becomes liable if the true owner suffers damage.

(1) A cheque is crossed generally where it bears across its face the words " and company " or any abbreviation thereof, between two parallel transverse lines, or two parallel transverse lines simply.

(2) A cheque is crossed specially when the name of a banker is included in the crossing, and the cheque is deemed to be crossed specially to that banker.

A holder of a cheque crossed " not negotiable " cannot give a transferee a better title than he himself has.

Of the following crossings, the last on the right is a special crossing and the remainder are general crossings.

	& CO.	NOT NEGOTIABLE	ACCOUNT PAYEE ONLY	X BANK, LTD.

Crown, The. The sovereign in her public capacity as a body politic. The Crown is the highest branch of the legislature. The term is synonymous with the executive and the fountain of justice and honour. The Crown is one and indivisible.

Crown debts. Debts due to the Crown. These debts have been invested with special privileges and priorities. See also PREFERENTIAL DEBTS.

Crown grant. The certificate of title to lands granted by the Crown.

Crown lands. The demesne lands of the Crown which are surrendered in consideration of the Civil List. The land revenues of the Crown are collected by the Crown Estate Commissioners.

Crown prerogative. See PREROGATIVE.

cum dividend. [with dividend]. When shares are sold " cum div." the dividend accrues to the purchaser.

cum rights. When shares are sold " cum rights," the buyer has the right to claim new shares which are about to be issued.

cum testamento annexo. [with the will annexed.] See ADMINISTRATION, LETTERS OF.

cumulative preference shares. Preference shares which are entitled to receive any arrears of dividend out of available profits in any succeeding year or years, in priority to dividends being paid on any other class of share.

currency. (1) The medium of exchange circulating in a country; (2) the period during which an instrument is in force. See also LEGAL TENDER.

current account. (1) A banking account; a drawing account at a bank to which sums and cheques paid in are credited and sums withdrawn are debited. See DEPOSIT ACCOUNT.

(2) In partnership, the account set up for each partner to which his share of profits is credited, and his drawings debited.

current assets. See ASSETS.

current liabilities. Liabilities to be met within a comparatively short period, *e.g.,* trade debts as distinct from long-term indebtedness such as mortgages.

curtilage. A court-yard or land adjoining a dwelling-house. See also MESSUAGE.

custodian trustee. A trustee who has the custody and care of trust property, but not its management. See Public Trustee Act, 1906. He is not a " bare trustee " (*q.v.*).

custom. A rule of conduct, obligatory on those within its scope established by long usage. A valid custom has the force of law. A custom to be valid must be certain and reasonable, obligatory, not repugnant to statute law, though it may derogate from the common law.

General customs are those of the whole country, as, *e.g.,* the general customs of merchants. Particular customs are the usage of particular trades. Local customs are customs of a certain locality.

custom of trade. A custom or usage of a particular trade or market, *e.g.,* a custom of the Stock Exchange, in accordance with which contracts will be deemed to be made.

customs clearance. Before goods can be released from the control of the Customs, entries must be prepared, original invoices produced at the local Customs House, and duty paid, if any.

customs drawback. See DRAWBACK.

customs duty. A revenue duty levied upon certain imports.

customs union. A group of countries with common external customs duties. Examples are the E.E.C. and E.F.T.A. countries.

cy près. [Near to it.] The doctrine that where a settlor or testator has expressed a general intention, and also a particular way in which he wishes it carried out, but the intention cannot be carried out in that particular way, the court will direct the intention to be carried out *as nearly as possible* in the way desired. The doctrine is particularly applied to charities. Thus if a paramount charitable intention appears, a charitable gift will not be void simply because there is no such institution as is specified in the gift, but the property will be used for some similar purpose resembling as much as possible the specified object.

The Charities Act, 1960, ss. 13 and 14, extends to some extent the scope of the doctrine: *e.g.*, the application *cy près* of surplus money, which would otherwise result abortively to unidentifiable donors, is allowed.

cybernetics. The study of control and communication mechanisms and processes in management and machines.

D

damage. Loss, harm or injury actually incurred or suffered to possessions or person.

damages. A sum of money adjudged to be paid by one person to another as compensation for a loss by the latter in consequence of a wrongful act or default committed by the former. The principle is that the injured party should be put as nearly as possible in the same position, so far as money can do it, as if he had not been injured. Damages may be described as follows:

Nominal damages. A small sum awarded in recognition of the invasion of a legal right of the plaintiff.

Real or compensatory damages are awarded as compensation for damage actually incurred or suffered.

Contemptuous damages. The smallest coin of the realm awarded to a plaintiff in a case which the jury consider should never have been brought.

Exemplary damages. A large sum awarded in a case where the defendant's conduct has been despicable, or has aggravated the injury caused by him.

General damages. Damages assessed as fair and reasonable compensation for the loss or damage incurred by the defendants; *e.g.*, for pain, suffering or disablement.

Special damages. Actual damage or loss which has to be proved in evidence: *e.g.*, medical expenses; loss of wages. See NUISANCE.

Measure of damages. The method by which real loss or damage is assessed.

Mitigation of damages. It is the duty of a person entitled to damages to reduce the damage he has suffered so far as possible.

Remoteness of damage. Damage for which the defendant incurs no responsibility, although it may have followed upon some act of his: as where the chain of causation has been broken, and his act is not the effective cause of the damage. For the defendant to be liable the damage must be such as could be reasonably forseeable as resulting from his act.

The rules as to damages are substantially the same in contract as in tort.

dangerous chattels; dangerous goods. Things which are specially likely to cause injury to those persons into whose possession they may come. The liability of a person who puts such things into circulation depends upon whether the appropriate degree of care has been exercised: there is a special duty to take precautions. A person who keeps a dangerous thing on his land is liable if it escapes and causes damage to others. A seller of goods known to be dangerous must warn the buyer of the danger of such goods. A consignor must take reasonable precautions when sending dangerous goods and give notice of their dangerous nature to the carrier. In addition, provisions have been made by various statutes relating to dangerous goods; *e.g.*, prescribing conditions under which they may be carried by sea, rail, etc., and imposing penalties for the posting of dangerous articles or substances.

dangerous premises. Property which is specially likely to cause injury to persons resorting to it. The liability to compensate persons injured is, in general, upon the occupier of the premises, not the owner. An occupier owes the same duty to all his visitors, except as modified by agreement or otherwise; *i.e.*, to take such care as is reasonable to see that the visitor will be reasonably safe in using the premises for the purpose for which he is invited or permitted by the occupier to be there. (Occupiers' Liability Act, 1957.)

data. (1) Facts from which deductions may be drawn.

(2) In computer usage the facts which are fed in, stored or extracted from the machine in any operation.

data processing. A systematic sequence of operations performed by a computer on data (*q.v.*) with the object of extracting information or of revising it.

days of grace. Days allowed for making a payment or doing some act after the time limited for that purpose has expired. Three days of grace are allowed for the payment of a bill of exchange, except those payable on demand or at sight.

de auditu. [By hearsay.]

de bonis non. [Of goods not administered.] LETTERS OF ADMINISTRATION (*q.v.*) granted where an executor or administrator dies before administration is completed.

de die in diem. [From day to day.]

de facto. [In fact.]

de jure. [By right.]

de minimis non curat lex. [The law does not concern itself with trifles.]

de son tort. [Of his own wrongdoing.] See EXECUTOR DE SON TORT.

dead freight. Freight payable by a charterer in respect of cargo not shipped.

dead reckoning. The position of a ship reckoned with regard to course and speed only from a previous position fixed by reference to celestial or terrestial objects, not allowing for effect of current or wind.

dead rent. The minimum rent payable under a mining lease, irrespective of whether minerals are won or not. Where the minimum rent payable exceeds the royalty payable on the amount of minerals extracted, that excess may be redeemed out of the royalties in a subsequent period when the royalties exceed the minimum rent. This right to redeem is generally limited to a certain period.

dear money. When the available supply of credit is small, and borrowing can only be made at high rates of interest.

death duty. See ESTATE DUTY.

death, presumption of. When a person has been absent, untraceable and not known to be alive for seven years or upwards, he may be presumed to be dead.

debasement. Debasing the coinage, by reducing the standard of fineness.

debenture. (1) An instrument, issued by a company or public body to a specified person as evidence of a debt or as security for a loan of a fixed sum of money at interest. It contains a promise to pay the amount mentioned in it. It includes debenture stock, bonds and any other securities of a company, whether constituting a charge on the assets of the company or not. Debentures take precedence of shares in a winding up. Debentures may be classified as:

Simple or naked debentures carrying no charge on the assets.

Secured debentures which may take the form of a fixed charge on certain assets of the company, or a floating charge over the whole or any of the assets of the company, or a combination of both.

Registered debentures are repayable only to the registered holders or their personal representatives. They are transferable in a similar manner to shares, *i.e.*, the transfer must be registered by the company before it becomes operative.

Bearer debentures are capable of being transferred from one person to another by simple delivery and without notice to the company.

Any charge on a company's assets for the purpose of securing an issue of debentures is required to be registered with the Registrar of Companies and such register shall be open to inspection on payment of the requisite fee. If the debt in respect of which the charge is given be satisfied, or the property charged be released from the charge or ceases to form part of the company's property, the Registrar may enter a memorandum of satisfaction, in whole or in part, or the fact that the property or part thereof has been released from the charge or has ceased to form part of the company's property, as the case may be.

Every balance-sheet shall show under separate headings in respect of any issue of debentures, the expenses incurred in connection with the issue, any sums paid by way of commission, and any sums allowed by way of discount so far as they are not written off. In addition, there shall be shown in the balance-sheet particulars of any redeemed debentures which a company has power to reissue, and in the profit and loss account the amount of interest payable on the debentures.

(2) An acknowledgment of indebtedness by the state or a public officer; *e.g.*, a certificate of right to drawback (*q.v.*) on goods duly entered, shipped and exported.

debenture stock. Stock representing money borrowed by a company or public body, and charged on the whole or part of its property. It is borrowed capital consolidated into one mass for the sake of convenience. It differs from debentures mainly in its divisibility, and in its time of payment, generally in the event of a winding-up. It is almost invariably secured by a trust deed, and the rights of the stockholders are primarily against the trustees of the deed. The trust deed will usually vest in these persons a legal charge over the property which is a security of the debenture-holders.

debit. The opposite entry to credit in a system of double entry book-keeping; it represents value received by the account debited.

debit note. A note in writing stating that the account of the person to whom it is sent is to be debited in respect of some transaction; *e.g.*, a claim for goods received short, goods damaged in transit, interest, and so forth,

debt. A sum of money due from one person to another. Debts are: (1) of record, *e.g.*, recognisances and judgment debts; (2) specialty debts, created by deed; (3) simple contract debts; (4) Crown debts; (5) secured debts, those for which security has been taken; (6) preferential debts (*q.v.*).

debtor. A person by whom money is owed to another person, called the creditor. See also BANKRUPTCY.

deceit. Fraud; the tort or civil wrong consisting of inducing a person to act in a manner whereby he sustains damage by wilfully or recklessly causing him to believe and act on a falsehood. It gives rise to an action for damages. See FRAUD.

decimal system. Of weights and measures, coinage, etc., with denominations rising by tens.

decipher. To put into plain language a message in cipher.

deck cargo. Cargo carried on the deck of a ship, *e.g.*, timber.

declaration. A statement which is treated as putting on record its contents; *e.g.*, a declaration of trust. See also DYING DECLARATION; STATUTORY DECLARATION.

declarations by deceased persons may be admissible in evidence (a) where against pecuniary or proprietary interests; (b) in the course of a duty; (c) as to public rights; (d) as to pedigree.

decode. To put a message in code into plain language.

decree. An order of a court pronounced on the hearing of a suit. See ABSOLUTE; NISI.

deduction at source. Tax on certain payments (dividends, interest, salaries and wages, etc.) must be deducted by the payer and accounted for by him to the Inland Revenue.

deed. A writing or instrument written or printed on paper or parchment, signed, sealed and delivered recording the agreement of the parties whose deed it is. A deed must be signed. It is not always essential that a seal be actually fixed, it being sufficient if the contract is expressed to be a deed, or to be signed, sealed and delivered. The attesting or witnessing of a deed is not normally essential, but it is usual in practice.

Certain contracts in order to be valid must be by deed, *e.g.*, leases exceeding three years, transfer of a British ship, and contracts not supported by consideration.

An escrow is a deed, otherwise fulfilling the above conditions, delivered to a third party pending fulfilment of certain conditions upon which it will take effect. See also DEED POLL.

deed of arrangement. See ARRANGEMENT.

deed of assignment. See ASSIGNMENT.

deed of covenant. A contract not supported by consideration to pay regular amounts to another for a period in excess of six years. The period of more than six years (usually seven is chosen) is necessary for the covenanted amount to be recognized by the Inland Revenue as a charge against income for purposes of income tax, but not surtax.

deed of gift. A deed transferring property by way of gift.

deed of inspectorship. A deed entered into by a debtor with all or some of his creditors for the purpose of carrying on or winding up his business. It is included in the definition of deed of arrangement in the Deeds of Arrangement Act, 1914. See ARRANGEMENT.

deed poll. A deed made by one party only, *e.g.*, a power of attorney or a deed for publishing change of name. It takes its name from the fact that such a deed was made on paper with a smooth or shaven edge. Contrast INDENTURE.

deemed. Where a certain state of things is to be assumed, although not necessarily actually so.

defacement. The illegal operation of decreasing the value of coin by punching, clipping, cutting, sweating, etc.

defamation. The publication of a false and defamatory statement respecting another person without lawful justification. A defamatory statement is one exposing him to hatred, ridicule or contempt, or which causes him

67

to be shunned or avoided, or which has a tendency to injure him in his office, profession or trade. It may constitute libel or slander.

A statement is to be construed in its natural and ordinary meaning; if not defamatory in such meaning, it must be construed in the special meaning, if any, in which it was understood by the person by and to whom it was published. There must be publication; *i.e.*, a communication by the defendant of the defamatory statement to some person other than the plaintiff. (Defamation Act, 1952.) See also LIBEL; SLANDER.

default. Omission of that which a man ought to do; not doing what is reasonable in the circumstances. To make default means to fail to meet some engagement on the due date.

default summons. A summary means of recovering a debt or liquidated demand in an inferior court.

defeasible. The term used to describe an estate or interest in property which is liable to be defeated or terminated by the happening of a future event.

defence. (1) A reason given by any person against whom a proceeding is brought, which, if established, shows that there is no case against him. In an action, the defence is the statement delivered by the defendant in reply to the plaintiff's statement of claim, where he proposes to contest it.

(2) The right which every person has to inflict death or bodily harm in order to defend himself or any other person from unlawful violence, provided that he inflicts no greater injury than is reasonably necessary.

Defence Regulations. Regulations, made in times of emergency by Order in Council, necessary or expedient for securing the public safety, the defence of the realm, the maintenance of public order, the efficient prosecution of any war in which Her (His) Majesty may be engaged, and for maintaining supplies and services essential to the life of the community. (Emergency Powers (Defence) Act, 1939.) They have been continued in force, as necessary, by later Acts.

defendant. A person against whom civil proceedings (other than by petition) or summary proceedings before justices are brought.

deferred annuity. An annuity payable after the lapse of a specified time. Should death occur in the meantime, the purchase money is not necessarily returnable.

deferred charges. Expenditure resulting in intangible benefits and which is written off out of profits within a few years of being incurred, *e.g.*, the preliminary expenses of forming a company.

deferred income. Income actually received before it has been wholly earned, *e.g.*, interest received in advance; the unexpired portion of insurance premiums. It is sometimes called deferred revenue or unearned finance charge. It must be spread over the whole period to which it relates for accounting purposes.

deferred liability. An amount owing but not due for a considerable period, such as a loan on mortgage, debentures, etc.

deferred repairs. Provision in accounts of undertakings for the expenditure necessary on repairs which have not been done at the accounting date.

deferred revenue expenditure. Revenue expenditure, the benefit of which is not limited to the particular period in which the expense is incurred, which is temporarily capitalised or carried forward as a current asset and recouped from the profits of subsequent periods.

deferred shares. Shares with the right to take the whole or a proportion of profits after a fixed dividend has been paid on the ordinary shares.

They are called founders shares when the vendors of a business take part or the whole of their consideration in such deferred shares.

deficiency. The amount by which the realisable value of the assets of a debtor or company falls short of liabilities.

deficiency account. An account accompanying a statement of affairs (*q.v.*) of a bankrupt or company in liquidation, setting out details of the financial transactions of the bankrupt or company over a period prior to bankruptcy or liquidation.

deflation. A check to inflation following contraction of credit and reduction in purchasing power.

defunct company. One which the Registrar of Companies has cause to believe is not carrying on business and which he has power to strike off the register of companies.

del credere agent. A mercantile agent who undertakes to make good any loss incurred with respect to persons with whom he contracts for his principal as regards payment only; *i.e., a del credere* agent undertakes to pay for goods accepted by the customers he procures, upon the buyer's failure to pay, but he does not guarantee that customers will not repudiate contracts in some other manner such as by refusal to accept goods. He is usually paid a higher rate of commission.

delegate. A person appointed as a representative to act at a meeting, usually within given limits, on behalf of others.

delegation. The entrusting to another of some duty by the person required to perform it.

delegatus non potest delegare. [A delegate cannot delegate]. A person to whom powers have been delegated cannot delegate them to another, except with the express or implied authority of the principal. But an agent can delegate his authority where unforeseen emergencies arise, or where such delegation is justified by the custom or usage of the business in which he is employed, or where the act is purely ministerial.

Trustees may appoint agents to do trust business, and are not responsible for their default, if employed in good faith. But a trustee may not delegate to others the exercise of his discretion, except where property is situated abroad, or where the trustee himself leaves the United Kingdom for a period exceeding one month. (Trustee Act, 1925, ss. 23, 25.)

delivery note. A document specifying the goods being delivered which is handed to the consignee of the goods.

delivery of a deed. Generally effected by the grantor saying at the time of signing and sealing the deed: " I deliver this as my act and deed." See also DEED.

delivery of bill of exchange. Transfer of possession, actual or constructive from one person to another. Every contract on a bill is incomplete and revocable until delivery.

delivery order. A written document signed by the owner of goods authorising the delivery of certain specified goods to the person named or to bearer.

demand draft. A bill of exchange payable at sight or on demand. No acceptance is needed, and no days of grace for payment are allowed.

demand, elasticity of. In economics, when a certain change in the price of a commodity produces a more than proportionate change in the amount demanded, the demand is said to be elastic. If the proportionate change in demand is less, the demand is inelastic, and if it is the same, the elasticity of demand is unity. For example, if the demand for a commodity increases from 100 per week to 200 per week owing to a fall in price from 5s. per article to 4s. 6d., the demand is said to be elastic; if the demand merely increases to 105 articles per week it is said to be inelastic.

demarcation dispute. A dispute between members of different trades, or between different trade unions, as to who ought to do a certain aspect of the work in hand. Such disputes are most likely to occur where there are several trades or unions involved on particular work and some of the functions of the work could be carried out equally efficiently by members of different trades or unions.

demise. A lease of land. Demise of the Crown describes the transmission of the kingship and its appurtenances, on the death of British monarchs, to their successors.

demurrage. (1) The detention of a ship or railway truck beyond the number of days—called lay days—allowing for loading or unloading. (2) The sum fixed by the contract of affreightment (*e.g.*, the charterparty) as payable to the shipowner or railway authority for such detention.

denomination. designation. *e.g.*, " Bonds will be issued in denominations of, £10, £20, £50, £100."

department store. A large retail shop having many departments, each of which specialises in a different class of goods.

dependency benefit. The benefit, pension or allowance payable to a person in respect of another person, child or adult, who is wholly or mainly maintained by him. (National Insurance (Industrial Injuries) Act, 1946.)

depletion. Diminution in quantity and value of an asset due to extraction; applied particularly to mining and quarrying operations.

deponent. The maker of a deposition or affidavit.

deportation. Banishment from the country. Deportation orders are made by the Home Secretary on the recommendation of the courts as regards aliens convicted of crime, or where he deems it for the public good.

Commonwealth citizens may also be deported from the United Kingdom if they are convicted of offences punishable with imprisonment and are recommended by the court for deportation (Commonwealth Immigrants Act, 1962).

deposit. (1) A payment to guarantee performance of a contract. In the event of the contract being performed, it goes in diminution of the purchase price; and
(2) A naked form of bailment where an article is deposited for safe keeping for the benefit of the bailor.

deposit account. An account kept at a bank upon which cheques are not drawn, withdrawals being made on due notice being given to the bank. Interest is payable on balances, usually by reference to bank rate.

deposit receipt. A receipt issued by a banker for a deposit made by a depositor. It usually contains the terms of the deposit. It is neither negotiable nor transferable. See PAYING-IN SLIP.

deposition. A statement on oath in a judicial proceeding.

depositors. Advertisements by finance companies, etc., for deposits from the public must disclose information as to the financial standing of the company seeking the deposits as required by the Board of Trade. Such companies may not describe themselves as banks or bankers unless recognised as such (Protection of Depositors Act, 1963).

depot. A storehouse for goods, etc., a station.

depreciation. Decrease in value.
(1) The word denotes any decrease in value or price, *e.g.*, of a currency, of capital and of capital assets.
(2) In accountancy parlance it is the regular charge against the income of a business for the decrease in value of a capital asset during its useful life, due to use and the passage of time. The depreciable capital value of an asset is usually taken as its original cost, sometimes as a recent revaluation and rarely as its replacement cost. See also AMORTISATION; DEPLETION; OBSOLESCENCE.

depression. A period of extensive decline in business activity attended by heavy unemployment.

design. See INDUSTRIAL DESIGN.

devaluation. A reduction in the value of a currency in relation to another currency or to an internationally accepted monetary metal. A devalued currency will buy less of the goods or currency of another country than it did prior to devaluation.

devastavit. [He has wasted (the assets).] Any violation or neglect of duty by a personal representative which makes him personally responsible to persons having claims on the assets, *e.g.*, creditors and beneficiaries.

development. For the purposes of the Town and Country Planning Act, 1962, development means the carrying out of building, engineering, mining or other operations in, on or under the land, or the making of any material change in the use of any buildings or other land. The Act further provides that certain operations and use of land shall not be development.

The Town and Country Planning General Development Order, 1963, authorises many forms of development.

Where permission for development is necessary application in due form has to be made to the local planning authority for " planning permission." See also the Town and Country Planning Act, 1963.

Development District. Grants may be made to assist the carrying on of industry in depressed areas known as development districts: see the Local Employment Acts, 1960, 1963.

deviation. Where a ship, without lawful excuse, deviates from the voyage contemplated by the policy, the insurer is discharged from liability as from the time of deviation, and it is immaterial that the ship may have regained her route before any loss occurs.

There is a deviation from the voyage where the course of the voyage is specifically designated by the policy and that course is departed from; or the course of the voyage is not specifically designated, but the usual and customary course is departed from.

The difference between " change of voyage " and " deviation " is that in the former the voyage contemplated by the policy is abandoned, whereas in the latter there is only a deviation, the contemplated voyage not being set aside.

See also DISPATCH; SEAWORTHINESS.

deviation, standard. A statistical term denoting the dispersion of individual values in a series from the average value.

differential. The difference in wages or wage rates between one type of worker and another, *e.g.*, skilled and unskilled. It is also applied to differences in wages between industries.

digital computer. A computer in which representation of data is done by means of digits. *Cf.* ANALOGUE COMPUTER.

dilapidation. (1) Disrepair.

(2) A sum paid at the end of a tenancy for the purpose of putting the premises in repair for the succeeding tenant. Repair means making good defects including renewal where necessary. The term is adopted from the ecclesiastical law as to benefices.

dilatory motion. A motion (*q.v.*) moved with the object of delaying the transaction of the business before a meeting; such motions may be for the adjournment of the meeting or to proceed with the next business.

diminishing returns, law of. The tendency for the average and marginal products (*q.v.*) of a factor of production (*q.v.*) to decline as more of that factor is used in relation to other factors.

diplomatic privilege. The immunity of the official representatives of a foreign State from local jurisdiction.

direct expenses. Those expenses, other than materials and wages, which have direct relation to and can be identified with a particular unit of production; *e.g.*, inward carriage on cement delivered to a contract site has direct reference to and is identifiable with that particular building contract.

direct taxes. Those assessed on and payable by individual persons, *e.g.*, income tax; as distinct from those (called INDIRECT TAXES) which are borne by persons other than those who make payment to the Commissioners; *e.g.*, purchase tax (*q.v.*). Direct taxes fall on income while indirect taxes are levied on goods and services.

directorate. The body of directors.

directors. Persons chosen by the members of a company to be responsible for the management of the business of the company: they are the officers of the company. Director includes any person in accordance with whose directions or instructions the directors of a company are accustomed to act, and any person occupying the position of a director, by whatever name called. Public companies must have at least two directors and private companies, one. Their rights and duties are regulated by the Companies Act, 1948, and by the articles of association of the company. See also ASSOCIATE DIRECTOR and GOVERNING DIRECTOR.

directors' report. A directors' report is required to be attached to every balance sheet laid before a company in general meeting dealing with:
    (a) the state of the company's affairs;
    (b) the amount, if any, recommended to be paid by way of dividend;
    (c) the amount, if any, proposed to be carried to reserves.
    The report shall deal so far as material for the appreciation of the company's affairs by its members with any change during the financial year in the nature of the company's business, or its subsidiaries, or in the class of business in which it has an interest, which can be disclosed without prejudice to the company or any of its subsidiaries. Any information which is required by the Companies Act, 1948, to be given in the accounts and is thereby allowed to be given in a statement annexed thereto, may be given in the directors' report instead of in the accounts. In such cases the directors' report shall be annexed to the accounts and the auditors shall report thereon so far as it gives this information.

disability. Legal incapacity; as inability to contract or sue. A disability may be personal; *e.g.*, to enter into a certain marriage, or physically to consummate it. A general disability is one attaching to all persons of a class; *e.g.*, infants, or aliens.

disaffirm. To deny; to repudiate.

discharge. To deprive a right or obligation of its binding force; to release a person from an obligation: thus payment discharges a debt. Rescission, release, accord and satisfaction, performance, composition, bankruptcy and merger are varieties of discharge.

discharged bankrupt. A bankrupt who has obtained an order of discharge made by the court or the annulment of a receiving order. An order of discharge releases the bankrupt from all debts provable in the bankruptcy (with a few exceptions) and also enables him to acquire property without its vesting in the trustee. The effect of the annulment of the receiving order is, in general, that the bankrupt is placed in the same position as if he had not been adjudicated, but is subject to any prior disposition duly made and acts done by the official receiver or trustee. See also UNDISCHARGED BANKRUPT.

disclaimer. The renouncing, generally, by deed, of rights, interests or office, to which a person is legally entitled: *e.g.*, the disclaimer of land burdened with onerous covenants, or unprofitable contracts, etc., by a trustee in bankruptcy; the disclaimer of a lease by a lessee.

discount. (1) A deduction from a gross amount: *e.g.*, cash discount, for prompt payment; trade discount (*q.v.*).

(2) To discount a bill means to sell or buy the bill before it is due for payment for the amount estimated to be its value at the date it is sold or bought.

(3) In regard to shares and loan stock, discount is the amount by which it has dropped below its nominal par value or issue price. Shares may not, in general, be issued at a discount.

discount market. That part of the money market whose principal business is the buying and selling of bills of exchange at a discount.

discount rate. The rate fixed by the Bank of England at which the bank will discount bills of exchange. See also BANK RATE.

discounted cash flow. A method of measuring the forecast return on a capital project, which takes into account the tax status of the project, its forecast, useful life and the effect of the timing of payments and receipts.

discovery. The obtaining by one party to an action or suit of information on oath from another party. It is of two kinds:

(1) discovery, by interrogatories, of facts relevant to the issue in the action, and within the knowledge of the party interrogated; and

(2) discovery of documents relating to the matters in question in an action, and in the possession of the party.

discretion. A man's own judgment as to what is best in a given case as opposed to a rule governing all cases of a certain kind. Thus a trustee has a discretion as to the management or application of the trust property. So a judge or court has a discretion in making orders or imposing conditions on litigants: *e.g.*, as to costs. A judge must exercise his discretion judicially, and if he proceeds on a wrong principle, his order may be set aside by the Court of Appeal.

discretionary trust. A trust under which the trustee has a discretion as to the application of the trust property; *e.g.*, a trust to distribute funds among such charitable objects as the trustees shall think fit.

74

discrimination. The practice of selling the same article or service at different prices to different buyers.

dishonour. A bill of exchange dishonoured by non-acceptance or after acceptance by non-payment.

dispatch. The condition in carriage of goods by sea that the ship will commence and complete the voyage within a reasonable time. See also DEVIATION.

disposable income. The gross income (normally of the applicant and his or her spouse) less deductions for income tax, rent, dependants, etc. (Legal Aid and Advice Act, 1949). In economics it is gross income less only direct taxes. See LEGAL AID AND ADVICE.

disposition. Every mode by which property can pass, other than by devolution; *e.g.*, by will.

dissolution. The putting an end to a legal relationship; *e.g.*, of a partnership or company, or of a marriage by a decree of divorce, etc. See DISCHARGE.

distrain. To levy distress (*q.v.*).

distress. The act of taking and holding goods, to enforce without the aid of legal proceedings, some duty; *e.g.*, payment of rent, or to remedy some wrong. A power of sale over the goods taken has to be annexed by statute to the right to distrain; as, *e.g.*, in the case of distress for rent.

distress damage-feasant. An occupier of land may seize any cattle, or other trespassing animals or thing, which are unlawfully upon his land doing damage there, and may detain them until payment of compensation for the damage done. There is no power of sale.

distribution. (1) The means by which goods are transferred from those who produce or manufacture them to those who use them.

(2) The division of the national income among those who contribute the different factors of production.

(3) For taxation purposes, the dividends paid by a company.

diversification. (1) Of a business endeavour, the production of several different articles in order that it should not depend unduly on the demand for one product.

(2) Similarly, the establishment of a greater variety of industry in a geographical area.

divest. To take away an estate or interest which has already vested.

dividend. (1) The amount of the profits of a company which is resolved by the directors to be divided amongst its members, usually expressed as a percentage of paid-up capital, or as an amount per share. If for any period a dividend is not declared by a company, the dividend is said to be passed. See also COVER.

(2) A payment under bankruptcy, deed of arrangement, or composition with creditors.

(3) A payment to creditors or shareholders, out of the assets of a company, in a liquidation.

dividend warrant. A cheque (invariably to order) issued to a shareholder as payment of a dividend (*q.v.*). Every dividend warrant must show the gross amount of dividend, the tax deducted therefrom and the amount of the net payment. Where double taxation relief is obtained the company's net effective rate of tax must also be shown.

division. Voting by means of separation into two groups for the purpose of counting of votes.

divorce. Dissolution of marriage, granted by the court on the petition of either the husband or the wife, for adultery, desertion, cruelty, incurable unsoundness of mind; or on the wife's petition, for rape or unnatural offences committed by the husband. Normally a petition cannot be presented in the first three years of marriage.

dock. (1) A place constructed for the berthing of ships and the loading and unloading of cargo; an artificial basin or inclosure provided with gates to keep the water at the proper level.

(2) The place in a criminal court in which the accused is placed when on trial.

dock warrant. A document issued by dock authorities certifying that goods therein enumerated are held in a dock warehouse on behalf of the person in whose favour the warrant is drawn.

document of title. (1) A document which enables the possessor to deal with the property described in it as if he were the owner, *e.g.*, a bill of lading; dock warrant, or a railway receipt.

(2) In respect of real property any deed or document being a material link in the chain of proof of ownership.

documentary bills. Bills of exchange accompanied by a bill of lading, invoice and insurance papers. Acceptance of the bill of exchange (and in some cases, payment of it) is necessary in order to obtain possession of the bill of lading (*q.v.*).

documentary credit. A letter of credit issued on condition that drafts drawn under it will be negotiated only if accompanied by invoices, bills of lading and insurance policies of value at least equal to the draft.

dollar. The standard unit of currency used in the United States of America. Many other countries have also adopted it for their currencies. It is a decimalised currency, unlike the pound sterling.

dollar premium. The premium which arises on purchase or sale of dollar stocks (*q.v.*) on a stock exchange in the U.K. and on investment outside the sterling area which is forced by exchange control regulations to go through the investment dollar pool.

dollar stocks. United States and Canadian stocks and shares.

domestic. Belonging to the house. A domestic servant is, properly, a servant living and sleeping in the house. Domestic service includes the work done by a school cleaner or office caretaker employed by a county council. Domestic purposes in an insurance policy may include boilers used for heating radiators in offices and showrooms.

domicile or **domicil.** The place of a person's permanent home; the country which a person chooses, or is deemed to have chosen, as his permanent home, there being the fact of residence and the intention of remaining. The civil status of a person, or his legal rights and duties (including capacity to marry) are determined by the law of his domicile. His political status, or nationality, is independent of domicile.

Domicile may be of origin or birth; or by operation of law, *e.g.*, of a woman on marriage, or infant child; or of choice.

dominion. The self-governing members of the British Commonwealth, which are not republics, *i.e.*, the Dominion of Canada, Commonwealth of Australia, and New Zealand. See also BRITISH COMMONWEALTH OF NATIONS.

dominion income tax relief. See now DOUBLE TAXATION.

dominion register. A branch share register which may be maintained in the U.K. by a company transacting business in any part of Her Majesty's dominions outside Great Britain or in the Channel Islands or the Isle of Man showing the members registered in the place where the principal register is maintained.

donatio inter vivos. See GIFT INTER VIVOS.

donatio mortis causa. A gift of personal property made in contemplation of death, to take effect only on the death of the donor, and accompanied by actual or constructive delivery of the property at the time.

Such gifts are liable to estate duty.

donee. One to whom something is given; *e.g.*, by will.

donor. One who gives something; *e.g.*, to charity.

dormant partner. A sleeping partner who takes no active part in the management of the firm whose profits are unearned for income tax purposes. See PARTNERSHIP.

double entry. The first principle of book-keeping (*q.v.*) systems. The dual aspect of a financial transaction is recognised by entering it twice; once, to the credit (*q.v.*) of the account which gives the value and again, to the debit (*q.v.*) of the account which receives the value.

double insurance. Where an insurance is a contract of indemnity, *e.g.*, fire insurance, and the insured takes out policies in two or more companies, which has the effect of over-insuring his property. The insured is only entitled to recover his loss once over.

double option. A put and call option (*q.v.*) taken out on a specified security at the same time.

double taxation. The assessment of the same income or profits both in the United Kingdom and under the laws of other countries including members of the Commonwealth. Relief may be granted under conventions entered into with the government of the country concerned.

down payment. A deposit against the total purchase price in a hire-purchase transaction. The minimum percentage of the purchase price which must be paid as a down payment is controlled by the government and is varied as an instrument of monetary policy.

draft. (1) A bill of exchange before acceptance. See also BANKER'S DRAFT. (2) A preliminary form of a document, which, when settled, is engrossed for execution.

draught. The distance from the lowest part of the ship to the water line at which the vessel is floating.

drawback. The refund of duty made on the exportation of goods for which customs duties and excise have been paid on importation.

drawee. The person to whom a bill of exchange is addressed.

drawer. One who signs a bill of exchange as the maker.

due date. The date on which a bill of exchange is due for payment; three days of grace must be added to the expressed period of the bill.

dumping. Placing goods on the market in large quantities at unprofitable prices or prices lower than those charged elsewhere. Anti-dumping duties have been imposed to limit or discourage the importation and sale of goods in unfair competition with home produced goods.

dunnage. Materials used in the stowage of cargo to prevent shifting or damage or to build up or separate the cargo.

duopoly. In economics, the situation in which two independent firms are selling an identical product in the same market.

durante minore aetate. [During minority.]

duress. Coercion by imprisonment, violence or threat. An agreement or promise made under duress will not be upheld.

Dutch auction. An auction where property is offered at a high price, which is reduced until accepted.

dying declaration. A statement, not on oath, made by a person since deceased, whose death is the subject of a charge of homicide. It must be shown that the deceased believed he was in danger of death.

dying deposition. A deposition of a person dangerously ill taken before a Justice of the Peace containing material information about some crime. It is admissible at the trial in the event of the witness's death, or of the impossibility of his giving evidence.

E

earned income. Income of an individual arising from the exercise of any office or employment or property attaching thereto; deferred pay and pensions in respect of past services of the recipient, or the husband or parent thereof, or to anyone else in respect of the services of a deceased employee; income arising from the carrying on by a person of a vocation, trade or profession, including woodlands; benefits under the National Insurance Acts where assessable; family allowances, and certain income from patent rights. Earned income is taxed more leniently than un-earned income.

earnest. A nominal sum given to a vendor as a token of good faith and/or in part payment for the purpose of binding the agreement.

earnings. (1) Of employees it means the amount of money received during a period for labour services.

(2) Of a company it refers to profits after deduction of direct taxation on profits, *i.e.*, corporation tax in the U.K.

earnings basis. The assessment to tax of the profits of a trade, business or profession on the basis of profits which have become due in the accounting period, irrespective of when payment is received; as contrasted with the cash basis, *i.e.*, that of actual receipts.

earnings yield. The earnings (*q.v.*) of a company in a period expressed as a percentage of the nominal, or market, value of the company's total issued ordinary share capital. See also PRICE EARNINGS RATIO.

easement. A right which the owner of land, the dominant tenement, enjoys in respect of other land, the servient tenement, *e.g.*, rights of way, rights to light and air, and to water.

econometrics. The systematic analysis of economic data with the aid of a computer, or by mathematical and statistical methods.

economic growth. Expansion in the national income or total volume of production of goods and services of a country.

economic planning. Central state planning to secure the optimum allocation of a country's resources in order to achieve economic objectives at which the government and people of the country are aiming.

economic policy. The general aims, or objectives, of a government in the economic sphere. A common denominator for all countries' economic policy could be said to be the maintenance of a high rate of economic growth (*q.v.*) in order to secure an improving standard of living for the people.

economics. The social science of the production and distribution of wealth.

education. Is one of the principal influences on the quality of a country's labour force and therefore on its capacity to produce goods and services.

effective tax rate. The average rate in the £ of direct taxation payable by an individual.

ejectment. The dispossessing by process of law of a person in wrongful possession of land or premises.

ejusdem generis. [Of the same kind or nature.] A rule of construction applicable where particular words are followed by general words; the general words are limited by the particular words.

election. Choice, as of representatives, directors, etc.

(1) Election at common law is the principle which puts a man to his election whether or not he will affirm a contract induced by fraud; or whether in a case of wrongful conversion he will waive the tort and recover the proceeds in an action for money had and received.

(2) Election in equity arises where there is a duality of gifts in the same instrument as by will; one of the gifts being to C of the donor's own property, and the other being to B of the property of C. The gift to C takes effect only if C elects to permit the gift to B also to take effect.

electricity. See UNITS OF MEASUREMENT.

electronic computer. See COMPUTER.

embargo. A prohibition from passing. To stop the movement of ships or goods. For example, the prohibition imposed in time of war by a belligerent State upon merchant ships against their leaving port. It is the equivalent of quarantine in the usage of the U.S.A.

embezzlement. The crime of converting to his own use, by a clerk or servant, of property received by him on behalf of his master. The distinction between embezzlement and larceny by a clerk or servant is that in larceny the thing stolen is taken out of the possession of the master, whereas in embezzlement the thing is appropriated while in possession of the servant, and before it has come into the possession of the master.

emblements. Crops and annual vegetable products growing on land. A right to emblements arises where the occupier of land has sown or planted growing crops and his occupation is determined by a cause beyond his control, e.g., where a tenancy at will is determined by the landlord. He then has the right to gather the crops after the end of his tenancy.

employer. Any person or corporation who engages the services of another person for hire. A person or corporation with whom a workman has a contract of service. Where an insured person is employed by two or more persons in the same week, the first of these is treated as the employer.

employer's liability. Although compensation for industrial injuries and diseases is dealt with by the National Insurance (Industrial Injuries) Act, 1946, the employer is still liable at common law for the injury to an employee caused by the negligence of himself or his servant. This may be insured against.

employment. Any trade, business, profession, office or vocation. For the purposes of the National Insurance Acts employment means gainfully occupied in employment in Great Britain, being employment under a contract of service. Insured persons pay weekly contributions at different rates, as (1) employed persons, (2) self-employed persons, or (3) non-employed persons.

Minimum periods of notice to terminate the employment of those who have been employed for a qualifying period, and matters connected with the giving of the notice, and also the requirement that employers are to give written particulars of employment, are provided for in the Contracts of Employment Act, 1963.

Provision is made for securing the health, safety and welfare of persons employed to work in office premises (q.v.), shop premises (q.v.) and certain railway premises by the Offices, Shops, and Railway Premises Act,

1963. In particular, there are general provisions as regards cleanliness, overcrowding, temperature, ventilation, lighting, sanitary conveniences, washing facilities, drinking water supply, clothing accommodation, sitting facilities, seats for the sedentary, floors, passages and stairs, cleaning and dangerous machinery, first aid and fire precaution. The Factories Act, 1961, is amended as necessary.

employment, full. The level of economic activity in a community at which every person who is prepared to work at prevailing wages can find employment.

enclosure. Something enclosed; *e.g.*, in a letter, or by a wall (as an enclosed town) or a fence (as an enclosed field).

encroachment. The unauthorised extension of the boundaries of land on to the land of another.

encumbrance. A charge or liability, *e.g.*, a mortgage.

end product. The completed product so far as a particular firm is concerned. Other firms may alter or add to the product before delivering their own end product.

endorse. Also INDORSE. To write one's name on the back of a document, especially a cheque.

endowment. The gift to a woman of a dowry. Money or property paid to a charitable, educational or religious institution for the furtherance of its activities generally, or some specified part thereof.

endowment funds. Pension and provident funds created for the benefit of employees.

endowment policy. A policy of assurance, insuring money to be paid on the survival for a specified period of the person assured, either with or without provision for the payment of money in the event of the death of that person before the expiration of that period.

enemy alien. See ALIEN ENEMY.

enfranchise. To make free or to confer a liberty. For example, to confer the right to vote.

engross, to. Copying a document from the draft, usually by typewriting, with words, dates and amounts set out in full, and with the testatum and attestation clauses.

engrossment. The formal document, as engrossed; *e.g.*, a deed or will, ready for execution.

entail. Interest in land such that it could only descend to children, grand-children, etc., of the tenant. See PERPETUITY.

entered. A ship is " entered in " when its arrival in port has been officially notified to the Customs, and " entered outwards " when the intention to begin taking cargo on board has been notified. When all formalities have been complied with to obtain the Customs permission to sail, the vessel is " cleared outwards." See ENTRY.

entrepôt trade. Trade consisting of the importing of goods for the specific purpose of export.

entrepreneur. One who undertakes on his own account the risk element of an industrial or commercial enterprise.

entry. (1) The act of going on land with the intention of asserting a right in it.

(2) Forcible entry is the offence of entering in a violent manner.

(3) The declaration to the Customs of the nature and quantity of ship's cargo.

(4) A brief memorandum in an accounting record.

equitable. That which is fair, reasonable or just; that which is in accordance with, or regulated, recognised or enforced by the rules of equity, as opposed to those of the common law. See also EQUITY.

equitable apportionments. Rules of apportionment formulated by the courts to secure an equitable adjustment between life tenant and remaindermen, as opposed to statutory apportionments derived from the Apportionment Act, 1870.

equitable assignments. Assignments which equity recognises as effective to transfer the property assigned. They are informal assignments which do not comply with the requirements of a legal assignment. The intention to assign must be made clear but the assignment need not be in writing. Notice to the debtor is not required but should be given to protect the assignee's interests. See ASSIGNMENT.

equitable charge. A security over property for a debt which charges the property in equity only.

equitable interests. Beneficial interests in property which is vested in another person as the legal owner; equitable interests as contrasted with legal interests. The prime example of an equitable interest is the interest of a beneficiary where the trust relationship exists; *i.e.*, where the trustee as legal owner has domain and stewardship over property exercised by him on behalf of the beneficiary. The rights of the owner of an equitable interest are liable to be defeated by a bona fide purchaser for value of the legal estate without notice of the trust or equitable interest.

A company is not bound to register notices of equitable interests, and such a notice cannot affect the company with any trust.

equitable lien. This exists where the person entitled to the lien has not possession but has the right to have the property of another applied to discharge certain specific liabilities; *e.g.*, a partner in a dissolution of partnership has an equitable lien to have partnership assets applied to partnership debts. See LIEN.

equitable mortgage. (1) Where there is a mortgage of an equitable interest in property; *e.g.*, the mortgage by a *cestui que trust* of his interest in the trust property, or the mortgage of an equity of redemption (*e.g.*, a second or subsequent mortgage).

(2) Where there is a mortgage of a legal interest which does not convey the legal estate to the mortgagee, *e.g.*, the deposit of title deeds or scrip with the lender.

equities. The ordinary shares of industrial and commercial companies on which dividends may be declared to the extent of the profits remaining after providing for fixed interest and dividends on loan capital and preference shares. On the Stock Exchange they are contrasted with gilt edged (*q.v.*).

Equity. The body of rules founded in fairness and justice which was evolved by the Lord Chancellors and the Court of Chancery to supplement the common law and also alleviate its harshness. Equity provided remedies and recognised rights unknown to the common law For example, the enforcement of trusts is dealt with entirely in equity since the common law recognised only the rights of the legal owner. The remedy of the common law courts was to give damages to a person whom it regarded as having suffered injury, whereas the courts of equity could, where justice required it, grant a decree of specific performance, or an injunction. In time the rules of equity became as fixed as those of the common law, and statute law became the only method of modification of those rules. Clashes had inevitably occurred between the systems of common law and equity, and it was finally established that the rules of equity prevailed over those of the common law.

Common law and equity are now administered concurrently by the courts, but matters of law which originated in Chancery are assigned to the Chancery Division.

In accountancy, equity is the term used to denote the net value of assets, *i.e.*, total assets less liabilities to outside persons. In the case of a partnership it denotes the total of capital and current accounts, and in the case of a company it denotes the total of share capital, and capital and revenue reserves.

equity of redemption. The equitable right which a mortgagor has to pay off the mortgage and redeem the mortgaged property, after the legal period for repayment of the loan has passed. The mortgagor has this right until he has been foreclosed, or until his right is barred by the Statutes of Limitations, or until the property has been sold by the mortgagee under a power of sale. The equity of redemption of a mortgagor is an equitable interest in the property.

equity shares. That part of the issued share capital which does not bear a fixed rate of interest.

ergonomics. Study of the efficiency of workers, of which Time and Motion Study is a part.

escheat. The reversion of land to the Crown on failure of next-of-kin of an owner dying intestate and without heir.

escrow. See DEED.

essence of the contract. A condition or provision in a contract without which the contract would not have been entered into, and breach of which brings it to an end.

estate. (1) Estate denotes the condition in life or circumstances of a person. The " three estates of the realm " are the Lords spiritual and temporal, and the Commons.

(2) The extent or nature of the interest which a person has in property, or the various modes of ownership of property, particularly in land. Thus there are estates of freehold or leasehold; for life or at will; absolute or conditional; in possession or in expectancy; vested or contingent; legal or equitable, and so on.

(3) The whole sum of the assets and liabilities of a person.

estate agent. An agent whose work mainly comprises the finding of buyers, tenants or sellers of property on behalf of owners or buyers. Remuneration is by commission based on the value of the transaction.

estate duty. The duty on property of deceased persons which actually passes on death, or is deemed so to pass; as where a gift was made by the deceased *inter vivos*, *i.e.*, within the five years preceding his death. Property passes when it changes hands. Estate duty is payable where the principal value of all property, real or personal, settled or not settled, exceeds £5,000 (Finance Act, 1963). The rates of duty range from a minimum of one per cent. to a maximum of eighty per cent. on estates exceeding one million pounds.

estate owner. Under the Property Acts of 1925 the estate owner is the person in whom the legal estate in land is vested, and conveyances of the land must be made by him. Estate owners comprise an absolute owner, trustees for sale, a tenant for life under a settlement, a mortgagor and personal representatives.

estimate. A contractor's statement of sums for which he will undertake specified work. See TENDER.

estimates, parliamentary. The civil estimates as presented to Parliament. See BUDGET.

estoppel. The rule of evidence or doctrine of law which precludes a person from denying the truth of some statement formerly made by him, or the existence of facts in which he has by words or conduct led others to believe and act upon.

(1) Estoppel by record. A person is not permitted to dispute the facts upon which a judgment against him is based.

(2) Estoppel by deed. A person cannot dispute his own deed; he cannot deny the truth of recitals contained in it.

(3) Estoppel *in pais*. Estoppel by conduct, *e.g.*, a tenant, having accepted a lease, cannot dispute his lessor's title.

(4) Quasi-estoppel is where a person makes a promise to another intended to affect their legal relations, and to be acted upon. If it is acted on, the promise stands good, although there is no consideration.

(5) Equitable estoppel is where a person acquiesces in a mistake by another so as to tacitly represent that the other is in order in proceeding as he does; *e.g.*, in building on the land of that person.

etc. (et cetera). And so forth.

et seq. (et sequentes). And the following.

European Economic Community. An economic and political association of six European countries, established in 1957 by the Treaty of Rome. The economic objective is to eliminate internal tariffs and establish a common external tariff.

eviction. The compulsory removal of persons from land or other property. Eviction orders are granted by the courts.

evidence. All the legal means, exclusive of mere argument, which tend to prove or disprove any matter of fact, the truth of which is submitted to judicial investigation.

(1) Oral. Statements made by witnesses in court under oath.

(2) Documentary. Documents produced for the inspection of the judge.

(3) Conclusive. Evidence of a fact which the court must take as full proof of such fact and which prevails over all evidence to disprove it.

(4) Direct. Evidence of a fact actually in issue; evidence of a fact actually perceived by a witness with his own senses.

(5) Circumstantial. Indirect evidence which is relevant, inasmuch as it establishes facts from which presumptions or conclusions may be drawn.

(6) Real. Evidence supplied by material objects produced for the inspection of the court.

(7) Extrinsic. Oral evidence given in connection with written documents.

(8) Hearsay. Evidence of a fact not actually seen or heard by a witness himself, but told to him by another person.

(9) Original. Evidence which has an independent probative force of its own, *e.g.*, an original document.

(10) Derivative. Evidence which derives its force from some other source, *e.g.*, oral evidence of the contents of a document.

(11) Parol. Oral evidence.

(12) Prima facie. Evidence of a fact which the court must take as proof of such fact, unless disproved by further evidence.

(13) Primary. Evidence which itself suggests that it is the best evidence, and which is required to be produced if available, *e.g.*, an original document.

(14) Secondary. Evidence which itself suggests the existence of better evidence, and which is rejected if primary evidence is available. For example, a copy of a document may not be put in evidence, if the original document is in existence and available.

ex capitalisation. An indication against a stock exchange quotation for a share that the share is being dealt in without benefit of a recent bonus issue or capital distribution.

ex cathedra. [From the chair.] With official authority.

ex concesso. [Admittedly.]

ex contractu. [From, or arising out of, a contract.]

ex curia. [Out of court.]

ex delicto. [From, or arising out of, an offence; from the crime.]

ex dividend. [Without dividend]. When stocks and shares on which a dividend has been declared, or is anticipated, are sold " ex dividend " the buyer is not entitled to the dividend. See CUM DIVIDEND.

ex gratia. [As of favour.] Implying absence of right.

ex officio. The description of one who by virtue of his office is entitled to occupy a certain position.

ex parte. In the absence of one side.
(1) Used in such phrases as an "*ex parte* statement," *i.e.*, a statement made by one side.
(2) An application in a judicial proceeding made (a) by an interested person who is not a party, *e.g.*, a trustee applying for directions as to administration of trust property, (b) by one party in the absence of the other.

ex post facto. Retrospective. *Lit.*, from what is done afterwards.

ex rights. A term used in describing the selling of shares so that the purchaser is not given rights to a new issue of shares about to be made to shareholders.

ex-ship contracts. Contracts for the sale of goods in which the seller's duty is to deliver the goods to the buyer from a ship which has arrived at the port of delivery. The buyer is not concerned with shipment.

ex warehouse; ex wharf. Where the vendor pays all charges up to and including discharge from warehouse, or delivery from wharf.

excess capacity. Facilities for producing more goods than are being demanded. It may result from over-investment in productive capacity or a falling off in demand.

exchange. Mutual transfer or conveyance of property: barter. See EXCHANGE, RATE OF; STOCK EXCHANGE.

exchange control. The system of government control, exercised by the Treasury largely through the Banks, over financial transactions between residents in this country and residents outside the sterling area, to prevent loss of capital and valuables. Provision was made for the acquisition of holdings of foreign currency, etc., and dealings in gold and foreign currency were restricted to authorised dealers. (Exchange Control Act, 1947.)

exchange equalisation funds. Funds, managed by the official monetary authorities, held partly in foreign exchange and partly in gold, which are used for intervention in the foreign exchange markets with the object of stabilising the exchange rate of sterling.

exchange, rate of. The rate which has to be applied to the currency of one country to convert it into the currency of another, *e.g.*, sterling to dollars. The rate at which drafts for payment in a foreign country in the currency of that country can be purchased for English currency at the relevant date. Rates may be at a discount, at par, or at a premium. Rates may be quoted for varying times, such as telegraphic transfer, sight, 30 days' sight, 60 days' sight, etc.

Exchequer. The "Account of Her Majesty's Exchequer " with the Bank of England into which are paid all government receipts and revenues. The fund so formed is called the Consolidated Fund, out of which are paid the sums necessary for the public service as authorised by Parliament, and subject to the control of the Comptroller and Auditor General.

exchequer bonds. Issued by the Treasury for fixed periods not exceeding six years, and either payable to bearer or registered at the Bank of England. Interest is fixed at the time of issue.

excise. A tax imposed on the production of certain commodities within the country, as distinguished from duties levied on imported goods. The excise is managed by the Commissioners of Customs and Exicse. The duties fall mainly under two heads: (1) On commodities, *e.g.*, beer, matches; (2) Licence duties issued to persons licensed to sell dutiable commodities; *e.g.*, distillers; brewers.

execute; execution. To execute is to complete or carry into effect. Thus to execute a deed is to sign, seal and deliver it. To execute a judgment or order of court is to carry it into effect or enforce it.

executed contract. A contract where one party has performed all that he is required to do according to the contract. A delivers one ton of coal to B; A has performed his part of the contract, and it remains for B to pay the price.

executed trust. A trust in which the limitations are complete and final; *e.g.*, where A conveys property to C for life and after his death to B absolutely.

executive. A person who is managerially responsible for a functional or general aspect of a firm's business. The Executive is the administrative branch or aspect of the Government.

executor (fem. **executrix**). An executor is the person to whom the execution of a will, that is, the duty of carrying its provisions into effect, is entrusted by the testator. The duties of an executor are to bury the deceased, to prove the will, to collect the estate, and, if necessary, convert it into money, to pay the debts in their proper order, to pay the legacies, and distribute the residue among the persons entitled. He may bring actions against persons who are indebted to the testator, or are in possession of property belonging to the estate.

executor de son tort. [Of his own wrong.] One who, being neither executor nor administrator, intermeddles with the goods of the deceased. When a man has so acted, he renders himself liable, not only to an action by the rightful executor or administrator, but also to be sued by the creditor or legatee of the deceased. He has all the liabilities, though none of the privileges, which belong to an executor or administrator.

executory. That which remains to be carried into effect.

executory contract. A contract where both parties still have obligations to perform under it. X agrees with Y to write up his accounts for fifteen guineas. Both considerations are yet to be performed and the contract is " executory."

executory interest. A future interest in real and/or personal property which does not depend upon the determination of prior particular estates; *e.g.*, a gift by will " to my son A on his becoming twenty-one."

executory trust. A trust raised by a stipulation or direction, in express terms or by necessary implication, to make a settlement upon trusts which are indicated, but not finally declared by the instruments containing the stipulation or direction.

Exemplification. An official copy of a legal document sealed by the court or a public officer.

exempt private company. See COMPANY.

exhibit. A document or piece of evidence which is identified in an affidavit or by a witness when giving evidence and sworn to for the purposes of the case.

exor. Executor (*q.v.*).

expatriation. (1) Banishment from one's own country.
(2) Loss of nationality by renunciation of allegiance, and the acquisition of a foreign nationality.

expense. Outlay of cash or other resources.

expense allocation. The process of distributing the expense items to appropriate jobs, contracts, services, processes or other unit of cost determination.

expert. Any person whose profession gives authority to a statement made by him; for instance, an engineer, valuer or accountant.
An expert witness is one who has made the subject on which he speaks a matter of particular study, practice or observation. A doctor is not qualified as an expert witness on all branches of medicine, nor a lawyer on all branches of law.

export entry. A printed form to be completed and lodged at the Customs office by a person desiring to export goods. The form shows the port of sailing, ship, date of sailing, destination, owner, marks and numbers, number of packages, description of goods, country of origin, weight, value, etc. The converse is IMPORT ENTRY, and the information is somewhat similar.

export sales. See C.I.F.; F.O.B.; EX-SHIP CONTRACTS.

export trade. The sale of a country's products abroad. The products consist of goods (visible items) and services (invisible items).

exporter. One who sells goods or services abroad either as principal or factor.

express. Express is contrasted with implied, thus direct communication is opposed to communication by implication, *e.g.*, an express trust, as opposed to an implied trust.

express trust. A trust created by clear words, *e.g.*, where A gives property to B in trust for C. A is called the author of the trust, or the settlor, testator, etc., according to the instrument by which the trust is created.

extant. Being or remaining in existence.

external debt. The amount that one country owes to others. Servicing (*i.e.*, periodic interest and repayment) the external debt is a major item in the balance of payments of a developing economy.

exterritoriality. Rights which, when conferred by treaty, give to a British subject abroad complete personal protection, assurance of satisfactory judicial tribunals, and such enjoyment of his property as British law would afford him for British property.

A person with diplomatic privilege (*q.v.*) enjoys exterritoriality as regards the country to which he is accredited.

extradition. The surrender by one government to another of a fugitive criminal accused or convicted of an extradition crime, *i.e.*, a crime which is not merely political. Treaties are made between countries containing reciprocal obligations to deliver up fugitive criminals.

extraordinary general meetings. Meetings held to transact some particular business of a company which it is desired to bring before the members. Notice of the special business must be stated in the notice calling the meeting. The meeting may be called by the directors and in some special circumstances by the members.

extraordinary resolution. See RESOLUTION.

extrinsic evidence. See EVIDENCE.

F

F.I.F.O. " First in, first out." A term used to indicate a basis for charging out materials for production purposes or for valuing stock on hand at a given date, under which it is assumed that the goods are used or sold in the order in which they were acquired.

F.O.B. See FREE ON BOARD.

face value. The nominal value written or printed on the face of bonds, notes, share certificates, debentures, and other documents, indicating their par value.

factor. A mercantile agent (*q.v.*).

factor of production. Resources used in the provision of goods and services are classified into the factors of land, labour, capital and management.

factory. A manufactory; premises with plant or machinery for the making of goods; a works. The Factories Act, 1961, consolidates the law relating to the safety, health and welfare of persons employed in factories. For the purposes of the Town and Country Planning Acts, factories are described as industrial buildings, either light, general or special. See also EMPLOYMENT.

factory cost. In cost accounting—total cost of producing goods ready to
  (1) transfer to finished stock warehouse or
  (2) transfer to finished parts stock.
In determining factory cost, that proportion of expenses of administration (such as directors' fees, office salaries, printing, stationery, telephone, etc.) which is deemed to be properly attributable to factory activity would be included, but factory cost excludes selling or distribution expense and general administration charges as well as any profit loading.

factum. (An act or deed.) See NON EST FACTUM.

fair average quality. A fair average of the quality of the various classes of a product in a specified mixture (*e.g.*, wheat).

fair comment. A fair comment on a matter of public interest or which is submitted to public criticism, is not actionable as defamation (*q.v.*). Comment is of the nature of criticism or opinion and must be distinguished from a statement of fact. Fair comment means comment honestly believed to be true, not inspired by any malicious motive, and not irrelevant.

fair wear and tear. The normal amount of depreciation to cover the use over a period of time of some form of property or other capital asset.

false imprisonment. The confinement of a person without just cause or excuse. There must be a total restraint of the person; and the onus of proving reasonable cause is on the defendant.

false oath; false swearing. See PERJURY.

false pretences. A false representation of fact. Obtaining goods, money, etc., by false pretences with intent to defraud is a criminal offence.

false trade description. A trade description which is false in a material respect as regards the goods to which it is applied, and includes every alteration of a trade description, whether by way of addition, defacement or otherwise, where that alteration makes the description false in a material respect, and the fact that a trade description is a trade-mark or part of a trade-mark, shall not prevent such trade description being a false trade description within the meaning of the Merchandise Marks Act, 1887.

family allowances. A small sum to which mothers are entitled in respect of their second and subsequent child. It is paid by the state.

farm subsidies. Price support for various farm commodities, *e.g.*, cereals and fatstock, plus grants on certain farm purchases, *e.g.*, fertilisers and improvements, which are paid by central government to the farmer or his agent.

fashion. Changes in the attitude of consumers towards goods which are available for sale. The unpredictable nature of fashion makes the anticipation of demand difficult for the producers of certain goods, *e.g.*, shoes.

faults, all. All the faults consistent with a thing being what it is described. A sale with " all faults " releases the vendor from responsibility for honest mis-statements capable of being detected by examination.

federal state. A composite state with a written constitution which apportions the sovereign power between a central or federal legislature on the one hand, and a system of local legislatures on the other, in such a way that each is sovereign within its prescribed sphere. The purpose is to reconcile national unity and power with the maintenance of state rights. The United States of America, for example, is a federal state.

federation. A form of union by which neighbouring independent states vest certain of their powers in a central body chosen by them jointly, called the Federal Goverment, leaving the local legislatures with limited functions only; *e.g.* Australia, Canada. See also FEDERAL STATE.

fee simple. The fullest interest a person can have in land amounting for all practical purposes to the ownership of the land itself. See also FREEHOLD ESTATE.

felony. Formerly every species of crime, a conviction for which occasioned the forfeiture of the lands or goods of the offender and the penalty for which was death (except petty larceny). The distinction between felonies and misdemeanours remains, (*q.v.*) but forfeiture and the death penalty for felony have been abolished.

feme covert. [A married woman.]

feme sole. An unmarried woman, *i.e.*, a spinster, widow or divorcee.

fiat. [Let it be done.] A decree or warrant of a judge or public officer in certain processes or proceedings.

fidelity guarantee insurance. An insurance taken out by an employer to indemnify himself against fraudulent embezzlement or fraudulent misappropriation of the employer's money by an employee.

fiduciary. The relationship of one person to another where the former is bound to exercise rights and powers in good faith for the benefit of the latter; *e.g.*, as between trustee and beneficiary. In commerce it is used as equivalent to unsecured, *e.g.*, a fiduciary loan. The fiduciary note issue is the issue of bank notes without any gold reserve to meet them, but backed by Government securities.

fi. fa. [*fieri facias*: that you cause to be made.] A writ of *fi. fa.* is a writ of execution on a judgment commanding the sheriff that out of the goods and chattels of the defendant he "cause to be made" the amount recovered by the judgment and (usually) costs. Under this writ the sheriff or his officer seizes the goods of the defendant, sells them by auction, and (if the defendant should not be made bankrupt or insolvent in the meantime) pays the proceeds into court. Such proceeds are then available to satisfy (in whole or in part) the plaintiff's claim. The wearing apparel of the debtor and things in actual use cannot be siezed under a *fi. fa.*

final judgment. A judgment determining the rights of the parties; as contrasted with an interlocutory (or intermediate) judgment. A final judgment may still be the subject of appeal.

finance. In a broad sense it is the factor of production (*q.v.*) known as capital. The requirements for finance of businesses vary with the type of trade and from time to time. All businesses require some permanent finance (fixed capital) and fluctuating amounts of short term finance (working capital).

Finance Act. An annual Act of Parliament (but there may be more than one in some years) which contains the government's fiscal alterations for the current year. Its provisions are founded on the Chancellor's budget proposals and on the Finance Bill.

finance house. A financial institution which specialises in the financing of hire purchase transactions, principally for retailers and their customers. A finance house obtains its finance from the commercial banks or from deposits by the public.

Finance Houses Association. Formed in 1945 with the object of protecting the interests of those engaged in hire-purchase or instalment-credit business.

finance market. Any organised market whose function is the provision of finance, *e.g.*, stock exchanges, discount market.

financial year. Of a business is the interval of a year which is habitually adopted for purposes of preparing the formal financial accounts. The year adopted by a particular business may run to any date and may be changed.

financier. A term usually applied to an individual, but it also relates to companies, who provides finance for business enterprises.

finding. A conclusion upon an inquiry of fact.

fire assessor. See ASSESSOR.

fire inquest. An inquiry held by a coroner into the origin and results of a fire, in the City of London only.

fire insurance. A contract of indemnity, in consideration of the payment of an annual premium, against loss by fire, the most common being:
(1) Specific policies. Where particular property is specifically insured for a certain sum, *e.g.*, a dwelling-house.

(2) "Blanket" or General Policies. Where different classes of property, *e.g.*, stock and machinery, are grouped and insured for one fixed amount. The value of any particular item is not stated separately.

(3) Floating Policies. Where property is covered in different places. For example, stock may be insured in store, at warehouse and in transit all under the one policy.

(4) Concurrent Policies. A concurrent policy may exist where two policies for fire insurance have been taken out in respect of the same property in different companies and one of the policies covers additional matter. For instance, where one policy is taken out to cover a building and another policy is taken out with another company to cover both building and contents. In the event of a total loss occurring the contents would be covered by the latter policy solely and the loss on the building would be borne rateably by the two insurance companies.

(5) Declaration Policies. Where the amount of stock varies to a great degree in quantity and value during the period covered by the policy, it is usual to cover such property by a declaration policy. At the time the policy is effected, the amount stated as the sum insured is considered the maximum risk during the period. At regular intervals, however, *e.g.*, monthly, declarations are given by the insured as to the amount of stock comprising the risk. In accordance with these declarations the premium is adjusted at the end of the period stated in the policy. Stock declaration policies are usually subject to average.

firm. (1) A partnership (*q.v.*). The style or title under which one or several persons carry on business. It is also frequently used of companies.

(2) In economics, an autonomous business unit.

firm name. The name under which the business of a firm is carried on. It may be the name of one or more members of the partnership or may be a fictitious name. A partnership may include the word "company" in its name but must not use the word "limited" as the last word in its name. The Registration of Business Names Act, 1916, applies to every firm and every individual carrying on business in the United Kingdom in names other than their own true surnames and to every company carrying on business under a business name which does not consist of its corporate name, and such firm, individual or company must be registered under that Act.

firm offer. An offer which does not lapse but remains open until revoked.

fiscal year. The financial year of the government, which for income tax purposes begins on April 6th and ends on April 5th of the next year. The illogical date arose from changes in the calendar.

fixed assets. See ASSETS.

fixed capital. See ASSETS; CAPITAL.

fixed charge. A charge on specific property as contrasted with a floating charge (*q.v.*).

fixed costs or expenses. Costs or expenses which, over a relatively short period, do not vary in amount despite variations in the volume of production, *e.g.*, rent, insurance and loan interest.

fixed liabilities. Long-term liabilities, *e.g.*, mortgages, debentures. See also DEFERRED LIABILITY.

fixed plant. Machinery and plant and other similar equipment placed in a definite position.

fixed trust. See UNIT TRUSTS.

fixtures. Personal chattels annexed to land, that is, fastened to or connected with it. Whatever is so annexed, as a general rule, becomes part of the realty, and the property in it immediately vests in the owner of the soil.

Tenant's fixtures are chattels annexed to land or houses, which are removable by the tenant. They are not distrainable for rent, but they may be seized in execution. They are:—

(1) articles either ornamental or of domestic convenience, of the nature of fittings rather than additions to the house itself, which can be removed entire without substantial damage to the fabric;

(2) trade fixtures, *i.e.*, fixtures erected for the purpose of carrying on some trade, business or manufacture. They may be removed although damaging the fabric.

flags of convenience. Ships registered in countries other than those to which they really belong, in order to avoid taxation, are said to be flying flags of convenience. Liberia and Panama are examples of countries which provide shipowners with flags of convenience.

flat. A separate and self-contained set of premises constructed for use as a dwelling and forming part of a building from some other part of which it is divided horizontally.

flat rate. Of interest is the current return on an investment, ignoring inflation, reinvestment or any premium over the purchase price which may be payable on redemption.

floating assets; circulating assets. See ASSETS.

floating capital. Current or circulating assets. See also ASSETS.

floating charge or security. An equitable charge on the assets for the time being of a going concern. It attaches to the subject charged in the varying condition it happens to be in from time to time. It is a charge in equity on the property for the time being in existence. It need not be over the whole of the assets of the company. It does not prevent a company from dealing with its property in the ordinary course of business, and only becomes a fixed charge when it crystallises; *i.e.*, when the company no longer is a going concern, or goes into liquidation (even for the purpose of reconstruction), or ceases to carry on business; a receiver is appointed, or the person entitled thereto, *i.e.*, the mortgagee, intervenes.

floating debenture. A debenture carrying a floating charge over assets.

floating policy. (1) One, in marine insurance, which is issued to cover all shipments of goods by the insured by any vessel between specified places. (2) One issued to factors or warehousemen to cover their limited interest in property of which they have charge. See also FIRE INSURANCE.

flotsam. Goods lost by shipwreck, or cast overboard, which remain afloat. If unclaimed, they belong to the Crown. See also JETSAM.

folio. (1) Leaf of paper, etc., numbered only on front.

(2) In bookkeeping, two opposite pages of ledger, etc., used concurrently; page of ledger, etc., used for both sides of account.

(3) Page number of printed book.

(4) Number of words, 72 or 90, taken as unit in reckoning length of document.

(5) A sheet of paper folded once, and so a book of that size.

football pool. A competition offering prizes for the forecast of future events; *viz.*, the results of football matches. The conduct of pool betting business is regulated by the Betting, Gaming and Lotteries Act, 1963. See also POOL BETTING.

forecasting. Attempting to forecast future sales and requirements is an essential function of business management.

foreclosure. When a mortgagor has failed to pay off the mortgage debt at the proper time, the mortgagee is entitled to bring an action in the court asking that a day may be fixed on which the mortgagor is to pay off the debt, and that in default of payment on that day the mortgagor may be foreclosed of his equity of redemption (*q.v.*); *i.e.*, he loses the property.

foreign attachment. See ATTACHMENT.

foreign bill. Any bill other than an inland bill (*q.v.*).

foreign companies (overseas companies). See COMPANY.

foreign exchange. The process of exchanging one currency for another. A foreign exchange market is where this process takes place. See EXCHANGE, RATE OF.

foreign sovereigns. They may sue, but may not be sued, against their will, in the English courts. See DIPLOMATIC PRIVILEGE.

foreign trade. International trade, which may be bilateral or multilateral; the latter being the best method of achieving an expansion in the level of world trade.

foreign-going ship. Ships sailing between the United Kingdom and foreign ports beyond Europe between the Elbe and Brest.

foreshore. The shore and bed of the sea and of any tidal water below the line of the medium high tide between the spring tides and the neap tides. The property in the foreshore is prima facie vested in the Crown.

forestalling. Avoidance of withholding tax by payment of artificially high dividends during the period of transition to a system of corporation tax for companies in the U.K.

forfeited shares. Shares in a company, the ownership of which is forfeited by the holder for non-payment of calls or other reasons, as provided for in the articles of association.

forfeiture. The loss of property as a penalty for some act or omission, *e.g.*, a forfeiture clause in a lease provides that on the breach of certain covenants the lease shall be at an end and the lessor may re-enter.

Contraband, or smuggled goods are forfeited to the Crown on seizure. Notice of seizure is given where the forfeiture is to be challenged in the courts.

forgery. Making a false document in order that it may be used as genuine, This includes the counterfeiting of seals and dies. Forgery with intent to defraud or deceive is punishable as a criminal offence. (Forgery Act, 1913.)

forwarding agent. An agent who attends to the collection, forwarding and delivery of goods.

founders' shares. Shares issued, usually as fully paid up, to persons who have promoted the formation of a company, or who have taken an active part in its formation, as remuneration for their services, or for some other consideration. In many cases the holders of founders' shares are entitled to the surplus profits after a certain fixed rate of dividend has been paid on all the other shares.

franc. The standard unit of currency for several countries, including France, Belgium and Switzerland, in Europe. Like most currency units it is decimalized.

franchise. (1) A liberty or privilege; especially the right to vote at a public election.

(2) A particular privilege or right; *e.g.*, the right to hold a market or fair, granted by the Crown, or acquired by prescription (*q.v.*).

franco price. Price of goods which includes delivery to buyer's warehouse.

franked investment income. Income which has already been subject to corporation tax before receipt.

fraud. A false representation of fact made knowingly, or without belief in its truth, or recklessly not caring whether it is true or false. It is a breach of the rules of fair dealing, with the object of gaining an unfair advantage.

(1) Actual fraud occurs where one person causes pecuniary injury to another by intentionally misrepresenting or concealing a material fact which, from their mutual position, he was bound to explain or disclose *e.g.*, where a person is induced to purchase a business by false accounts of its profits.

(2) Constructive fraud may exist where there is no wrongful intention, but the court will not enforce a transaction if it is unconscionable; *i.e.*, against conscience.

Fraud entitles the injured person to avoid the transaction induced by the fraud (*e.g.*, in the case of a contract, to have it rescinded) or to recover damages for the injury; it gives rise to a defence to any action brought by the fraudulent party to enforce the contract or other transaction, but it does not make it void *ab initio*.

Fraud may constitute a criminal offence; *e.g.*, fraudulent statements made by a director of a company in a prospectus.

fraud on a power. Exercising a legal power of appointment of property for some purpose other than that intended.

Frauds, Statute of. The Statute of Frauds (29 Car. 2, c. 3) was passed to prevent fraud, by requiring that certain transactions should be evidenced by a note or memorandum in writing: notably those in regard to land, and, in general, to sales of goods of the value of £10 or more, and to certain other contracts.

The provisions in regard to land were superseded by the Law of Property Act, 1925, and those as to goods by the Sale of Goods Act, 1893, s. 4.

By the Law Reform (Enforcement of Contracts) Act, 1954, section 4 of the 1893 Act was repealed, and as to contracts, only the provision that contracts of guarantee should be evidenced by writing, was left still in force.

fraudulent conversion. The offence committed by a person who has received or been entrusted with the property of another, who fraudulently converts it, or the proceeds, to his own use or the use of another.

fraudulent misrepresentation. See MISREPRESENTATION.

fraudulent preference. A debtor commits an act of bankruptcy if he makes a conveyance of property which would be void as a preference or fraudulent preference under the Bankruptcy Act, 1914, or any other Act. Any preference whether fraudulent or not is avoided in certain circumstances. See PREFERENCE, FRAUDULENT.

free alongside ship. (f.a.s.). Includes all charges (including wharfage and porterage) up to but not including hoisting on board.

free and open market. A market such as the Stock Exchange where all may trade and transactions are made publicly.

free enterprise. An economic system, also called capitalism, adopted by a country in which individuals are free to own capital and undertake economic activity within the laws of the country. In most countries some economic activity is under the control of the state and the system is then known as a mixed economy.

free goods. Customs non-dutiable goods.

free of capture and seizure. A clause in a Lloyd's marine insurance policy, reading thus: Warranted free of capture, seizure, arrest, restraint, or detainment, and the consequences thereof, or of any attempt thereat (piracy excepted) and also from all consequences of hostilities or warlike operations, whether before or after declaration of war.

free of particular average. See AVERAGE.

free on board. Under a " free on board " (F.O.B.) contract it is the duty of the seller to put the goods on board the ship named by the buyer, and to pay the expenses incurred thereby, and to make a reasonable contract of carriage for their transport to the buyer. The property in the goods passes to the buyer, and they are at his risk, once the goods have been put aboard ship, but it is the duty of the seller to notify the buyer of the shipment to enable him to insure the goods: if the seller fails to do so the goods will be at his risk.

free trade. Trade unhampered by national tariffs.

freehold estate. An interest in land (an estate in fee simple) which amounts to full ownership of the land. See LEASEHOLDS.

freight. The charge for transporting goods by air, land or sea; in particular, the price paid to a shipowner for the carriage of goods to their destination. It is only payable on such delivery.

friendly society. A society which as part of its ordinary business provides benefits during sickness or other infirmity, or in old age, or in widowhood, or for orphans, registered under the Friendly Societies Act, 1896.

fringe benefits. A supplementation of monetary wage payments with other benefits. Examples of fringe benefits are holidays with pay, pensions, expense accounts, luncheon vouchers and provision of a car. Although fringe benefits have a monetary value it is largely intangible and usually goes tax-free. The attraction of fringe benefits is therefore greatest to those with high money incomes liable to high rates of direct taxation.

full age. The age of 21 years. See INFANT.

full employment. See EMPLOYMENT, FULL.

functional classification. Classification of expenditure of an enterprise according to the purpose or function served, *i.e.*, according to the functional responsibilities operative in the organisation, *e.g.*, printing of advertising matter would be classified under selling or marketing expense rather than under general administrative charges as printing or stationery.

functions of money. Principally money serves as a medium of exchange. Its other functions include measurement as a unit of account, a method of payment, a store of value and a standard for deferred payments.

fund. Actual cash resources of a particular kind, *e.g.*, money in a drawer or bank, or a particular category used by a person in making up his accounts.

fundamental disequilibrium. Occurs when a country's official rate of exchange is out of line with its real value in relation to other countries. The result of such disequilibrium appears in the country's balance of payments and the remedy is to make an adjustment to the country's official rate of exchange.

funded debt. Long-period loans floated by the government. Ten to fifteen years is the least of the long-term periods in this respect.

funding operation. Generally speaking it is the replacement of floating, revolving or short-term debt with a fixed loan debt over a definite period.

funds statement. A statement showing the sources from which an enterprise has derived additional funds during a given period and the ways in which those funds have been applied. Also known as a Movement of Funds statement.

further education. Education beyond the normal or basic limits of age or accomplishment which are required by the state. In the long term the effect of further education is to improve the quality of a country's labour force.

future estate. An estate limited to come into existence at some future time, *e.g.*, a contingent remainder.

future goods. Goods to be manufactured or acquired by the seller after the making of a contract of sale. See GOODS.

future property. Property which will be caught by, or subject to, a covenant presently made, when it comes into possession at a future date, *e.g.*, a covenant to settle after-acquired property on the trusts of a marriage settlement.

futures. Dealings in " future " goods, securities, etc., *i.e.*, goods not yet manufactured or produced or not yet arrived; securities bought or sold for future delivery. In general, such dealings, although embarked upon with the object of pecuniary gain through speculation, have the important economic function of minimising extreme fluctuations in the prices of goods or securities involved.

G

gaming. The playing of a game of chance for winnings in money or money's worth. Contracts relating to gaming or wagering are void and no action can be brought for recovering any money or stakes alleged to be won on any wager.

Under the Betting, Gaming and Lotteries Act, 1963, gaming is lawful provided (1) that the game offers equal chances to all players; (2) that no stake money is applied otherwise than by way of winnings; and (3) that no charge is made for taking part in the game. Members of a bona fide club, however, may, apart from their annual subscriptions, take part in gaming on payment of a fixed sum fixed before gaming begins. See also BETTING; WAGER.

garnishee. A debtor who has been ordered to pay the debt to a person who has obtained a judgment against the debtor's original creditor. See also GARNISHEE ORDER.

garnishee order. An order made by a judge upon the application of a judgment creditor, attaching debts owing or accruing due from third persons to the judgment debtor, the object being to prevent the debtor from collecting the money and to make it directly available to the creditor to satisfy the debt.

Gazette. In England the *London Gazette*. In Scotland the *Edinburgh Gazette*. The *Gazette* contains Proclamations, Orders in Council, Statutory Instruments (*q.v.*), appointments to public offices and matters of which the public must be given formal notice, *e.g.*, dissolutions of partnership bankruptcy proceedings, resumptions of land, etc. It is admissible in evidence for many purposes.

gearing. The relation between prior charge capital and the equity capital; *i.e.*, between the loan and preference capital on the one hand, and ordinary capital on the other. High gearing means that the prior charges are large in relation to the equity, and therefore that they absorb a large proportion of earnings.

general average. See AVERAGE.

General Commissioners. Members of the public who are appointed by the Lord Chancellor for different areas of the country to act in a judicial capacity to hear appeals from certain assessments and decisions of the Inspector of Taxes.

general meeting. It is necessary for all companies to hold each year at intervals of not longer than fifteen months (except in the case of a newly incorporated company) what is called an annual general meeting. At these meetings the shareholders are afforded an opportunity of hearing of the company's progress and, if necessary, of criticising the directors' stewardship. A report is submitted by the directors, accompanied by a revenue or profit and loss account and a balance-sheet and group accounts if applicable, and after this report has been formally received, a dividend (if any) is declared, directors elected, auditors appointed and their remuneration determined. *Cf.* EXTRAORDINARY GENERAL MEETINGS.

general strike. A total withdrawal of labour in a country by organised or general labour. Such a strike completely dislocates the economic life of an industrial society.

gift. A gratuitous grant or transfer of property. For a valid gift there must be an intention to give and such acts as are necessary to give effect to the intention, *e.g.*, delivery; or it may be made by deed. Equity will not construe an imperfect gift as a declaration of trust.

gift inter vivos. A gift (*q.v.*) made by one living person to another. *Cf.* DONATIO MORTIS CAUSA.

gilt-edged securities. Investments, usually carrying a fixed rate of interest, which are considered to have a very low risk of non-payment of interest or redemption moneys, when due, *e.g.*, Government Stocks.

giro. See POSTAL GIRO.

gloss. A commentary on some aspect of the law.

glossary. A list of unusual, obsolete, dialectal, or technical terms with definitions or explanations.

go-slow tactics. An alternative to strike action, it involves workers going slow, or working to rule, in their tasks.

going concern. A business in actual operation and working order. One in which the transfer of ownership would effect no interruption of business. A valuation of a business on the basis of a going concern is higher than on a break-up value.

gold clause. A provision in an international contract, relating to payment, inserted with the object of rendering the contract immune from any currency regulations or depreciation which may affect the contract while it is in force.

gold reserves. That part of a country's total reserves for its currency which is represented by holdings of gold.

gold standard. A country is said to be on the gold standard when (i) its central bank buys and sells gold at fixed prices, (ii) movement of gold into and out of the country is unrestricted, and (iii) the unit of currency is based on a given weight of gold of a given fineness.

golden handshake. Substantial compensation for loss of office paid to an executive of a company on being displaced. The Finance Act, 1960, imposed income tax on sums, in general, in excess of £5,000.

good faith. A thing is done in good faith when it is, in fact, done honestly, whether it be done negligently or not.

goods. All chattels personal other than things in action and money, including emblements, industrial growing crops and things attached to, or forming part of, the land which are agreed to be severed before sale or under the contract of sale. Chattels (*q.v.*) personal are tangible moveable property.

Specific Goods are those identified and agreed upon at the time of sale; for example, a Bentley car.

Future Goods are those to be manufactured or acquired by the seller after the making of the contract of sale.

goodwill. Every advantage of the reputation, connection and earning capacity of a firm as built up over a period of trading.

Originally goodwill was interpreted solely in terms of the attitudes of customers or clients, as in its definition as the probability that old customers will continue to resort to the old place of business or continue to deal with the firm of the same name. In later years, however, there has been a tendency to regard goodwill more broadly as " the value of all the favourable attitudes impinging upon the concern, including, with customers, the employees and other groups associated with the enterprise." (W. A. Paton: *The Accountants' Handbook* (America)). The *Accountants' Handbook* also points out that the mere presence of favourable attitudes and relationships does not imply the existence of goodwill as an asset, since every business involves such attitudes and relationships in some degree. It is only when these factors are persistent and unusual that they come to have an economic significance. Further, goodwill as a recognisable asset arises only when there is a possibility of transfer. It is often calculated as an assessment of the present value of the estimated future profits of a business in excess of a normal return on its assets.

governing director. A director (*q.v.*) given autocratic powers of directing the policy of a company. Sometimes appointed when a person converts his business into a company.

government stocks. The loan stock issues made by the British Government, colloquially known as gilt-edged stocks. Examples are Consols (Consolidated Stocks) and Treasury Stocks.

governor, colonial. The representative of the Crown in a colony or dependency. The powers and functions of a Governor are regulated by Ordinance or Statute.

governor-general. The official in charge, actually or nominally, of the administration of an area, usually with Governors or Lieutenant-Governors under him. In the British Dominions he is now generally at the head of a self-governing community associated freely with other communities in allegiance to the Queen, and represents or behaves like a constitutional monarch, *e.g.*, the Governors-General of Australia, Canada, New Zealand.

grading. Many commercial commodities are subdivided into classes or grades by reference to their quality, size, etc.

graduated pension. The national pension scheme which started in April, 1961, under which people in employment pay contributions which are graduated according to earnings. Employers pay an amount equal to that of their employees.

grant. See CROWN GRANT.

gratuity. (1) A present, usually in monetary form, made in recognition of service rendered; a tip. It includes any money gratuitously paid, whether it is paid in one sum or in instalments.

(2) A bounty given to soldiers, and others, upon retirement or to mark some special occasion.

Gresham's Law. Propounded by Sir Thomas Gresham (1519-1579) stated that bad money will always drive out good money, but never the reverse. In a bi-metallic system the standard coin possessing the lower market value will remain in circulation while the stronger coin will be retained as bullion. Where a mono-metallic system is in use the lighter coins will circulate while the heavier will be retained.

gross. (1) The total or whole; the full amount without deduction. Converse: NET.

(2) Twelve dozen.

gross annual value. See ANNUAL VALUE.

gross income. The total income of an individual before payment of direct taxation.

Gross National Product. The total monetary value of the production (goods and services) of a country in a year.

gross profits. See PROFIT.

gross receipts. Total receipts before deduction is made for expenses.

gross weight. Weight of both goods and package.

gross yield. The return on an investment represented by the gross interest or dividend, before deduction of withholding tax.

ground rent. The rent reserved when land is leased to a person with a condition that he erects certain buildings thereon. It is usually small in comparison with the rent of the same land when built on, and is usually reserved only in the case of long leases, *e.g.*, 99 years.

group of companies. Several companies which are associated the one with the other because of their common source of control and/or ownership by a company, individual or group of shareholders.

growth stock. A stock exchange equity stock on which the public expects the earnings and dividends to grow faster in the future than on other available comparable equity stocks. Stocks which are believed to be growth stocks will be on sale at current yields lower than average because of the expectancy of higher than average future benefit.

guarantee. A contract whereby one person (the guarantor or surety) promises another (the creditor) that he will answer for the debt, default or miscarriage of a third person (the principal debtor) in consideration of some benefit received by the principal debtor from the creditor. A contract of guarantee must be evidenced in writing. See also INDEMNITY.

guarantor. See GUARANTEE.

guardian. A person having the right and duty of protecting the person, property or rights of one who is without full legal capacity or otherwise incapable of managing his own affairs, *e.g.*, a minor, a lunatic.

guardian ad litem. A person appointed to defend an action or other proceeding on behalf of a person not permitted by law to act for himself, *e.g.*, a minor, a lunatic. See also NEXT FRIEND.

H

H.I.F.O. "Highest in, first out." A basis for charging out materials for production purposes or for valuing stock on hand at a given date, under which it is assumed that the goods are used or sold in the order of highness of cost; *i.e.*, the dearest goods are disposed of first.

habeas corpus, writ of. [You have the body.] A prerogative writ which constitutes a means of safeguarding the liberty of the individual by preventing unwarranted imprisonment. It is directed to the person having the control or custody of any other person, directing him to bring up the body of the person in his control or custody before the court making the order. It thus enables a person to be brought before the court to learn why he is imprisoned and thereafter to be dealt with according to law, *e.g.*, by being released if wrongly held or obtaining an early trial.

habendum. The clause in a conveyance which indicates the estate to be taken by the grantee. Formerly it commenced " To have (habendum) and to hold (tenendum)."

hammered. Denotes the expulsion of a member of the Stock Exchange who is unable to fulfil his obligations to pay for securities bought or to deliver shares sold.

Hansard. An official report of the proceedings in Parliament—so called from the name of the compilers during a long period.

harbour dues. Amounts paid by owners of ships, or merchandise being loaded or unloaded, for the purpose of maintenance of the installations in a harbour. They are variously described as tonnage rates, berthing charges, inward and outward harbour rates, buoyage rates, etc.

hard currency. A strong currency, *i.e.*, one for which there is a strong demand in relation to the available supply. The exchange rate for a hard currency will tend to stand above parity.

hardware. A colloquial computer term for the machinery as opposed to the programming (*q.v.*) or method of use.

hawker. One who travels from place to place or house to house carrying or exposing goods for sale by retail. These activities are regulated by statutes providing for the issue of licences.

hearsay evidence. See EVIDENCE.

hedging. Attempts to minimise risks of price variations, *e.g.*, by contracting to buy or sell on a specified date in the future at an agreed price.

heir. A person who succeeds by descent. One who inherited property by descent on the intestacy of its owner. The Administration of Estates Act, 1925, abolished descent to heirs. The word " heirs " is, however, still to be construed as formerly when it is used after 1925 in deeds or wills, but it will give corresponding equitable interests only in property.

hereditament. A term signifying any interest in land which orginally descended to the heir. The term includes a few rights unconnected with land, but it is used as the widest expression for real property of all kinds. It appears in the phrase " lands, tenements and hereditaments " in deeds relating to land.

An incorporeal hereditament covers rights such as fishing rights.

hidden reserve. A reserve which is not apparent from the published accounts of a company. The creation of hidden (or secret) reserves was prohibited by the Companies Act, 1948, except in the case of banking, shipping and insurance companies.

High Court of Justice. The High Court of Justice consists of the Lord Chancellor, the Lord Chief Justice, the Master of the Rolls, the President of the Probate Division, the Lords Justices of Appeal, and the Judges of the Queen's Bench, Chancery, and Probate, Divorce and Admiralty Divisions.

high seas. The open sea as opposed to " territorial waters." The latter, for general purposes, may be said to be the sea extending for three miles from the shore of a maritime state or country; such state or country regards these waters as part of its territory. A twelve-mile limit is claimed by certain states.

highway. A passage which is open to the public for passing and repassing. It includes all roads, bridges (other than county bridges), carriageways, bridleways, footways, causeways, churchways, pavements and public rivers. The right of the public, once acquired is permanent and inalienable except by Act of Parliament.

highway code. Directions for the guidance of persons using roads, which may be varied, amended, revoked or added to, as the Minister of Transport thinks fit.

hire. (1) To procure the temporary use of personal property or the temporary services of a person or persons for payment or other consideration. (2) To grant the same. (3) The price or consideration paid therefor. *Cf.* BAILMENT; LEASE.

hire-purchase. A hire-purchase agreement is a contract whereby one person (the owner) delivers goods to another person (the hirer) on conditions providing for the payment of a periodical rental, the option of ultimate purchase; a power to the hirer to return the goods and, in certain circumstances, the right of re-possession by the owner.

The fact that the property is not to pass until the final payment has been made does not of itself necessarily constitute a contract a hire-purchase agreement. Although one party to a hire-purchase agreement agrees to sell, the other party does not agree to buy. Until the total amount is paid the property in the goods remains with the owner, so that the hirer cannot give a good title to third parties under a sale without the concurrence of the owner.

In the case of motor-vehicles it is usual for the " buyer " to select the car, etc., from the " seller," who then sells outright to a finance company, who then enters into a hire-purchase contract with the " buyer." There is then no contract of sale between the " buyer " and the " seller."

The Hire-Purchase Act, 1965, applies to hire-purchase and credit-sale (*q.v.*) agreements where the total sum payable does not exceed £2,000. The Act provides, *inter alia*, that the cash price must be stated, a memorandum of agreement must be signed by the hirer and by or on behalf of the other parties, and a copy sent to the hirer within 7 days. Certain conditions and warranties are implied. The hirer can determine the agreement and return the goods on payment of one-half the hire-purchase price. When one-third of the price has been paid the owner can only regain possession of the goods by action.

hoarding. (1) The accumulation of stocks or money, beyond ordinary day-to-day needs. (2) A board for the display of bills or advertisements, subject to the Control of Advertisements Order.

hold. The interior space in a ship below decks used for cargo stowage.

holder, of bill of exchange. The payee or indorsee of a bill or note, who is in possession of it, or the bearer thereof.

holder in due course. A holder who has taken a bill, complete and regular on the face of it, under the following conditions:

(1) that he became the holder of it before it was overdue, and without notice that it had been previously dishonoured, if such was the fact; and

(2) that he took the bill in good faith and for value, and that at the time the bill was negotiated to him he had no notice of any defect in the title of the person who negotiated it.

Until the contrary is proved, every holder is deemed to be a holder in due course. This applies to all holders except the original payee. The rights of a holder in due course are not affected when the acceptor or other party has been induced to sign the bill by fraud.

holding company. A company which has a controlling interest in another company (a subsidiary company), either through its holding more than one half of its equity shares, or through its share holdings and power to appoint the directors. Some holding companies conduct normal business operations as well as controlling subsidiaries, while the assets of others consist almost exclusively of shares in subsidiaries. The former have been described as operating holding companies, the latter as pure holding companies.

holding out. Representing oneself to be of a certain capacity (*e.g.*, a partner in a firm) when this is not the case. If others accept and act on this assumption the person holding out is estopped or prevented by law from denying the representation. Similarly a person may render himself liable as principal for the acts of another whom he " holds out " as his agent.

A person who holds himself out as one qualified as, *e.g.*, a legal or medical practitioner renders himself liable to penalties.

holograph. Wholly written. A document entirely in the handwriting of the person from whom it proceeds—*e.g.*, a holograph will is one entirely in the testator's handwriting.

home ownership. Many people make their major investment when they buy their own homes. Home ownership is usually made possible by means of an advance on mortgage from a building society and it is encouraged by concessions in the taxation of individuals.

honorarium. A voluntary payment for services rendered, *e.g.*, an honorarium to an unpaid secretary, which cannot be sued for at law. Counsel's fees are deemed an honorarium.

honorary. A position held either without rendering services, or without receiving emoluments; *e.g.*, an hon. member who pays no subscription, or an hon. secretary who does secretarial work without pay.

honour, payment for. To pay a bill " for honour " is to pay it for the sake of saving someone's (usually the drawer's) business reputation.

horizontal integration. Of an industry or a group of companies means that specialisation is undertaken at one stage of production. *Cf.* VERTICAL INTEGRATION.

hot money. Volatile capital which is moved from centre to centre seeking a more rewarding, or safer, currency to hold.

hotchpot. Where a fund is appointed to be divided amongst a class and one of the class has already received a special or appointed share, that person may be required to add his special share to the fund, for the purpose of computing the share of each beneficiary, before it is distributed; he is then said to bring his special share into hotchpot.

House of Lords. The Upper House of Parliament. It is also the Supreme Court of Appeal for Great Britain; by convention, the appellate jurisdiction is exercised only by members who hold or have held high judicial office, and these members sit in a Committee, called the Appeals Committee.

householder's or houseowner's comprehensive insurance policy. The cover granted, subject to the terms and conditions of the policy, comprises various contingencies relating to building and contents of private dwellings, private boarding houses and residential flats; *e.g.*, fire, burglary and theft.

Housing Societies. Associations for the construction of dwelling-houses by the members as a voluntary service. (Housing Act, 1961.)

husband and wife. The relationship of husband and wife which begins on marriage ceases on death or dissolution of marriage by decree of divorce or nullity. At common law husband and wife were regarded as one person, and that person was the husband. However, equity modified the common law in favour of the wife, who now has the same rights to her property as a single woman. See MARRIED WOMEN.

A husband is not liable for his wife's contracts, except those entered into as his agent or for necessaries (*q.v.*), and a married woman is liable for her own torts. At common law, husband and wife could not sue each other in tort, but now each of the parties to a marriage has the same right of action in tort as though they were not married, except that proceedings may be stayed if unwarranted, or if they concern questions of property (Law Reform (Husband and Wife) Act, 1962, s.1).

Money or property derived from a housekeeping allowance belongs to the husband and wife in equal shares (Married Women's Property Act, 1964).

hydrocarbon oils. These are light oils; *e.g.*, motor spirit, and heavy oils; *e.g.*, paraffin and diesel oils. They are subject to customs duty on importation. They are known as fuel oils.

hypothecation. (1) The pledging of a ship and/or her freight or cargo by the master as security for borrowing for the use of the ship. The transaction is known as bottomry (*q.v.*), the master pledging the ship as above and undertaking repayment on completion of the voyage. Failing this the debt is lost. Hypothecation of the cargo only is known as *respondentia*. Hypothecation is also used for pledging or charging generally.

I

I.O.U. [I owe you.] An admission of indebtedness. It is not a negotiable instrument and does not require to be stamped.

idem, ad. [Of the same mind.] Agreed: a necessary element in a valid contract.

ignorantia facti excusat. [Ignorance of fact excuses.]

ignorantia legis neminem excusat. [Ignorance of the law excuses nobody.] This is still generally true of English law, but innocence may be taken into account in awarding punishment.

illegal. An act which the law directly forbids, as to commit a murder, or to obstruct a highway, is illegal.

illegal contracts. The law will not enforce certain contracts, which are void, by reason of illegality. A contract may be illegal at common law as contrary to public policy (*q.v.*), *e.g.*, a contract to commit a crime or a tort, and certain contracts in restraint of trade. Where two people together hold the common design to use something for an unlawful purpose, so that each participates in the unlawful purpose, that contract is illegal in its formation, and ignorance of the law is no excuse.

Contracts made in breach of statutory provisions are, as a rule, also illegal.

illegitimate. Born out of lawful wedlock and not legitimated. See LEGITIMACY; LEGITIMATION.

immediate parties. As regards bills of exchange those who are in immediate contact, *e.g.*, the indorser and his immediate successor, and the indorser and his immediate predecessor; also the drawer and the acceptor. The acceptor and payee as between themselves are remote parties (*q.v.*).

immobility of labour. The reluctance or refusal of displaced labour to move into employment which is available in another area.

imperfect. A contract, trust, etc., which is lacking in some requisite so that it is not legally enforceable.

import duty. See CUSTOMS DUTY; *cf.* EXCISE.

import entry. See EXPORT ENTRY.

import licence. A licence has to be obtained to import goods which are the subject of quota or exchange control restrictions.

import quotas. Used as an alternative, or in addition, to import duties to restrict the quantity of a commodity which may enter a country in a given period and to protect the home production of that commodity. A proportional share of the allowed total is allocated to suppliers.

import substitution. A policy of replacing imports with home produced goods. To the extent that the policy succeeds there is an improvement in the trade balance and balance of payments.

importers. Those who import goods, generally used in the sense of merchants or agents importing goods from abroad.

impost. A tax or duty, particularly on imports. See Import Duties Act, 1958.

imprest system. A system of disbursing by means of advances and refunds, *e.g.*, the system of advancing a petty cashier a lump sum, which he accounts for periodically, and is refunded with the amount spent. The petty cash account therefore remains consequently in debit only for the original amount advanced. The system is often adopted in the case of branches of a business which are advanced a certain amount to pay expenses and are then reimbursed by head office for the amount expended.

improvements. Operations on land (*e.g.*, clearing, fencing, erection of buildings) which increase its value.

The improvements of agricultural land for which a tenant can claim compensation under the Agricultural Holdings Acts, 1948, 1958, are divided into three parts, (1) Those for which the consent of the landlord is necessary, *e.g.*, planting orchards, or hops; (2) Those for which the consent of the landlord or the approval of the Agricultural Land Tribunal is necessary, *e.g.*, permanent or semi-permanent improvements such as buildings, permanent fencing, or land drainage; (3) Those for which no consent is necessary, *e.g.*, mole drainage, protection of trees, liming, etc.

Capital moneys may be expended on improvements under the Settled Land Act, 1925.

in bond. Goods on which duty has not been paid and which are placed in a store or warehouse approved by the Customs and Excise Commissioners, where security for duty has been given. See BONDED GOODS.

in camera. The hearing of a case in private, *e.g.*, in court with the public excluded; or in the judge's chambers.

in curia. [In court.]

in extenso. [At full length.]

in flagrante delicto. [In the very act.] Caught in the act of adultery or crime.

in forma pauperis. [As a poor person.] See now LEGAL AID AND ADVICE.

in futuro. [In the future.]

in loco parentis. [In the place of a parent.] Where a person is invested with all or some of the rights and duties towards a child that a parent has by virtue of relationship, he stands for all or some purposes *in loco parentis* towards the child. A person may assume the position, *e.g.*, by adoption, or have it delegated him, *e.g.*, a schoolmaster.

in pari delicto, potior est conditio possidentis. Where the circumstances are such that the court will refuse to assist either party, the party in possession will not be disturbed.

in pari materia. [In an analogous case.]

in personam. Rights which avail only against a particular person or persons Rights of action in contract or in tort are of this kind. *In personam* is contrasted with *in rem* (*q.v.*).

in re. [In the matter of.]

in rem. A phrase used in describing an act, proceeding or right available against the world at large, as opposed to *in personam* (*q.v.*). A right of property is a right *in rem*. An admiralty action is a proceeding *in rem* when the ship itself is arrested and adjudicated upon.

in situ. [In its own place; in its original position.]

in statu quo. [Properly, *in statu quo ante*; in the position in which one was before.]

in terrorem. A condition in a will or gift which is intended to frighten or intimidate the donee. The condition is void if it is annexed to a gift of personal property and if it is either in total restraint of marriage or forbids the disputing of the will. To be valid the condition should be followed by a gift over.

in toto. [Entirely; wholly.]

in transitu. [In course of transit.] See STOPPAGE IN TRANSITU.

incendiarism. Arson.

incentive. Any tangible or intangible inducement with a view to achieving better results in some sphere, *e.g.*, to workers to produce more, to individuals to save, to industry to export more, etc.

inchmaree clause. A special clause inserted in marine insurance policies to cover losses to the hull or machinery of a vessel caused through negligence of the master, engineers, mariners, etc., or through explosion, breakages or any latent defect in the machinery or hull. In order to recover the loss, the owners of the ship must not be guilty of negligence. The clause is almost universally inserted in policies on steamships.

inchoate. In an early stage; incomplete.

incidence of taxation. The way taxation comes to be paid by those who are unable to recoup themselves from anyone else. The incidence of direct taxation is on those who earn the income, but indirect taxation may be passed on, in whole or in part, to the consumer.

income. That which comes in. The receipts of an individual or corporation as a result of personal exertion, business, investments, etc. Income is contrasted with capital in the sense that fruit is contrasted with the tree that produces it.

In economics, the revenue of a person or firm over a given period available after provision for the maintenance of capital intact. See CAPITAL; EARNED INCOME.

income bond. Sometimes issued on the funding of arrears of dividend on preference shares. Repayment is from future profits of the company over a number of years.

income tax. Is an annual tax on income imposed by the yearly Finance Acts, which also amend the consolidating Income Tax Act, 1952. The scope of the tax is, in general, on income which arises in the United Kingdom, or which accrues to residents in the United Kingdom, except for certain income not received here. The Schedules of charge, which also apply for Corporation Tax on company profits, are as follows.

Schedule A. The annual value of lands and houses (totally abolished after 1963–1964).

Schedule B. Amenity lands and woodlands (abolished, except as to commercial woodlands, 1962–1963).

Schedule C. Interest and dividends payable out of public revenue.

Schedule D. Case I: profits from trades or businesses.

Case II: profits from professions or vocations.

Case III: interest, annuities and other annual payments.

Case IV: income from foreign and colonial securities.

Case V: income from foreign and colonial possessions.

Case VI: other annual profits or gains not otherwise charged.

Case VII: short-term capital gains (*q.v.*).

Case VIII: rents and other receipts from land, less certain deductions (from 1964–65).

Schedule E. Emoluments from employments, offices and pensions, and " fringe benefits " such as rent-free living accommodation.

Schedule F. The gross amount of company distributions (dividends and certain other payments).

Returns must be made of income to H.M. Inspector of Taxes. Assessments to tax may be appealed against to the General or Special Commissioners and thence to the High Court by Case Stated. See also COMMISSIONERS OF INLAND REVENUE; PAYE; RELIEFS, INCOME TAX; SHORT-TERM GAINS; SPECIAL COMMISSIONERS OF INCOME TAX.

incomes policy. An attempt to check the inflationary spiral through Government supervision and control of rises in money income caused by wage awards, dividend increases, etc. The object is to contain the rise in money incomes within the real rise in national income.

incorporation. The merging of an association of persons into a separate distinct body politic, or artificial person, or corporation, by the Crown or by virtue of a special or general Act of Parliament.

incorporeal hereditament. See HEREDITAMENT.

incorporeal property. Property which is intangible, which has no body or substance, *e.g.*, an annuity—a right to receive a yearly payment; as opposed to tangible or corporeal property, *e.g.*, a motor-car.

increasing returns. If, in a particular industry or firm, the application of additional factors of production (*q.v.*) yields a more than proportionate return, the industry or firm is said to be in a state of increasing returns.

indemnity. A form of contract arising where a person (who thereby becomes primarily liable) undertakes to compensate another for loss he may suffer as a result of a transaction with a third party. This contract need not be evidenced in writing. Contrast GUARANTEE.

indent. An order for goods especially from overseas; orders for goods for importation, usually taken by an agent, called an indentor, for overseas firms or manufacturers. Indenting means placing an order for goods with a local agent of an overseas seller.

indenture. A deed to which there is more than one party. Formerly a deed to be executed by two parties was written in duplicate on one sheet of parchment which was then torn or cut with serrated or indented edges. The copies could thus be readily identified by comparing the edges. See DEED POLL.

independent contractor. One who is employed under a contract for services; he is his own master and does not work under the control of the employer. See also MASTER AND SERVANT.

index numbers. A series of numbers by which changes in the magnitude of phenomena, such as prices, productivity, stocks, etc., can be measured from time to time or from place to place; *e.g.*, the retail prices index. The standard is 100 as at a particular date.

indictment. The written charge upon which a person is tried before a jury. See FELONY.

indirect taxation. Taxation of goods or services and therefore taxation of expenditure rather than income. Purchase tax is an indirect tax; so is excise duty.

individual. A natural person, as opposed to an artificial person such as a company or corporation.

indorse. Literally to write the signature of a person upon the back of something, *e.g.*, a bill.

indorsee. The person to whom something (*e.g.*, a bill of exchange) is indorsed; *i.e.*, made payable by indorsement.

indorsement. A writing on the back of an instrument. It is a means of transference of bills of exchange, bills of lading, etc., and the writing need not necessarily be on the back of the instrument to be operative. An indorsement may be

(1) In blank, where the person to whom the instrument is payable merely signs and delivers the instrument to another.

(2) Special, where the name of the transferee is specified.

(3) Restrictive, *i.e.*, where further transfer of the bill is prohibited: " Pay D only " or " Pay D for the account of X " or " Pay D or order for collection."

(4) Conditional, *i.e.*, where the indorsement contains some conditions, *e.g.*, " Pay Clive Jones upon the surrender of a bill of lading for 10 bales of wool." The payer of a bill may disregard any conditions in any indorsement and the payment is valid even if the conditions have not been fulfilled. See also CHEQUES; SANS RECOURS.

indorser. The person by whom a document, *i.e.*, a bill of exchange, is indorsed.

industrial and provident society. A society for carrying on any industries, businesses or trades authorised by its rules, whether wholesale or retail, including dealings with land, and banking. A bona fide society, consisting of seven persons at least, when registered under the Industrial and Provident Societies Act, 1893, becomes a body corporate with limited liability, and regulated by its rules.

industrial arbitration. See ARBITRATION, INDUSTRIAL.

industrial award; industrial agreement. Conditions of employment in various trades, industries and callings are fixed by industrial awards or industrial agreements. An award is made in a trade dispute by the members of an industrial court, to whom the matter has been referred by the Minister of Labour under the Industrial Courts Act, 1919. An agreement is made between employers and employees and requires to be filed in accordance with statutory provisions. See AWARD.

Industrial Bankers' Association. An association of the smaller finance companies, formed to prescribe a strict code of conduct, and to ensure a reasonable degree of liquidity, and an adequate excess of assets over external liabilities, of its members.

industrial design. A design applicable in any way or by any means to the purpose of ornamentation, pattern, shape or configuration of an article, or to any two or more of those purposes. Copyright in a design, which must be new or original and not published before the application for registration, may be obtained by registration under the Registered Designs Act, 1949. It begins on the date registration takes effect and continues so long as the registration remains in force. Such copyright gives the exclusive right to apply the design or authorise its application to articles in respect of which it is registered. See also COPYRIGHT.

industrial disease. A disease due to the nature of the insured person's employment, or the risk of a particular occupation, and not common to all persons. Industrial injuries benefit is payable.

industrial life assurance policy. A policy upon human life the premiums in respect of which are received by collectors of the company which issued the policy by means of house to house visits (Industrial Assurance Act, 1923).

industrial relations. Relations between management and labour or their respective representatives.

industrial union, organisation, association, etc. A body comprising a number of employees (*e.g.*, a trade union) banded together to act for the benefit of employees in matters of dispute or negotiations with their employers; or a number of employers banded together for the protection of employers' interests. See also TRADE UNION.

industry. The manufacture of products by firms employing capital and labour in factories and works. The word " industry " is also used to describe all the industries within an economic system.

infant. A person under the age of 21 years. He becomes of full age from the first moment of the day preceding the 21st anniversary of his birth. An infant has not full legal capacity.

inferior court. See COURT.

inflation. Occurs when purchasing power consistently outpaces the supply of goods and services, which results in increased prices. The causes vary and include expansion in credit, full employment and restricted supply of goods. All countries which enjoy full employment undergo a degree of inflation and attempt to control it through their monetary, fiscal and economic policies.

information. A step by which certain criminal and, in some inferior courts, civil proceedings, are commenced.

infra. [Further on, lower down.]

infringement. Interference with, or violation of, the right of another, particularly the right to a patent, industrial design or copyright. The remedy is an injunction to restrain future infringements, and recovery of the damages caused or profits made by the past infringements.

ingot. A bar of metal cast in a mould. One speaks of ingots of gold and silver, and of bars of the baser metals.

ingress. Entry.

initial allowance. One of the forms of capital allowance (*q.v.*) allowed to a business under the taxing statutes as a set-off against profits before depreciation. The initial allowance is granted on the investment in certain capital assets at a rate which varies with the type of the asset and according to whether it is new or second-hand.

injunction. A remedy, for damage suffered or prospective, by which a party to an action is required to do or refrain from doing a particular thing. An injunction is either mandatory (to do something), *e.g.*, to take down a wall obstructing light; or restrictive (to refrain from doing something), *e.g.*, to stop wrongfully infringing a copyright, and may be interlocutory, *i.e.*, limited in time (*e.g.*, until trial of the action), or perpetual.

injury. An actionable wrong, irrespective of actual damage.

inland bill. A bill which is, or on the face of it purports to be (1) both drawn and payable within the British Isles; or (2) drawn within the British Isles, upon some person resident therein. Unless the contrary appears on the face of the bill, the holder may treat it as an inland bill.

inland revenue. (1) Revenue from taxes under the management of the Inland Revenue; *e.g.*, estate duty, income tax, stamp duties, surtax, corporation tax.

(2) General description of the body of government employees who conduct the day-to-day administration of the tax law.

innkeeper. The owner or occupier of premises who holds out that he will provide food and lodging for travellers.

innocent misrepresentation. See MISREPRESENTATION.

innovation. In economics, the introduction of a new process, product or technique which provides avenues for profitable investment.

Inns of Court. The independent, self-governing societies of Lincoln's Inn, Gray's Inn, Inner and Middle Temples, with the exclusive right of calling members to the Bar.

innuendo. The allegation by the plaintiff in an action for defamation of the real meaning of the words used by the defendant, which were not on the face of them derogatory.

input. Data which is transferred from external store, or peripheral equipment, of a computer to an internal store. The term is also used to describe the process of transferring the data.

inquest. An inquiry by a coroner (*q.v.*).

inquisition. An official investigation or inquiry; a formal document recording the result of the inquiry; *e.g.*, a coroner's inquisition, *i.e.*, certificate in regard to the proceedings at an inquest (Coroners Act, 1887).

insanity. (1) For purposes of the criminal law, the test of insanity, according to the McNaghten Rules, is at the time of the commission of an act was the accused labouring under such a defect of reason from disease of the mind as not to know the nature and quality of the act he was doing; or if he did know it, did he know it was wrong?

(2) An insane person may repudiate a contract if he was so incapable at the time of entering into it as not to know what he was doing, and the other party knew of his condition. He is, however, bound to pay for necessaries.

(3) If an insane person has lucid intervals, he has the full legal capacity of a normal person during those intervals.

(4) An insane person cannot make a valid will.

(5) A marriage entered into by a person who is insane at the time is void.

(6) A petition of divorce may be presented, either by a husband or wife, on the ground that the respondent is incurably of unsound mind, and has been continuously under care and treatment for at least five years immediately preceding the presentation of the petition.

inscribed stock. Stock for which no actual documents are issued, but in respect of which the holders' names are inscribed in the register of the issuing authorities; *e.g.*, in the register of the Bank of England. Such stock can be transferred only by the holder or his attorney under power by signature.

insolvent. A person who is unable to pay his debts as they become due. Insolvency usually results in arrangement proceedings, or in the administration of the insolvent estate in bankruptcy, or (in case of death) by the court.

inspectorship, deed of. See DEED OF INSPECTORSHIP.

instalment. A payment on account.

instalment credit. See HIRE-PURCHASE and CREDIT SALE AGREEMENT.

instrument. A formal legal document in writing, *e.g.*, a deed or will.

insurable interest. In order to take out a policy of insurance, the insured must have an interest in the safety of the subject-matter insured, or be prejudiced by its loss. No insurance may be made on the life of a person, or on any other event, unless the person for whose benefit the policy has been made has an insurable interest in such life or event. The object of the rule is to prevent infringement of statutory provisions relating to wagering and to prevent fraud.

insurance. A contract whereby a person, called the insurer (or assurer), agrees in consideration of money paid to him, called the premium, by another person, called the insured (or assured), to indemnify the latter against loss resulting to him on the happening of certain events. The policy is the document in which is contained the terms of the contract. Insurance is a contract *uberrimae fidei* (of the utmost good faith) and of idemnity only, except in the case of life and accident insurance and certain other specific instances when an agreed sum is payable. See also ASSURANCE.

insurance agent. Although employed by an insurance company, if the agent becomes the amanuensis of the proposer, he becomes his agent, and his knowledge as such will not be imputed to the company.

insurance broker. An agent who arranges policies of insurance on behalf of his clients with insurers; *e.g.*, at Lloyds (*q.v.*).

insurance policy. A document, which must be stamped, upon which the insurance indemnity is written, accompanied by the conditions and the risks undertaken.

insurance premium. The consideration, usually payable annually by the party insured to the insurance company, for undertaking the risks set out in the policy.

intangible assets. Items in a balance sheet which represent investment by the business in assets which give an intangible benefit, *e.g.*, goodwill and preliminary expenses. *Cf.* INCORPOREAL PROPERTY. See ASSETS.

integration. Specialisation within an industry or group of companies in single processes (horizontal integration (*q.v.*)) or successive processes (vertical integration (*q.v.*)).

intensive cultivation. Application of relatively high quantities of other factors of production to land in order to achieve a high yield from a scarce supply of land.

intention. To have a purpose in mind to reach a desired objective. The general rule is that a person is responsible for the natural and probable consequences of his acts whether he intended them or not. In tort, a person is liable for the foreseeable damage resulting from his own acts, whether it is a direct or indirect consequence of his acts, and even if it is greater in amount than could have been foreseen.

In criminal law wrongful intention is, in general, an essential ingredient in the more serious offences. See MENS REA.

inter alia. [Among other things.]

inter se [Among themselves].

inter vivos. [Between living persons.]

interest. (1) A right, claim or share in some specific property, *e.g.*, life interest in land.

(2) Money agreed to be paid in consideration of money lent, calculated in proportion to the amount and period of the loan. Interest is not payable on a debt, except where there is an agreement to pay it. The agreement may be expressed, or implied from the course of dealing between the parties or from trade custom. Interest is payable on overdue bills of exchange; judgment debts; money obtained by fraud, and where it is recoverable by virtue of a statutory provision.

interest on companies' capital. Where any shares are issued by a company for the purpose of raising money to defray the expenses of the construction of any works or buildings, or the provision of any plant, which cannot be made profitable for a lengthy period, the company may pay interest on the capital paid up for that period, and may charge amounts so paid as part of the cost of construction of the work or buildings or the provision of plant.

interim dividend. Payment of an equity dividend to shareholders of a company as part of the total dividend for the financial year, before the results of the year's trading are completely known.

interlocking directorships. A form of association (*q.v.*) between companies whereby individuals act as some or all of the directors of otherwise separate companies and thereby, possibly, impose a measure of common policy for those companies.

international law, public. That body of rules which by custom or treaty civilised nations regard as binding upon themselves in their relations with one another, and whose violation gives the injured party a right to redress. International law is law of imperfect obligation because there is no recognised common superior to enforce it. See also PRIVATE INTERNATIONAL LAW.

international monetary fund. An international monetary authority to which member countries contribute fixed quotas of their currency and gold. Its purpose is to assist countries through temporary difficulties in their balance of payments by allowing borrowing from the fund.

interpleader. A legal proceeding whereby a person in possession of property in which he claims no interest, but to which two or more other persons lay claim, may summon the claimants before a court, and have their respective claims determined. See also STAKEHOLDER.

interrogatories. Written questions put by one party to an action to the other, on matters arising in the action, to be answered by affidavit.

intervener. A person who interposes himself in proceedings in the Probate, Divorce and Admiralty Division with leave of the court. Any person can intervene in a suit for divorce or dissolution by showing cause against a decree nisi.

intestacy. Total intestacy occurs where a person dies leaving no will, or one which is invalid or ineffectual, *e.g.*, because it is improperly executed, or witnessed, fails to dispose of the testator's property or the testator survives all his beneficiaries. Partial intestancy is where a will disposes of part only of the testator's property. On an intestacy, property is distributed according to rules laid down in the Administration of Estates Act, 1925, as amended by the Intestates' Estates Act, 1952.

intestate. One who dies without leaving a will.

intra vires. [Within the power of.] See ULTRA VIRES.

invalid. Void; of no legal effect.

inventory. A detailed list. In book-keeping a list of goods, plant, buildings, etc., on hand at a particular date, together with any relevant information, *e.g.*, trading stock on hand at balancing date.

invest. To apply money in the purchase of some property from which interest, rent or profit is expected, and which is to be held for the sake of the income which it will yield.

investigation. A systematic search or inquiry. Investigations may be undertaken in business for several purposes, including:

(1) to report on the financial position and earning capacity of a business to prospective investors;

(2) to report on the economic and commercial viability of a proposed investment or course of action;

(3) on behalf of the proprietors of a business into a known or suspected fraud;

(4) for the purpose of giving expert advice in legal or arbitration proceedings;

(5) on behalf of the Board of Trade to investigate the affairs of a company in manner provided for under the Companies Act, 1948.

investment. The application of resources to the creation of new capital (*q.v.*); every mode of application of money which is intended to return interest or profit.

A company holding investments in other companies (which are not subsidiaries) must show in its balance-sheet under separate headings the aggregate amounts respectively of the company's (1) trade investments; (2) quoted investments (other than trade investments); (3) unquoted investments (other than trade investments).

There must be shown by way of note or statement annexed to the balance-sheet if not otherwise shown, the aggregate market value of the quoted investments (other than trade investments) where it differs from the amount of the investments as stated, and the stock exchange value of any investments of which the market value is shown (whether separately or not) and is taken as being higher than their stock exchange value. See also AUTHORISED INVESTMENTS; TRADE INVESTMENTS.

investment allowance. An allowance against taxable profits for investment in certain new capital expenditure. The allowed deduction from profits is calculated as a percentage of the capital investment. Investment allowance is not deducted from the cost of the capital investment for the purpose of calculating capital allowances (*q.v.*).

investment bank. A bank which specializes in providing long-term capital for commercial and industrial concerns. Investment may take the form of fixed interest or equity capital. Financial advice and underwriting services are additional services which will usually be available to the bank's clients.

investment grant. Capital grants paid in cash by the government on investment by industry in certain types of capital asset. The system replaced that of investment allowances (*q.v.*); in contrast to which it is more selective and the benefit does not depend on profits being earned.

investment trusts. A term which is usually applied in the U.K. to investment trust companies. Such companies have a fixed capital structure and invest in a range of quoted securities. Their shares are traded on a stock exchange similarly to those of other companies. The quoted price of their shares almost invariably represents a discount on the underlying value of the investment trust based on the market value of the shares which it owns in other companies. *Cf.* UNIT TRUSTS.

invisible imports and exports. Items of international trade other than in tangible goods, *i.e.*, services such as shipping and insurance charges, interest payments on international loans, expenditure by foreign tourists, etc.

invitee. A person invited to enter premises of an occupier with his consent, on business in which he and the occupier have a common interest, *e.g.*, a customer entering a shop. It is the duty of the occupier of premises to take reasonable care that the invitee will be reasonably safe in using the premises for the purpose for which he is invited to be there (Occupiers' Liability Act, 1957). See LICENSEE.

invoice. A statement giving particulars of goods purchased by or indented for a customer; *viz.*, the goods, prices, quality, quantity, charges, and the marks on cases or packages.

ipso facto. [By that very fact.]

ipso jure. [By the law itself.]

irredeemable. A term used for undated stocks or debentures which are, in effect, permanent loans.

irrevocable. Not revocable, that which cannot be rescinded; *e.g.*, an irrevocable letter of credit (*q.v.*).

isolated transaction. A single transaction of purchase and sale, or one purchase and many sales, not made in the course of carrying on a business. It may, however, be liable to income tax as being trading.

issue. (1) Children, grandchildren and all other lineal descendants; (2) a matter in dispute between parties; (3) to publish; (4) to allocate shares in a company to applicants, or the shares so issued.

issued capital. Capital actually issued as distinct from nominal or authorised capital of a company.

issued generally. Shares, etc., issued to persons who are not existing members or debenture-holders of the company.

issuing house. A financial concern whose business is the making of public issues of shares, or stock, on behalf of limited companies.

J

Jerque note. The inward clearing bill issued by the Waterguard officer to the ship's master after which stores and cargo for the outward voyage may be taken on board.

jetsam. Goods which are cast into the sea and there sink and remain under water. If unclaimed they are the property of the Crown. *Cf.* FLOTSAM.

jettison. The throwing overboard either from a ship or aircraft of goods from necessity to lighten the vessel or aircraft in a storm, or to prevent capture or for other sufficient cause.

jobbers. Dealers in stock and shares on the Stock Exchange whose function is to "make a price"; *i.e.*, to quote to stockbrokers the prices at which they will respectively buy or sell particular stocks and shares. Their profit is called the "jobbers' turn"; *i.e.*, the differences between the prices at which jobbers buy and sell.

joint. Liabilities, benefits, etc., which are shared; *e.g.*, joint tenants; joint tortfeasors. See PARTNERSHIP.

joint account. A bank account owned by two or more persons jointly; the survivor is entitled to the balance. It may be operated by either or any of the persons, or as may be arranged.

joint account clause. Where two or more persons advance money and take the security to themselves jointly, each is in equity deemed to be separately entitled to his proportion of the money, so that on his death it passes to his personal representatives and not to the|surviving co-lender or co-lenders. This rule made it usual, in cases where money was advanced jointly, to insert in the mortgage deed, etc., a clause stating that the money belonged to the lenders on a joint account in equity as well as at law, and that the receipt of the survivors or survivor, or his personal representatives, should be a full discharge for any moneys due on the security, to enable the surviving mortgagee to give a receipt to the mortgagor for the whole of the mortgage money.

joint and several obligation; joint and several liability. An obligation or liability entered into by two or more persons, jointly and severally, so that each is liable severally, and all liable jointly, and a creditor or obligee may sue one or more severally, or all jointly, at his option.

joint demand. When an increased consumption of one commodity brings about an increased demand for another, the two goods are described as being in joint demand. For example, increased purchases of safety razors increases the demand for razor blades.

joint obligation; joint liability. A bond or covenant or other liability entered into by two or more persons jointly; each is liable for the full amount but all must be sued upon it together.

joint products. Separate and distinct goods or services necessarily produced in the same process: *e.g.*, gas and coke; wheat and straw.

joint stock company. The large partnerships or companies which existed prior to the first Companies Act in 1825. See COMPANY.

joint tenancy. The tenancy of land created by vesting property in two or more persons by the same conveyance in the same right and title. The share of a holder vests on his death in the survivor or survivors. The four unities necessary for there to be a joint tenancy are: unities of possession, interest, title and time. Joint tenancies may be ended by partition amongst the joint tenants. Although property is held at law by joint tenants, they may hold in equity as tenants in common.

Where property is owned in common by two or more persons and it is not stated how it is held, there is a presumption that they hold as tenants in common (*q.v.*).

Similar rules apply to co-ownership of personal property, the words joint owners and owners in common being used.

joint tortfeasors. Two or more persons who jointly commit a tort or civil wrong: they must, in fact or law, have committed the same wrongful act. Joint tortfeasors are jointly and severally responsible for the whole damage. At common law a judgment obtained against one joint wrongdoer released all the others, even if it was unsatisfied. One joint tortfeasor has a right of contribution or indemnity from another joint tortfeasor.

joint venture. A special form of partnership for a particular purpose. It may, *e.g.*, consist in a joint consignment of goods, or a joint underwriting of an issue of shares.

journal. Originally in bookkeeping parlance the book(s) of original record into which the routine recurring types of transaction were entered. Nowadays the journal more usually contains entries of transactions of a particular rather than a general nature.

journal entry. A memorandum of a transaction, recorded in the journal, indicating the two aspects (debit and credit) involved and the ledger accounts to which the entry must be transferred (or " posted "). Any transaction can be recorded in the form of a journal entry.

judge. An officer of the Crown who sits to administer justice according to law.

judgment. The decision or sentence of a court in a legal proceeding. Also the reasoning of the judge which leads him to his decision, which may be reported and cited as an authority if the matter is of importance, or can be treated as a precedent.

judgment creditor. One in whose favour a judgment for a sum of money is given against a judgment debtor.

judgment debtor. One against whom judgment is given for a sum of money, for which his property is liable to be taken in execution at the instance of the judgment creditor.

Judicial Committee of the Privy Council. See PRIVY COUNCIL.

judicial proceeding. Proceedings before any court, tribunal or person having by law power to hear, receive or examine evidence on oath.

jurisdiction. The power of a court or judge to entertain an action or other proceeding. Territorial jurisdiction means the district or limits within which the judgments] or orders of a court can be enforced or executed.

jurisprudence. The science of law; the principles on which legal rules are based.
Jurisprudence is used, incorrectly, as synonymous with law.

jury. A body of twelve men and women summoned and sworn to decide questions of fact in a judicial proceeding. Juries still officiate in the higher criminal courts, but they are seldom required in the civil courts.

justice. The establishment of right between men. In practice, justice means justice according to law, so that there may be uniformity. To the lawyer, it is more important that justice should be certain, rather than ideally just.
A judge of the High Court is addressed as Mr. Justice ——. See JUDGE.

justices of the peace. Persons appointed by the Crown for the conservation of the peace and for the execution of other duties in the county or borough to which they are appointed. The appointment is usually for life. Their duties are:
(1) judicial, being those in which they carry out the functions of a judge, *e.g.*, the summary trial of a minor offence, and
(2) ministerial, where they act as servants under some statute, *e.g.*, in committing for trial an accused person against whom a prima facie case has been made out; administering an oath to a person swearing an affidavit; taking a statutory declaration or issuing certain summonses, warrants and other processes in matters within their jurisdiction.

K

kaffirs. South African gold mining shares.

keep house. The act of bankruptcy which a man commits when he begins to keep to his house and denies himself to his creditors.

key industry. An industry which affects many others and therefore the whole of a country's economy. The power industries are examples of key industries.

kite-flying. Dealing in accommodation bills (*q.v.*) to raise money.

knight. The lowest title of dignity. It is not hereditary. Knights are of the following orders: Garter, Thistle, St. Patrick, Bath, St. Michael and St. George, Star of India, Indian Empire, Royal Victorian, British Empire and Knight Bachelor.

knock for knock. An agreement between two insurance companies under which each insurance company pays its own insured what he is entitled to under his policy, and does not insist on his bringing an action against the party insured by the other company.

L

labour. A factor of production (*q.v.*), it consists of human effort, both manual and otherwise.

laches. Negligent or unreasonable delay in assserting or enforcing a right; *e.g.*, the holder's omission, without lawful excuse, to perform his duties with reference to a bill of exchange.

lagan or ligan. Goods cast into or sunk in the sea, but made fast to a cork or buoy in order that they may be found again. If unclaimed they belong to the Crown. *Cf.* FLOTSAM; JETSAM.

laisser faire. [Let things be.] A state of the economy where the individual is free to carry on business and conduct himself with the minimum of state control, as opposed to state planning and restriction.

land. Any ground, soil or earth whatsoever, whether dry or under water, including all buildings on the land, and also everything attached to the land. In economics it is one of the factors of production (*q.v.*) for which there is a substantial demand and a limited supply. It includes the column of air above it, and extends downwards to the centre of the earth.

Land Registry. The office where the three registers kept are (1) the property register which describes the property and refers to matters such as easements and overriding interests; (2) the proprietorship register which states the nature of the title; and (3) the charges register (Land Registration Act, 1925), See also REGISTERED LAND; REGISTER OF TITLE.

Land tax. This was levied according to the quota to be raised from each parish. Provision was made for its redemption, which became compulsory by the Finance Act, 1949. Land tax was finally abolished by the Finance Act, 1963.

landed cost. The cost of purchasing goods including all charges incurred up to the time of landing them in the country of destination. For example, the landed cost of goods bought in England and shipped to Australia would comprise their purchase price in England, the cost of transport to the port of shipment, insurance and freight charges to Australia, landing charges and duty in Australia.

landlord and tenant. The relationship of landlord and tenant is created by contract (by words, writing, *e.g.*, a tenancy agreement; or deed, *e.g.*, a lease) whereby a tenant occupies the landlord's house or land subject to certain conditions such as the payment of rent, etc. The landlord has a right to distrain for rent in arrear.

Lands Tribunal. A board appointed under the Lands Tribunal Act, 1949, being a mixed board of lawyers and expert valuers to decide questions arising under the Town and Country Planning Acts, *inter alia*; or the War Damage Act, 1943; and appeals from local valuation courts, or as to water rates, etc.

lapse. The termination of a right or privilege through disuse. A legacy lapses where the legatee dies before the testator. There is an exception where a child or other issue of the testator dies before the testator, leaving issue who are living at the testator's death; in such case unless a contrary intention appears in the will, the legacy passes as if the child, etc., had died just after instead of before the testator.

larceny. The crime consisting of wrongfully taking and carrying away personal goods of another, with the intention of permanently depriving the owner of them.

last in, first out. A method of stock valuation which assumes that issues to production are made from the last available stock to have been purchased. The system is abbreviated to LIFO.

law. A law is an obligatory rule of human conduct. The law in force in a country is the sum total of such rules.

law merchant. The custom of merchants derived from the body of mercantile usage which governed the relations of traders throughout Western Europe. It was in early times enforced in special courts, but it was gradually recognised by the common law courts, and become assimilated into the general law. The rule is now that once a general mercantile custom has been proved in the courts it becomes binding in all future cases. This source of common law rules is not closed, and as any new custom becomes generally recognised amongst merchants and is proved in the courts, it becomes part of the common law. Parts of the law merchant have been codified by statute, *e.g.*, the law relating to bills of exchange. See also MERCANTILE LAW.

law report. A published account of a legal proceeding, giving a note of the principles of law involved, statement of the facts, the arguments on both sides, and the reasons the court gave for its judgment. To be authoritative, it should be signed by a barrister, or issued by the Stationery Office.

Law Society. The professional body for solicitors in Great Britain.

lay days. The time allowed to charterers of vessels for either loading or unloading, applied sometimes to both, but usually to loading. If described as "running lay days," they mean consecutive days; if as "working lay days," they mean working days only, and Sundays and holidays would not count.

lay-by system. A method of purchasing goods, mainly from retail stores, and paying for them by instalments. Until the final instalment is paid possession of the goods is retained by the seller. Contrast HIRE PURCHASE.

leading case. A judicial decision of special importance as settling the principles of a branch of law. See also PRECEDENT.

leading questions. Questions which directly or indirectly suggest to a witness the answer he is to give: such are questions embodying a material fact and admitting the answer " Yes " or " No "; *e.g.*, " Were you at 3 p.m. in your shop? " The alternative non-leading form of this question is " Where were you at 3 p.m. ? " The general rule is that leading questions are allowed in cross-examination but not in examination in chief.

lease. A grant of the possession of real property to last for a fixed period, or at will, and usually with the reservation of a rent. The person who grants the lease is called the lessor, and the person to whom it is granted the lessee. A lease must be for a less estate or term than the lessor has in the property, for if it comprises his whole interest it is a conveyance or assignment and not a lease.

Where a person who is himself a lessee grants a lease of the same property to another person for a shorter term, it is called an underlease or sublease or a derivative lease.

leasehold. Land held under a lease. A leasehold estate is personal estate, and is an interest in land which may be of any duration; *e.g.*, one month, six years, 99 years, or determinable at will.

ledger. One of the account books in a system of double entry bookkeeping, it contains a summarised and classified record of entries made in books of original entry (journals).

legacy. A gift of personal property by will. The person to whom the property is given is called the legatee or donee, and the gift is called a bequest.

(1) A specific legacy is a bequest of a specific part of the testator's personal estate, *e.g.*, My gold watch given to me by A.

(2) A demonstrative legacy is a gift of a certain sum directed to be paid out of a specific fund, *e.g.*, £100 out of my Consols.

(3) A general legacy is one payable out of the general assets of the testator, *e.g.*, £100. See ABATEMENT OF LEGACIES.

(4) A pecuniary legacy is a legacy in money. Annuities are included in legacies.

legal aid and advice. Legal aid is assistance in bringing or defending a claim or proceedings in a civil court, if the applicant's disposable income or capital is within certain limits. Assistance is either free, or a contribution is called for. Similarly, an applicant who qualifies can obtain advice from a solicitor for a nominal sum (Legal Aid and Advice Acts, 1949, 1960).

Legal aid in criminal cases has been assimilated to the provisions with regard to civil cases.

legal costs. See BILL OF COSTS; TAXATION OF COSTS.

legal mortgage. See MORTGAGE.

legal tender. Tender or offer of payment in a form which a creditor is obliged to accept. Copper coins are legal tender up to a shilling, silver coins up to 40 shillings; notes are legal tender for any amount. (Currency and Bank Notes Act, 1928.) A creditor is not obliged to give change. For a tender to be effective, the debtor must seek out his creditor and tender, unconditionally, the amount of the debt.

legatee. One to whom a legacy is given.

legislation. An act being the expression of the will of a competent legislature, whether it lay down a general rule or be no more than a privilege. The promulgation of rules which have the force of law, emanating from an authority duly authorised by the legislature.

legitimacy. The condition of being born in lawful wedlock.

legitimation. A child born out of wedlock is legitimated by the subsequent marriage of its parents, unless the child was born when either parent was married to a third person (Legitimacy Act, 1926). That Act has been extended to cases where either one or both parents were married when the child was born (Legitimacy Act, 1959).

lessee. One to whom a lease is granted.

lessor. One who grants a lease.

letter of allotment. See ALLOTMENT.

letter of credit. An authority by one person to another to draw cheques or bills of exchange (with or without a limit as to amount) upon him, with an undertaking to honour the drafts on presentation. An ordinary letter of credit contains the name of the person by whom the drafts are to be negotiated or cashed: when it does not do so, it is called an open letter of credit.

Revolving letter of credit—One in which, after notice of drawing against it is received by the issuing bank, the balance available for drawing against reverts back or " revolves " to its original amount.

Irrevocable letter of credit—One which cannot be withdrawn or revoked before the expiry date named in the credit, unless by agreement of all parties.

Circular letter of credit—A document in two parts issued by a banker to enable a customer to obtain moneys from the banker's agents while travelling. The two parts of the document are: the credit itself, which states the total amount of money to be made available and provides for indorsement of the various amounts drawn from time to time, and a letter of indication, for identification of the bearer, and which includes his specimen signature.

letter of hypothecation. See HYPOTHECATION.

letter of indemnity. A letter stating that the writer will indemnify the person to whom it is addressed against loss which may arise from some specific act undertaken for the writer's benefit or on his behalf. See INDEMNITY.

letter of licence. An instrument authorising a debtor or any other person to manage, carry on, realise, or dispose of a business with a view to the payment of debts. It is included in the definition of deed of arrangement in the Deeds of Arrangement Act, 1914. See ARRANGEMENT.

letter of offer. The acceptance of an offer of a contract made by letter dates from the posting of the letter of acceptance.

letter of renunciation. A document executed by an existing shareholder who is entitled to a new issue of shares, assigning to a grantee the rights to those shares.

letter of request. A letter accompanied by the requisite information from a personal representative of a deceased shareholder addressed to the company requesting that he be registered as the holder of the shares held by the deceased. In most companies a transmission form is used. See TRANSMISSION.

letter of rights. A letter from a company informing a shareholder that he is entitled to apply for further shares at a specified price. The shareholder can either take up the shares or sell his " rights " through his broker.

letters of administration. See ADMINISTRATION, LETTERS OF.

letters of marque. See MARQUE, LETTERS OF.

levy. To raise or impose; *e.g.*, a tax or duty.

lex domicilii. The law of the place of a person's domicile (*q.v.*).

lex loci contractus. [The law of a place where a contract is made.] This is generally the proper law of the contract, *i.e.*, the law by which the contract is to be interpreted. It governs capacity to enter into a contract.

lex mercatoria. [The law merchant (*q.v.*)].

lex non scripta. [The unwritten law.] The common law, being that derived from judicial decisions and customs.

lex scripta. [The written law.] Statute law.

liability. (1) The condition of being actually or potentially bound or obliged in law or equity; *e.g.*, liability to abate a nuisance. (2) An obligation; that for which one is liable, *e.g.*, a debt. See CURRENT LIABILITIES; FIXED LIABILITIES; CONTINGENT LIABILITY; LIMITED LIABILITY.

libel. Defamation (*q.v.*) by means of writing, prints, pictures or some other permanent form. Libel may also be a crime if it is such that it is a danger to the public peace, *e.g.*, because it is blasphemous, obscene or seditious or threatening or abusive. See SLANDER.

liberty. (1) A privilege enjoyed by a particular person or body of persons; freedom granted to do an act otherwise wrongful.

(2) A place which enjoys a franchise (*q.v.*) or is exempt from the ordinary law in certain respects.

licence. (1) An authority to do something which would otherwise be wrongful or illegal. An agreement permitting the licensee to enter upon or do some other act in relation to the land of the licensor which would otherwise be unlawful.

(2) The certificate of permission issued by an authority to do something requiring to be specifically authorised: *e.g.*, a driving licence. See also LETTER OF LICENCE.

licensee. One to whom a licence (*q.v.*) is given. At common law, the occupier of premises is under no obligation to a licensee to make them safe for use by him: the licensee must take them as they are: but the occupier must not lead the licensee into a trap or concealed danger. Nor must the occupier or his servants negligently harm the licensee. Under the Occupiers' Liability Act, 1957, the occupier owes the common duty of care to licensees. See also INVITEE.

lie. An action " lies " if on the facts it is competent in law to institute it.

lien. A right to possession or application of the property of another by reason of a payment or duty owed by that other. Liens may be—

(1) possessory:

    (a) general—*e.g.*, where a solicitor retains a client's deeds against payment of a general account.

    (b) particular—*e.g.*, where a solicitor retains deeds to a property against payment for a lease he has drawn up in respect of that property.

(2) Equitable—where the person entitled to the lien has not possession but has the right to have the property of another applied to discharge certain specific liabilities, *e.g.*, a partner in a dissolution of partnership has an equitable lien to have partnership assets applied to partnership debts.

(3) Maritime—where a ship and its cargo are charged with the payment of a liability arising from a maritime adventure. See SALVAGE.

(4) Statutory—where the lien is conferred by statute, *e.g.*, the lien of a master or seamen on a ship for wages (Merchant Shipping Act, 1894). Under the Sale of Goods Act, 1893, an unpaid seller has an implied lien on the goods, even though the property in them may have passed to the buyer.

life annuity. A yearly sum payable to a person during his life; in practice by periodical payments, *e.g.*, monthly. See ANNUITY.

life assurance. This is a contract to pay a certain sum of money upon the death of a person, or on the happening of some other specified event connected with the life of a person, in consideration of the due payment of certain premiums. It is not a contract of indemnity.

The most common types of life assurance are:

Whole life. Where the proceeds of the policy are payable on the death of the person insured.

Endowment. Where the proceeds of the policy are payable on the insured attaining a certain age, or in the event of the prior death of the insured.

Annuity. Where the proceeds of the policy are payable in the form of fixed income, either yearly, quarterly or monthly.

The premiums may, in respect of the above policies, be payable either for the whole term of the policy; for a stated number of years, or in a lump sum at the commencement, in which case the policy is known as a single premium policy. See also ASSURANCE.

life tenant. A person who holds property beneficially for his lifetime.

light dues. Amounts payable by the owner of a ship for the purpose of maintenance of lighthouses and navigation marks.

lighter. A boat (usually flat-bottomed) used in loading, unloading and transporting cargo of an ocean going ship.

limitation, statutes of. The statutes which prescribe the periods within which proceedings to enforce a right must be taken. They bar the right of persons who, through ignorance or neglect, have failed to exercise their rights for stated periods. They are of two kinds: (1) when, on the expiration of the time, the remedy is barred but not the right, *e.g.*, no action may be brought on a simple contract after six years; (2) when on the expiration of the time the right is barred, as where a person has been out of possession of land for a certain period.

The time limits in certain cases for bringing legal proceedings claiming damages in respect of personal injuries or in respect of a person's death, or for claiming contribution between joint tortfeasors are extended by the Limitation Act, 1963.

limited liability. The liability of a shareholder in a limited company only extends to the amount remaining unpaid (if any) on his shares. See CALL; COMPANY.

limited owner. The owner of an interest in property less than the full fee simple, *e.g.*, a tenant for life.

limited partner. A partner other than the general or active partners. Limited partners contribute to the partnership assets a specified amount in money or money's worth, and enjoy immunity from liability beyond the amount so contributed. They take no part in the management of the firm, and have no power to bind the firm. They may, however, inspect the books and advise. A limited partnership must be registered with the Registrar of Companies and must consist of one or more general partners who are responsbile without limitation for the partnership debts. (Limited Partnership Act, 1907.)

lineal ancestor; lineal consanguinity; lineal descendant. See COLLATERAL CONSANGUINITY.

liquid assets. Cash or property of a readily realisable nature, *e.g.*, Government securities. See ASSETS.

liquid reserve. A reserve backed by liquid assets.

liquid securities. Securities readily realisable. See LIQUID ASSETS.

liquidated. Fixed or ascertained. A debt is liquidated when paid, and a company when wound up. See also WINDING UP.

liquidated damages. See DAMAGES.

liquidation. The process of winding up a company. See WINDING UP.

liquidator. A person appointed to carry out the winding up of a company. The duties of a liquidator are to get in and realise the property of the company, to pay its debts, and to distribute the surplus (if any) among the members. A liquidator may be appointed in a voluntary winding up. or in a winding up by the court; in the latter case, the liquidator cannot as a rule take any important step in the winding up without the sanction of the court.

liquidity, international. The availability of credit or foreign currencies is required to finance international trade. The extent of international liquidity depends partly on the balance of payments and reserves position of trading countries and partly on the policy pursued by the International Monetary Fund.

lis alibi pendens. [A suit pending elsewhere]. The plaintiff must elect which of two or more suits he will proceed with; the others will be stayed or dismissed.

list price. The recommended price at which an article is for sale, usually by retailers.

listed stock. Securities which may be dealt in on the Stock Exchange. A security quoted on the Stock Exchange is said to be " listed." Before the Stock Exchange will " list " stocks or shares, application must be made to the committee, and all its conditions, which are designed to protect the public, must be complied with.

litigation. Contesting a suit at law. Litigants are the parties to the dispute.

Lloyd's. Lloyd's originally was the name of the coffee house in the City of London where those interested in ships and insurance used to meet. Lloyd's was incorporated in 1871. It is the centre for amassing the latest information regarding ships all over the world. It consists of brokers, underwriters and " names." The brokers bring in all kinds of insurance risks as well as marine. They deal with underwriters who decide the risks, premiums and conditions which they will accept. The underwriter, however, in accepting risks, acts on behalf of a syndicate of named persons. Some members of it may be insurance brokers; the rest are either gentlemen who are prepared to risk £75,000 each or businessmen who can bring in annual premiums of not less than £1,500; they need not stake more than £3,500. Lloyd's accounts are kept open for three years.

Lloyd's Registry of Shipping. The institution which surveys and classifies ships. The Registry publishes annually Lloyd's *Register of British and Foreign Shipping* containing the names and description of merchant vessels. See also A1 AT LLOYD'S.

loading. (1) An additional insurance premium charged in order to cover some expense or adverse factor. In life insurance the premium may be loaded to meet additional risks owing to the occupation (*e.g.*, publican) or ill-health of the person insured.

(2) An addition to cost: synonymous with burden, oncost, overhead.
(3) An additional element in fixing standard wages: *e.g.*, "weight for age." See BASIC WAGE.

load-lines. Marks on the hull of a ship indicating the maximum depths to which the ship can be loaded safely in various prescribed circumstances. See also PLIMSOLL MARK.

loan. An amount of money made available by one person (the lender) to another (the borrower) over a period of time in exchange for repayment during or at the end of the period and interest at an agreed rate on the outstanding principal sum.

local authority. A body charged with exercising the functions or powers bestowed on them by law in respect of a local government area. See LOCAL GOVERNMENT.

local government. The system of administration of local services by the division of the country into areas, each controlled by a council. The local government areas are parishes, rural districts, urban districts, boroughs, county boroughs and counties.

lock-out. A closing or partial closing of a business, factory, etc., by an employer, or the dismissal of some or all of the employees for certain purposes; *e.g.*, forcing employees to agree to some term or condition of employment, or to aid another lock-out, etc.

loco. A locomotive. Light locomotives are vehicles the weight of which exceeds $7\frac{1}{4}$ tons, but not $11\frac{1}{2}$ tons, unladen. Heavy locomotives are vehicles exceeding $11\frac{1}{2}$ tons in weight, unladen.

loco citato (loc. cit.). In that part of the work which has just been referred to.

loco price. The ex-warehouse price of goods.

locum tenens. [One who holds the place of another.] One who lawfully executes the office of another.

locus in quo. [The place in which.] The place where it is alleged a thing has been done or happened.

locus poenitentia. [A place of repentance.] The chance of drawing back from something agreed on.

lodger. A person who occupies rooms in a house of which the general possession remains in the landlord, as shown by the fact that he retains control over the street (or outer) door.

log; log book. A volume in which is entered a record of happenings in and to a ship, aircraft or motor vehicle.

London. Provisions with respect to its local government and the functions of local authorities in the metropolitan area are contained in the London Government Act, 1963.

London Gazette. See GAZETTE.

long or short. One who purchases securities enough and to spare is said to be "long" of them. One who sells securities which he does not own, is said to be "short" of them. See also BULL and BEAR.

long room. The room in the customs house where public business is transacted.

long-term. A liability or security extending over a term of years; *e.g.*, mortgages, debentures.

loss. Where costs pertaining to a given transaction or activity have not been fully recovered in the form of benefits derived: a deficiency.

loss assessor. See ASSESSOR.

loss leader. When an item of goods, or a range of goods, is offered for sale by a retailer at a price which represents a loss to him in order to tempt customers in to buy it and potentially other goods which are on sale at a profit, the item which shows a loss is known as the loss leader.

loss of profits insurance. A policy of insurance which compensates the insured for loss of earning power resulting from the interruption of business in consequence of, usually, fire. The ordinary fire policy does not cover consequential losses.

lost or not lost. A clause inserted in policies of marine insurance in order to overcome the possibility of the policy being avoided should the subject-matter have been destroyed, without the knowledge of the parties, at the time the policy is effected. If at the time of effecting the policy the insured was aware of the loss and the insurer was not, the policy is void.

lot. " Drawing lots " is a method of determining a choice by chance as in the determination of debentures or bonds for redemption.

lots. Goods or parcels of land put up for sale by auction (*q.v.*). See also ODD LOTS.

lottery. A distribution of prizes by lot or chance without any substantial use of skill. Lotteries are in general illegal, by the Betting, Gaming and Lotteries Act, 1963. However, small lotteries incidental to certain entertainments, private lotteries, certain small lotteries conducted for charitable, sporting or other purposes, and lotteries of Art Unions, are exempt from this provision. Certain newspaper prize competitions are restricted by that Act.

lunacy. Insanity (*q.v.*); unsoundness of mind (*q.v.*).

lunatic. This term was replaced by " person of unsound mind " in 1930; now superseded by " person mentally disordered" (Mental Health Act, 1959). A criminal lunatic is now called a Broadmoor patient. See INSANITY; UNSOUNDNESS OF MIND.

M

magistrate. A judicial officer who sits as a court of inferior jurisdiction in criminal or quasi-criminal matters, called a magistrates' court. Justices of the Peace are honorary magistrates: a stipendiary magistrate is a salaried officer appointed to act in lieu of the ordinary justices in populous places; *e.g.*, Manchester. Metropolitan magistrates sit in the several London Magistrates' Courts, the principal one being at Bow Street. See Magistrates' Courts Act, 1952.

magnetic store. A computer store which uses magnetisation for the representation of data.

mail order. An order sent by post to traders who specialise in supplying goods by post.

maintenance. (1) The keeping of fixed assets in good order to enable them to discharge the function for which they were acquired, *e.g.*, premises, plant and machinery.

(2) The supply of the necessaries of life for a person. A maintenance clause in a deed of settlement is the provision of income for such a purpose.

(3) The allowance made by order of the court to a woman for her support or in respect of the children of the marriage, to be paid by her husband following a decree of divorce or nullity.

(4) The allowance made to a woman for her support and that of the children of the marriage in summary proceedings before magistrates. Orders may be made by magistrates obliging employers to deduct maintenance payments from the wages of their defaulting employees.

(5) Maintenance is intermeddling with litigation in which the intermeddler has no concern: the tort committed by a person who, having no interest in civil proceedings, and with no lawful justification, assists one of the parties, with money or otherwise, to institute, prosecute or defend the action. It is actionable at the suit of the other party on proof of special damage.

It is sufficient justification that the defendant was actuated solely by charitable motives, but it is no defence that the maintained proceedings were successful.

Contracts cannot be enforced which infringe the law as to maintenance. See also CHAMPERTY.

making-up price. The price at which stocks and shares are closed in one Stock Exchange account and carried over to the next account.

mala fides. [Bad faith.] See BONA FIDE.

malfeasance. The doing of an unlawful act, *e.g.*, a trespass.

malice. Ill-will. Malice in fact is where an act is done with a wrongful intention. Malice in law is where a wrongful act is done intentionally without just cause or excuse. See also MURDER.

malicious injury to property. Damage done to property deliberately or wantonly: it is an offence (Malicious Damage Act, 1861).

malicious prosecution. The institution of criminal proceedings against another maliciously and without reasonable and probable cause, by which that other suffers damage to his fame, person or property; provided that the proceedings terminate in the other's favour, so far as that may be possible.

man of straw. One who is incapable of justifying any financial credit that may be reposed in him.

managed trust. See UNIT TRUSTS.

management. The conduct of a business. The directors of a company have control of the management of a company, but they are controlled in the exercise of their powers by shareholders in general meeting. The quality of management may be improved by experience and education in Management Studies.

managing director. A director (*q.v.*) appointed to be in charge of the management of a company, where the company's articles so admit. Subject thereto, the powers and duties of a managing director are as contained in his contract of service with the company. His office terminates if he ceases to be a director. See MANAGEMENT.

mandamus. An order issued by the court to compel the performance of a duty directed to the person or body which is empowered by law to perform it; *e.g.*, a public officer, or an inferior court.

mandate. (1) A direction, request, or authoritative command. Thus a cheque is a mandate, by the drawer to his banker, to pay the amount to the transferee or holder of the cheque.

(2) The authority, conferred on " advanced nations " by the Covenant of the League of Nations, Art. 22, to administer former enemy colonies and territories which were inhabited by peoples not yet able to stand by themselves, applying the principle that the well-being and development of such peoples forms a sacred trust of civilisation. They were called mandated territories, and are now held on trust from the United Nations.

mandatory injunction. See INJUNCTION.

manifest. Usually means a statement of a ship's or aircraft's cargo showing marks, numbers, description of goods, shippers' and consignees' names, etc., but there is also a " passenger manifest."

manufacturing. The process of converting primary products into manufactured goods.

manufacturing account or statement. A statement summarising the costs over a given period of the manufacturing processes undertaken by an enterprise and exhibiting the cost of goods produced, usually in terms of elements such as cost of materials, labour and manufacturing overhead expenses.

margin. (1) The difference between the amount of a loan and the total value of the securities, which must be kept up by the borrower in the event of any depreciation in the value of the securities.

(2) Stock Exchange term for money put up by a client in part payment of the purchase of a stock. The broker finances the balance of the purchase money.

marginal cost. The increase in total cost resulting from an increase of one unit of production.

marginal land. In economics, land whose cultivation for a particular purpose yields no more than the minimum return to capital and labour required to keep it in its present use.

marginal product. The increase of total production resulting from the employment of one additional unit of a factor of production (*q.v.*).

marginal relief. Relief from imposts, *e.g.*, income tax, estate duty, at levels which only marginally exceed the inferior level (of income etc.) at which a lower rate of tax etc. applies.

marginal revenue. The increase in total revenue resulting from an increase of sales by one unit.

marginal utility. See UTILITY, MARGINAL.

marine insurance. A marine insurance contract is a contract whereby the insurer undertakes to indemnify the assured (who may be the owner of a ship, cargo, or freight), against marine losses, that is, the losses incident to marine adventure. Marine adventures occur, for example, when the ship or freight is exposed to maritime perils, such as perils of the sea, fire, water, pirates, seizures, etc.

The main types of marine insurance policies may be classified as follows:—

(1) OPEN OR FLOATING POLICY. One in which the particulars of the goods and ships are subsequently declared but in the meantime the policy describes the insurance in general terms. The declarations are usually made on special forms for each shipment and it is necessary, unless the policy otherwise provides, to make the declarations in the order of the shipments. A further point is that all consignments of goods covered by the policy must be declared, as the omission of any shipment would be a ground for avoiding the policy.

(2) VALUED POLICY. One in which there is specified the agreed value of the subject-matter. The value stated is conclusive for the purpose of partial or total losses (except in the case of fraudulent overstatement of value) but is only prima facie for the purpose of a constructive total loss.

(3) UNVALUED POLICY. One in which there is not specified the value of the subject-matter insured, but which leaves the insured value to be subsequently ascertained. The subject-matter is, however, specified.

(4) VOYAGE POLICY. One which covers the subject-matter from one place to another, *e.g.*, Sydney to Auckland. This type of policy may be linked with a time policy, and is then sometimes referred to as a MIXED POLICY.

(5) TIME POLICY. One which covers the subject-matter for a specific period of time, not exceeding twelve months. A time policy may contain an agreement to the effect that, in the event of the ship being at sea or the voyage being otherwise not completed on the expiration of the policy, the subject-matter of the insurance will be held covered until the arrival of the ship at her destination, or for a reasonable time thereafter not exceeding thirty days. See INCHMAREE CLAUSE.

(6) MIXED POLICY. A voyage policy which is linked with a time policy.

marine survey. An inspection of a ship, etc., carried out by a marine surveyor. It may be in connection with the acceptance of a risk, *e.g.*, to the hull, furniture, machinery, etc., of the ship; or in connection with a marine loss, *e.g.*, damage to the ship or cargo.

maritime lien. See LIEN.

maritime perils. See MARINE INSURANCE

mark. This includes device, brand, heading, label, ticket, name, signature, word, letter, numeral, or any combination thereof (see Trade Marks Act, 1938).

mark-down. A reduction in valuation of securities; or in the selling price of goods, etc.

mark-up. An addition to cost price for gross profit to arrive at the selling price.

marked cheques. Cheques " marked " by the banker upon whom they are drawn to indicate that they will be paid in due course.

market. (1) Market or fair is a franchise or privilege to establish meetings of persons to buy and sell, derived either from Royal grant or from prescription (implying such grant). (2) Dealers in different classes of commodities and securities congregate together on an Exchange and are known as a market.

market, open, sale in. The valuation of property by reference to the price it would fetch on a sale between a willing seller and a willing buyer in competition with others.

market overt. [Open market.] Where goods are sold in market overt the buyer acquires a good title even though the goods are stolen, provided he buys in good faith and without notice of any defect of title. This is an exception to the general rule that a buyer takes no better title than his vendor. This applies generally in the City of London, but to places outside the City of London only in the market place on market days.

market research. An analysis of demand for a certain product in order to determine the marketing and production policy for that product.

marketing. The means by which a product is sold and distributed to customers.

marking. Details of a stock exchange transaction may be marked when the deal takes place. The markings for the previous day appear in the Stock Exchange Official List.

marque, letters of. Letters of licence granted by the Sovereign, as part of the prerogative to pass the marches or limits of a country for the purpose of making reprisals wherever his subjects are oppressed and injured by those of another State, and justice is denied by that State to which the oppressor belongs. The object is to seize the bodies or goods of the subjects of the offending State, until satisfaction be made.

marriage settlement. See SETTLEMENT.

married women. Formerly man and wife were one in law, and that one was the husband. A husband became on his marriage entitled to all personal property of his wife (including that acquired after marriage) and to a life interest in her realty. The position of a married woman is now the same as that of a single woman or man. (Law Reform (Married Women and Tortfeasors) Act, 1935.) A married woman may pledge her husband's credit for necessaries (*q.v.*). See also HUSBAND AND WIFE.

Restraints upon the anticipation or alienation attached to the enjoyment of the property of married women were abolished by the Married Women (Restraint upon Anticipation) Act, 1949.

marshalling. (1) As between creditors. Where there are two creditors of the same debtor, and one creditor has a right to resort to two funds of the debtor for payment of his debt, and the other creditor has the right to resort only to one fund, the court will order the first creditor to be paid out of the fund against which the second creditor has no claim, so far as that fund will extend, so as to leave as much as possible of the second fund for payment of the second creditor. If the first creditor has already paid himself out of the second fund, the court will allow the second creditor to stand in his shoes and resort to the first fund to the extent to which the second fund has been exhausted by the first creditor.

(2) As between beneficiaries. The order in which the assets of a deceased person are to be applied for the payment of his debts regulates the administration of the assets between the persons beneficially entitled to the deceased's estate, but does not affect the rights of the creditors themselves, who may resort indiscriminately to all or any of the assets. If any beneficiary is disappointed of his benefit under the will through a creditor being paid out of the property intended for that beneficiary, he may recoup himself by resorting to any property which ought to have been used to pay debts before his property was resorted to.

(3) In accounting. A term used to express the arrangement of assets in a balance sheet according to a selected basis of classification.

martial law. The supersession of ordinary law and the temporary government of a country (or parts of it) by military tribunals; the assumption by officers of the Crown of absolute power exercised by military force for the suppression of an invasion and the restoration of order. It is proclaimed by the Crown or by notice by the military authorities. There is, however, no provision in the English legal system for martial law; and acts done in pursuance of it require to be legalised subsequently by an Act of Indemnity.

mass production. The production in large quantities of standardised products with the primary object of reducing cost and expediting production.

master and servant. The relation which exists when one person, for pay or other valuable consideration, enters into the service of another and devotes to him his personal labour. The master must have the right to control the manner in which the servant shall act, and the servant is bound to obey the reasonable commands of the master to do acts within the scope of his employment. A clerk is a servant, but an opera singer is

137

not. A master is liable for the act or default of his servant committed on his express authority, or in the course of and within the scope of his employment on the ground of implied authority. A servant has implied authority to do all things necessary to protect his master's property entrusted to his care.

An independent contractor is not a servant, and the employer is not liable for default, except where (1) the work is unlawful; or (2) it must be done in a certain way by statute and the contractor fails to do it in that way; or (3) the work is likely to cause injury, when the employer is bound to see that necessary precautions are taken.

A master has an action for damages against one who entices away his servant without just cause, or who injures him whereby he loses his services. A master owes a duty to his servant at common law to use due care for his safety. Although compensation for industrial injuries or industrial diseases are provided for by the National Insurance Acts a worker's common law rights remain.

A servant is entitled to customary holidays and notice determining his employment. A servant wrongfully dismissed, i.e., without such notice or wages in lieu, is entitled to sue the master for breach of contract. He may also sue on a *quantum meruit* (*q.v.*) for work actually performed.

mate's receipt. The receipt given by the mate for goods shipped on board, which is later given to the master of the ship so that he may sign the bills of lading for the goods.

matrimonial causes. Suits for divorce, nullity of marriage, judicial separation, etc. (Matrimonial Causes Act, 1965.) These matters are dealt with by the Probate, Divorce and Admiralty Division of the High Court of Justice, subject to rights of appeal to the Court of Appeal and the House of Lords. Questions of separation and maintenance are dealt with by courts of summary jurisdiction.

mature. A bill or other instrument which has become due.

maxim. A concise phrase stating, in a few words, an established principle of law. They derive their source and sanction from antiquity, from judicial recognition, and from acceptance and use by great legal writers; e.g., " *delegatus non potest delegare*," (*q.v.*); " *de minimis non curat lex* " (*q.v.*) (the law does not concern itself with trifles).

Mayor's and City of London Court. It was formed in 1921 by the amalgamation of the Mayor's Court of London and the City of London Court. It is virtually a county court for the City of London, actions are commenced by a plaint; but otherwise the procedure is substantially that of the High Court.

Measure (ecclesiastical). The Church Assembly under the Church of England Assembly Powers Act, 1919, prepares and passes Measures relating to any matter concerning the Church of England for submission to Parliament for approval.

measure of damages. See DAMAGES.

measure of value. Money is the common denominator in terms of which is estimated the value of all other goods, as well as being a medium of exchange.

measurement. See UNITS OF MEASUREMENT.

mechanisation. The use in production of high quantities of machinery in relation to labour. It should not be confused with automation.

meeting. See GENERAL MEETING.

memorandum of association. The document which in effect, is the charter of a company and defines and limits its objects and powers. It regulates the company's external affairs. Every memorandum must state of a company limited by shares or guarantee: (1) the name, with "Limited" as the last word; (2) the country of situation of the registered office; (3) the objects; (4) that the liability of the members is limited; (5) the amount of the share capital (if any) and its division into fixed shares.

The memorandum must be signed by seven or more persons, or two or more if a private company (and their signatures attested) opposite the number of shares they each agree to take. Tables B. C. D. & E. of the Companies Act, 1948, give models of memorandum of association of various kinds.

mens rea. [Guilty mind.] An evil intention, or a knowledge of the wrongfulness of an act. There is a presumption that it is an essential ingredient in every crime. Many minor statutory offences, however, are punishable irrespective of the existence of *mens rea*; the mere doing of the act forbidden is sufficient unless otherwise provided. But if a particular intent or state of mind is an ingredient of a specific offence it must be proved.

mental disorder. Mental illness, arrested or incomplete development of mind, psychopathic disorder, etc. (Mental Health Act, 1959.) See INSANITY; UNSOUNDNESS OF MIND.

mercantile agent. A factor. An agent having in the customary course of his business authority to sell goods, or to consign goods for sale, or to buy goods, or to raise money on the security of goods.

He can give a good title to a purchaser without notice of his want of authority.

mercantile law. A name conveniently applied to the body of rules, enforced by the courts, which regulate the relations of merchants, traders and others engaged in commercial transactions. It usually comprises the law relating to contract, partnership, companies, agency, bills of exchange, carriers, carriage by sea, insurance, sale, bottomry and respondentia, debt, guarantee, stoppage *in transitu*, lien and bankruptcy. See also LAW MERCHANT.

merchandise marks. The forging or false application of trade marks, or the application of false or misleading trade descriptions (including their quality or fitness) is an offence, unless there was no intention to defraud (Merchandise Marks Acts, 1887 to 1953).

merchant bank. Deriving their name from the development of their banking activities (principally the acceptance of bills of exchange) out of their merchanting business, merchant banks now also undertake many of the functions of commercial and investment banks.

merchantable quality means that the goods must be of saleable value; that is of some use for the purpose for which such an article is ordinarily used and in such condition and of such quality that a reasonable man acting reasonably would, after a full examination, accept them in performance of the contract.

merchant's risk. Goods carried at merchant's risk and properly jettisoned, give rise to a claim by the charterers for a general average contribution. See AVERAGE.

merger. (1) That operation of law which extinguishes a right by reason of its coinciding with another and greater right in the same person, *e.g.*, a life estate is merged in or swallowed by the reversion when the two interests come into the hands of the same person.

(2) A right of action on a simple contract debt is merged in a judgment for it so that no further action may be brought on the debt, but only on the judgment. A special characteristic of the debt, however, such as being a preferential claim in bankruptcy, is not lost merely because judgment is obtained in respect of it.

(3) In equity, merger is a question of intention. If the benefit of a charge on property and the property subject to the charge vest in the same person, then equity will treat the charge as kept alive or merged according to whether it be of advantage or not to the person entitled.

(4) The combining of two or more companies. See AMALGAMATION.

mesne. Middle, intervening or intermediate.

mesne profits. Profits realised by one not entitled to do so, between certain dates; *e.g.*, where a tenant remains in possession after his tenancy has expired, he is liable for the rents and profits for that period.

messuage. House; it includes outbuildings, courtyards, etc.

metric system. The decimal system adopted in most European countries and elsewhere for the measurement of length, money, weight, etc. Multiples of the unit of measurement are obtained by multiplying the unit by ten, one hundred, etc. It is often referred to as the decimal system.

middle price. The mean between the buying and selling prices of a jobber or dealer on the Stock Exchange, of a stock on a particular day.

middleman. An intermediary between buyer and seller or producer, such as an agent, broker, factor or wholesaler.

minimum subscription. Where shares are offered by a company to the public, the minimum subscription is the minimum amount which, in the opinion of the directors, must be raised by the issue of such shares to provide for (1) the purchase price of any property which is to be defrayed, wholly or partly, out of the proceeds of the issue; (2) the preliminary expenses, and commission payable to persons who have agreed to subscribe or procure subscriptions for shares; (3) the repayment of any moneys borrowed in respect of any of the foregoing; (4) the working capital; and the amounts to be provided for the foregoing out of other sources than the proceeds of the issue. The minimum subscription must be raised before the allotment of shares.

minor. A person under the age of twenty-one years. See INFANT.

minority interest. A term which may be used in consolidated balance sheets of holding companies to represent the book value of those shares and interests of subsidiary companies which are not held by the holding company, or other member of the group.

In company law there is protection of minority interests. A representative action may be brought on behalf of dissentients to restrain the company from doing an illegal or *ultra vires* act, or where there is a fraud on the minority, or to restrain the company from acting on resolutions which were not validly passed. An alternative description is interest of outside shareholders.

mint. A place where money is manufactured under public authority. " The Mint " is the Royal Mint in London. Mint condition means unsoiled, unused and in perfect condition.

minutes. Records kept in a minute book of proceedings at a meeting; *e.g.* of directors or shareholders in general meeting of a company, or of the committee of a society or club.

misadventure. An accident for which no one is liable.

miscarriage. A failure of justice.

misdemeanour. An indictable offence not amounting to a felony (*q.v.*).

misdescription. An error, mistake or mis-statement in the description of property. A misdescription affecting the title, value or character of land in a contract of sale may be substantial, so that the property purchased is not that which it was intended to purchase, or slight, so that compensation in money would be proper.

Substantial misdescription is a defence to an action for specific performance, and a ground for rescission; the purchaser cannot be compelled to take the property. The purchaser may, however, at his option, generally compel specific performance of the contract with an abatement of the purchase price. The vendor cannot enforce the contract where he has been guilty of fraud (*q.v.*) or misrepresentation (*q.v.*).

misfeasance. The improper performance of a lawful act, *e.g.*, where there is negligence or trespass. Misfeasance proceedings are brought against officers of a company, or a liquidator, where it appears in a winding up that they have failed in their duty at the expense of the company.

misrepresentation. A false representation or statement made by one of the parties to an intended contract, as to some matter relating to the contract, with the object and result of inducing the other party to enter into the contract.

(1) A fraudulent misrepresentation is one made knowingly, or without belief in its truth, or recklessly without caring whether it is true or not. The injured party may (i) refuse to be bound by the contract, and where necessary, bring an action for its rescission; (ii) take advantage of the contract, and sue for fraud, claiming such damages or loss as he has sustained; (iii) successfully defend any attempt to enforce the contract against him;

(2) an innocent misrepresentation is one made in the honest belief in its truth. The injured party may rescind the contract or refuse further performance of it, but cannot, as a general rule, sue for damages.

Misrepresentation renders a contract voidable, but not void. The party misled can enforce the contract, which remains binding, or he can treat it as at an end.

mistake. (1) In contracts. As a general rule, a person is bound by an agreement unless he can show that there is a mistake of fact of such a nature that it prevents the existence of a true agreement, when the contract will be void. Such mistakes are as follows:

(a) mistake as to the nature of the contract;

(b) mistake as to the identity of the other party to the contract;

(c) mutual mistake as to the existence of the subject-matter;

(d) mutual mistake as to the identity of the subject-matter;

(e) mistake of the intention of one party known to the other party.

A mistake of law is not sufficient to have a contract set aside.

(2) Money paid under a mistake of fact may be recovered, as money had and received to the use of the person paying it; but money paid under a mistake of law is not recoverable, except where paid to an officer of the court, or in case of fraud.

(3) A mistake in a written document may be rectified on application to the court.

(4) Mistake is usually no defence to an action of tort.

(5) In criminal law, a mistake of law is no excuse, but a mistake of fact (which if true would have justified the act) is a good defence.

mixed economy. This term is used of the economy of a country in which state and private ownership and production are both present.

moiety. One of two equal parts into which a thing is divided; one half.

monetary policy. Part of a government's overall economic policy, carried out in conjunction with the central bank, its object is to control demand through control of credit and to stabilise the value of the national currency. A country's monetary policy is not flexible, being largely determined by the balance of payments position.

money. Popularly, money may mean wealth.

In economics, the essential features of money are (a) that it should be acceptable as a medium of exchange (which implies liquidity); (b) that it should serve as a measure of value, and (c) that it should serve as a store of value. Anything that performs these functions is money.

In law, "money" may be variously construed, according to the context and surrounding circumstances; particularly in wills; *e.g.*, as cash in hand or in the bank, or as invested.

money market. Where dealings in short-term credit are effected in the City of London. The market consists of banks, discount companies, insurance companies, trustee companies and Savings Banks.

money order. An order from one post office, where money is deposited to enable that money to be paid to a specified person, usually at another post office. In the United Kingdom the sender is required to complete a form of requisition, and himself sends the order, but where the money is to be paid in British possessions or foreign countries a receipt only is given to the sender, and the post office makes all arrangements with the paying office for notification and payment to the payee. Money orders may also be telegraphed.

moneylender. Every person whose business is that of moneylending and who advertises and announces himself and holds himself out in any way as carrying on that business (but not including pawnbrokers, registered societies, etc.) must take out a licence.

The court may on proceedings taken by a moneylender to recover a loan, reopen a transaction appearing to be harsh and unconscionable. Loans at interest in excess of 48 per cent. are presumed to be harsh and unconscionable. Loans at compound interest are prohibited. (Moneylenders Acts, 1900 to 1927).

monometallism. See BI-METALLISM.

monopoly. (1) The exclusive control of the supply of some commodity.

(2) The Monopolies Commission has the duty of investigating and reporting on the existence of monopolies in the industries referred to it by the Board of Trade. (Restrictive Trade Practices Act, 1956.)

month used in statutes or in deeds, documents, orders, etc., may mean either a lunar month of 28 days or a calendar month (*q.v.*). It means a calendar month unless the contrary intention appears.

moratorium. The general postponement of payment of debts authorised by statute in an emergency.

mortgage. A conveyance of, or charge over property, by the borrower, the mortgagor, in favour of the lender, the mortgagee, by way of security for the repayment of a debt or money lent, with interest. A mortgage is essentially a conveyance of an interest in property with a provision for redemption; *i.e.*, on repayment of the loan interest and costs the conveyance becomes void, or the property must be reconveyed.

By the Law of Property Act, 1925, mortgages can only be made by (1) a lease for a term of years absolute, subject to a provision for cesser on redemption, or (2) by a charge by deed expressed to be by way of legal mortgage. See also EQUITY OF REDEMPTION.

mortgagee. The lender: see MORTGAGE.

mortgagor. The borrower: see MORTGAGE.

motion. (1) A proposed form of resolution. A motion becomes a resolution when " passed " by a meeting.

(2) An application to a court or a judge for an order directing something to be done in the applicant's favour.

multilateral trade. Free trade between nations. The greater the freedom of international trade the greater will be the tendency for the total amount of such trade to increase.

multiple shops. A chain of retail shops under common management and in the same trade. The geographical spread of such shops may mean that the chain establishes a national reputation for quality and price, which the consumer will expect to find in all branches.

multiplier. In economics, the ratio between a given increase in new investment and the ultimate increase in national income resulting from it.

murder. The crime of unlawful homicide with malice aforethought; as where death is caused by an unlawful act done with the intention to cause death or bodily harm, or which is commonly known to be likely to cause death or bodily harm. Death must result in a year and a day. The burden of proving malice (either express, or by implication) rests upon the prosecution. (*Woolmington* v. *D.P.P.* [1935] A.C. 462.)

mutatis mutandis. [With the necessary changes.]

mutual dealings. In bankruptcy, where there have been mutual debts, mutual credits, or other mutual dealings between a bankrupt and a proving creditor, an account is taken and only the balance is claimed or paid.

mutual life assurance company. A life assurance company in which there are no shareholders; the profits belong to the assured and are distributed amongst them as bonuses.

mutual wills. Wills made by two persons who leave their property to each other, so that the survivor of them takes; *e.g.*, by a man and his wife.

N

name, change of. A person may change his surname simply by the adoption of a fresh name. This may be evidenced by executing a deed poll, which may be enrolled at the Central Office of the Supreme Court, or the College of Arms. See ALIAS.

A company may change its name by special resolution, with the approval of the Board of Trade.

name day. The second day of the Stock Exchange settlement.

narration. The explanation accompanying a journal entry.

narrow seas. Seas running between coasts not far apart.

narrower-range investments. Trustees are empowered to invest in narrower-range investments (a) which are authorised by the Trustee Investments Act, 1961, (b) only on their taking proper advice.

national assistance. Monetary payments to those on small incomes to enable them to meet their expenses and attain a minimum standard of living. The funds are provided out of central government resources and not by means of contributions.

national debt. The total debt of the Government raised by borrowings. (National Debt Act, 1870.)

national income. The gross total of income earned in a community during a given period by the owners of the various productive factors, *i.e.*, the sum of wages, profits, rents and interest. It is also equal to the value to the final purchaser or consumer of all goods and services produced by members of the community.

Net national income is the value of final production less replacement of capital worn out in the productive processes during the period.

national insurance. Compulsory state insurance covering health insurance, old age and retirement pensions, unemployment insurance and industrial injuries insurance. Contributors fall under one of three categories, *i.e.*, (1) Employed persons; (2) Self-employed persons; (3) Non-employed persons. Each pays a different rate of contribution and certain minimum contributions are necessary for eligibility to benefit. A state graduated pension scheme was operative from 1961 from which employers could contract out if they provided at least equivalent benefits under a private pension scheme. See EMPLOYMENT; SELF-EMPLOYED; NON-EMPLOYED; GRADUATED PENSION.

national savings. Personal savings which are lent to the state through various media provided for such saving, *e.g.*, National Savings Certificates, Premium Bonds, Defence Bonds, etc.

National Trust. The National Trust for places of historic interest and natural beauty was incorporated by the National Trust Act, 1907.

nationalisation. The taking over by the state of the ownership and operation of an industry either by a statutory authority, such as the National Coal Board, or a Government Department, such as the Postmaster-General's Department.

nationality. The character or quality arising from membership of some particular nation or state, which determines the political status and allegiance of a person. A " stateless " person is one destitute of nationality. See BRITISH SUBJECT; DOMICILE; NATURALISATION.

natural justice. The rules and procedure to be followed by quasi-judicial bodies, as opposed to the strict procedure of purely judicial tribunals. Such bodies must act fairly, bona fide, without bias, giving each side the opportunity of stating its case, and not hearing one side while refusing to hear the other.

Proceedings which are not purely administrative will be quashed if these rules are violated.

natural persons. Human beings, as distinguished from artificial persons or corporations recognised by the law, *e.g.*, companies.

naturalisation. The process whereby an alien may acquire British nationality. Application for naturalisation may be made to the Home Secretary, who has power to grant a certificate of naturalisation on the taking of an oath of allegiance. The certificate may be revoked.

The qualifications are: (1) 12 months' continual residence in the United Kingdom; (2) 4 years' residence in the United Kingdom out of the last seven preceding that 12 months; (3) good character; (4) sufficient knowledge of English; and (5) an intention to reside in the United Kingdom. (The references to United Kingdom above extend to British Possessions, and Crown Service.) See British Nationality Act, 1948.

navicerts. A pass or certificate issued by a belligerent exempting a neutral ship or her cargo from contraband control.

necessaries. (1) Things vital to a person's existence such as food, clothing, and also such things as may be suitable to the particular condition in life of the person and to his requirements at the relevant time. Infants can make a binding contract to buy necessaries. A wife as agent of necessity (*q.v.*) may supply herself and her children with necessaries on her husband's credit either during cohabitation or after separation through the husband's fault, but she forfeits the right if she has committed adultery.

(2) Such things as are fit and proper for the service in which a ship is engaged, and such as the owner, being a prudent man, would have ordered if present. The master may hypothecate the ship for necessaries supplied abroad so as to bind the owner.

negligence. (1) Carelessness: and attitude of mind where there is indifference to obvious risks. (2) Conduct consisting of the omission to do something which a reasonable man would do, or doing something which a prudent and reasonable man would not do.

Negligence is the tort consisting of the breach of duty to take care to avoid acts or omissions which can be reasonably foreseen as likely to injure persons who are so closely and directly affected as ought reasonably to be in contemplation. Such persons can sue for damage suffered by them as ought reasonably to be foreseen as likely to ensue.

negotiable instrument. An instrument which, by the custom of merchants passes by delivery so as to give a bona fide holder for value a good title. It is a document evidencing an obligation, of such a nature that the mere delivery of it may operate as a complete legal transfer, of both document and obligation, and the possession of which, upon such transfer, may enable the transferee to hold the document and enforce the obligation evidenced by it notwithstanding any defect in, and free from any limitation of, or equity attaching to, the title of the transferor.

No notice of such transfer need be given to the party liable on the instrument. A holder in due course can sue in his own name. The most important negotiable instruments are bills of exchange (*q.v.*) cheques (*q.v.*), and promissory notes (*q.v.*). The law with respect to them is now contained in the Bills of Exchange Act, 1882.

There are other instruments, dealings with which are regulated by statute and/or custom, *e.g.*, bearer debentures, bills of lading (*q.v.*), dock warrants, warehouse certificates, and certain government bonds which are negotiable as being an instrument transferable by one person to another by indorsement or mere delivery, but may be wanting in the essential feature of giving the transferee a good title irrespective of the title of the transferor.

negotiate (1) To transfer for value by delivery, or indorsement followed by delivery; (2) To bargain.

nem. con; nemine contradicente.   [Without opposition; no one saying otherwise.]

nem. dis; nemine dissentiente.   [No one dissenting.]

nemo dat que non habet.   [No one gives who has not.]   No one can give a better title than he himself has.   See NEGOTIABLE INSTRUMENT.

net or nett.   Not subject to deduction.   Contrast GROSS.

net annual value.   See ANNUAL VALUE.

net estate.   All the property of which a testator has power to dispose by will (otherwise than by virtue of a special power of appointment) less the amount of his funeral, testamentary and administration expenses, debts and liabilities, and estate duty payable out of the estate on his death.

net proceeds.   The net amount issuing out of any particular matter or venture. It is generally applied to the net balance due to the consignor in respect of a particular consignment, after deducting from the gross proceeds all expenses and commission.

net profit (or loss).   See PROFIT.

new issues.   One of the principal functions of the capital market is to provide means for additional capital to be raised by making public issues of stocks and shares.   Many new issues require a prospectus.

new streets.   Before new buildings are erected on private roads, the likely cost of street works must be paid to the highway authority, or provided for. (New Streets Acts, 1951 and 1957).

new towns.   They were created by development corporations under the New Towns Act, 1946, with a view to containing the growth of the large conurbations.

next friend.   A person appointed to bring an action or other proceeding on behalf of a person under incapacity; *e.g.*, a minor.   See also GUARDIAN AD LITEM.

next-of-kin.   The nearest relative or relatives (if in equal degree.)   The person or persons entitled to the estate of a person on his death intestate.   See INTESTACY.

nisi.   [unless.]   A decree, order, rule, declaration, or other adjudication of a court which takes effect unless the person affected by it shows, within a certain time, some reason why it should not take effect.   See RULE.

nisi prius. [unless before.] Originally this meant a trial at Assizes, but more generally it means a trial before judge and jury of a civil action in the superior courts.

nominal capital. See CAPITAL.

nominal damages. A small sum given for the violation of a legal right where no actual damage has resulted.

nominal partner. A person who allows himself to be represented as a partner.

nominal value. Face value, not necessarily real or actual value.

nominee. A nominated person. The name of a person ǀentered in a company's share register who represents another person, the true owner.

non compos mentis. [Not of sound mind.] See UNSOUND MIND, PERSON OF.

non est factum. (It is not his deed.) The old common law defence which permitted a person who had executed a written document in ignorance of its character to plead that notwithstanding the execution " it is not his deed." (see *Foster* v. *Mackinnon*, L.R. 4 C.P. 711.)

The defence that there has been a mistake as to the very nature of a document which has been signed.

non sequitur. [It does not follow.]

non-employed. Not gainfully occupied in employment. See NATIONAL INSURANCE.

nonfeasance. Neglect or failure to do some act which ought to be done, *e.g.*, the failure of a highway authority to keep in repair the highway.

non-resident. The liability of an individual or company to U.K. taxation is determined by a combination of domicile and residence. Non-residents are not liable to U.K. taxation on income derived from outside the U.K. and on certain income from U.K. sources.

non-voting shares. A term applied to equity shares which share in the profits of a company, but which carry no votes and therefore have no control over the management or destiny of a company.

no-par value. Shares which are of no nominal value but represent that proportion of the company's net assets which remain after deducting the nominal value of other classes of share. Such shares can be issued at any price and their value in the balance sheet adjusted to conform with changes in net asset values. Their use has not been authorised in the U.K.

norm. A rule or pattern; an authoritative standard.

normal cost. (1) A standard cost (*q.v.*). Cost under ordinary or usual working conditions. (2) The lowest average cost of production under given conditions of plant and equipment.

not negotiable. The crossing of a cheque which destroys its negotiability. The cheque can still be transferred from one person to another but subject to any defect in the title of a prior transferor. See also CROSSED CHEQUE; NEGOTIABLE INSTRUMENT.

When written across a bill of exchange these words prohibit transfer (Bills of Exchange Act, 1882, s. 81 (1)).

notary public. A public officer whose chief duties are certifying deeds and documents, noting and protesting foreign bills, etc. The office is one of great antiquity, and the acts of a notary are recognised throughout the civilised world. See PROTEST.

notice. Knowledge, cognisance. At law a person's rights or liabilities may be affected by his having had or not having had notice of certain facts, *e.g.*, where a purchaser takes land in good faith and for value, without notice of a prior equitable charge, he does not take subject to that charge.

Notice may be (1) actual or express, where it is given in plain words either orally or in writing; or (2) constructive, where knowledge is presumed or imputed from the circumstances of the case; *e.g.*, where knowledge would have been obtained if proper enquiries had been made.

notice of dishonour. The notice to be given by the holder of a bill of exchange within the specified times, in order to preserve his rights against other parties to the bill. See DISHONOUR; NOTING.

notice of motion. The necessary notice which must be served beforehand. See MOTION.

notice to quit. Where there is a tenancy of land or tenements from year to year, month to month, or other like indefinite period, a notice to quit by the landlord, or notice of intention to quit by the tenant, is required to enable one party to determine the tenancy without the consent of the other.

noting. (1) A minute or memorandum made by a notary on a bill of exchange which has been dishonoured. It consists of his initials and charges and the date, and, in the case of foreign bills, is preparatory to a formal protest. See Bills of Exchange (Time of Noting) Act, 1917, s. 1.

(2) The marking of particulars of leases, mortgages, caveats, etc., on a certificate of title.

novation. The substitution for one party to a contract of a new or another person. A tripartite agreement whereby a contract between two parties is rescinded in consideration of a new contract being entered into on the same terms between one of the parties and a third party. In the case of a change in the membership of a partnership firm, the creditors of the old firm will usually be deemed to have accepted the new firm as their debtor by continuing to trade with the new firm as with the old.

noxious trade. See OFFENSIVE TRADE.

nudum pactum. [A bare agreement or promise.] One made without consideration and upon which, unless it be under seal, no action will lie.

nuisance. (1) Private nuisance is a tort or civil wrong done to one who is unlawfully annoyed, prejudiced or disturbed in the enjoyment of his property, *e.g.*, where a neighbour's roof drain overhangs and discharges water on his land. The remedy for a private nuisance is either by abatement (*q.v.*) or by action for damages, or an injunction (*q.v.*).

(2) Public nuisance is where a person is prevented from exercising

149

O.C.D.—6

a right to which he is entitled as a member of the public, *e.g.*, where an obstruction is unlawfully placed on a public road.

The remedy for a public nuisance is either by abatement or action by public authorities, *e.g.*, a local authority. Where the nuisance amounts to a criminal offence, the wrongdoer may be prosecuted. If special damage is caused to an individual by a public nuisance he has an action for damages or injunction against the wrongdoer.

nulla bona. The sheriff's return to the writ of fi. fa. (*q.v.*) of " no goods."

null and void. Of no legal effect; a nullity, *e.g.*, an agreement for an illegal consideration. It cannot be enforced, and, in general, money paid under it cannot be recovered by the payer.

nuncupative will. An oral testamentary declaration. See WILL.

O

oaths. An appeal to God to witness that what a party says is the truth, or that which he promises to do he will do, *e.g.*, the oath of allegiance (*q.v.*) to the Crown; the oath taken by witnesses in court, or a deponent when swearing an affidavit, etc. See AFFIRMATION.

obiter dictum. [A saying by the way.] An observation by a judge on a legal question suggested by a case before him, but not essential to the decision of the case before him. See PRECEDENT.

objects clause. The most important clause of a company's Memorandum of Association it sets out the business activities in which the company takes power to act. Anything which a company does which exceeds the powers conferred on it by its objects clause and elsewhere is "*ultra vires*" and therefore invalid.

obligation. (1) A bond (*q.v.*). (2) A duty; the relationship between two or more persons under the binding force of the law, where one or more may be compelled to act, or abstain, by the other or others. See CONTRACT.

obligee. One to whom a bond (*q.v.*) is made.

obligor. One who binds himself by a bond (*q.v.*).

obsolescence. Going out of use; becoming out of date, hence the decline in the service capacity of an asset, *e.g.*, new inventions and improvements may cause a machine otherwise in good condition to become obsolete and therefore valueless before its " natural " life is ended; the decline in value of stock on hand due to a change in consumer demand.

occupation lease. A lease made for the purposes of personal occupation of premises.

odd lots. Shares less in number than the normal unit of trading; *i.e.*, less than a marketable parcel. (Stock Exchange.)

offensive trade. A trade, business, etc., of an objectionable or noxious nature, *e.g.*, tanning, slaughtering, soap-making, boiling down meat, crushing bones; trades giving off offensive smells, or likely to cause lead or other poisoning.

offer. Offer and acceptance are essential for the formation of a contract. An offer is a proposal to enter into a contract; it is an offer of a promise made on condition of receiving a reciprocal promise, or performance. An offer may be express or implied from conduct. It must be communicated to the offeree.

The acceptance of the offer must be absolute and unqualified, in writing or by words or by conduct; but must be communicated to the offeror, while the offer is still in force, except in cases where the offer has to be acted on. The contract is complete on receipt of the acceptance, except in contracts by post; when the offer may be accepted by post. An offer can be revoked before acceptance, but is irrevocable after acceptance.

An offer must be distinguished from a mere invitation to treat, *e.g.*, where a person calls for tenders in respect of certain work. See also CONTRACT; FIRM OFFER.

offer for sale. This arises when a company allots an issue of shares or debentures to an issuing house which then invites the public to buy from it at a higher price than that which it paid the company. The offer for sale by the issuing house is a prospectus.

office copy. A copy of a document or official record made by authority and indicating that it is a copy so made, either by affixing a seal or by a statement to that effect; *e.g.*, an office copy of an order of court.

office premises. A building, or part, used solely or principally as an office or for office purposes (*q.v.*).

office purposes. Administration, clerical work (*q.v.*), handling money, telephone and telegraph operating (Offices, Shops and Railway Premises Act, 1963). See also EMPLOYMENT.

official assignee. See OFFICIAL RECEIVERS.

official list. The Stock Exchange daily list of quotations and of the prices at which bargains have been made in stocks and shares.

official rate of exchange. The rate of exchange for a country's currency which has been fixed by that country's government acting through its monetary authority. On the foreign exchange market (*q.v.*) dealings occur usually within a narrow margin from the official rate of exchange.

Official Receivers. Officers of the Bankruptcy Court who are appointed for each district, their duties being, in general, to supervise and effect the realisation and administration of the estate of the debtor, of which they take charge. They have to investigate and report on the prior conduct and dealings of the bankrupt and the present position of his estate. They conduct the public examination of the bankrupt. The official receiver is trustee of the estate of a bankrupt in the absence of an appointed trustee in bankruptcy.

Official Referees

Official receivers are also appointed for the purpose of winding up companies.

Official Referees. Officers of the Supreme Court, who enquire and report on such questions, and try such matters and issues as may be referred to them by a judge or master: in particular, the investigation of accounts and inventories, the conduct of arbitrations and the assessment of damages.

omnibus clause. A clause covering many different objects or matters.

omnium. The aggregate of certain portions of different stocks in the public funds.

oncost. An alternative description of overhead (or fixed) expenditure by a business organisation.

on demand. See AT SIGHT.

one man company. A private company in which the shares are held substantially by or on behalf of one person. See COMPANY.

onerous. Property or rights which, by reason of the burdensome duties or covenants attaching thereto partake of the nature of liabilities rather than assets; e.g., land burdened with onerous covenants, shares subject to calls. Such property may be disclaimed by a trustee in bankruptcy.

onus of proof. See PROOF.

open account. An active account; one which is still current.

open cheque. One not crossed, payable either to bearer on presentation at the bank, or to order on presentation. See also CROSSED CHEQUE.

open contract. One which contains only the price, the names of the parties, and the description of the property sold.

open cover. A proposal to insure before the goods to be insured are shipped.

open market operations. The action of the Bank of England in buying or selling Government securities in the money market for the purpose of curtailing or expanding the volume of credit, or of varying the ruling rate of interest. By selling securities the Bank can absorb a given amount of funds; by buying securities it can put more funds into the market.

open order. An order given to a stockbroker or agent or warehouseman for the purchase of stock, shares or commodities during a certain period—usually a short one.

open policy. See MARINE INSURANCE.

open shop. A business which will give employment to people irrespective of whether they are members of particular trade unions or of any trade union. The opposite state is the closed shop where only those who are members of particular unions are employed.

operating expenses. Direct expenses incurred by an enterprise in the course of its normal activities, and contributing to the generation of operating revenue.

152

operating profit. See PROFIT.

operating revenue. The revenue derived from those activities for which an enterprise is primarily organised and which normally form the chief source of revenue, *e.g.*, for a trading or manufacturing business, sales of merchandise.

operational research. The systematic examination of a business problem in order to find the best balanced solution for improved performance.

operative part. The part of an instrument which carries out the main object as opposed to recitals (*q.v.*).

opere citato; op. cit. In the work just referred to.

option. (1) A right of choice.

(2) A right acquired under an agreement whereby for valuable consideration one person gives to another a right to enter into a specified transaction within a period limited in the agreement. If the option is not exercised within the period limited it lapses, *e.g.*, option of purchase contained in a lease.

(3) A method of speculating in order to limit losses, if any. For the purposes of the Stock Exchange, options are of three classes; the put, the call, and the put and call. The purchase of an option gives the purchaser the right to buy or sell shares at a certain price on a certain future date. The put gives the right to sell, the call to buy, and the put and call to do either.

order (for payment). A cheque or bill payable " to order " is payable to the person named as payee or his " order," *i.e.*, the person to whom he assigns the right to collect the amount of the bill or cheque. See CHEQUE.

order-in-council. A formal order made by the Queen, or in the Dominions by a Governor-General or Governor; in the case of the Queen, made at a sitting of the Privy Council and in the other cases at a sitting of the Executive Council; it must be countersigned by at least two persons present at such meeting.

ordinary shares. See SHARE.

outcrop (mining). An orebody seen above the earth's surface.

output. (1) The quantity and/or value of goods produced during a stated period.

(2) The opposite of input (*q.v.*) in computer terminology.

outworker. An employee working outside the precincts of the factory.

over-capitalised. A company is said to be over-capitalised when the current or expected amount of profit is insufficient to yield a normal return on its paid-up share capital.

over-riding commission. The remuneration of a district agent who supervises the work of the agents in his district. He is paid by a commission on all business done by those agents.

over-trading. This is said to occur when a business has expanded its turnover beyond what can be achieved with its existing resources of fixed and working capital.

overdraft. The amount a customer of a banker has been permitted by the banker to draw in excess of the money paid in; security for repayment is usually demanded.

overdue. A bill of exchange of which the time for payment has passed; or a bill payable on demand which appears to have been in circulation for an unreasonable length of time. Anyone taking an overdue bill takes it subject to the equities of prior holders.

Overseas Trading Corporation. A term used in taxation of a company whose residence was in the U.K. but whose trading was conducted elsewhere. The advantages of such tax status were eliminated by the introduction of a corporation tax system in the U.K.

overspill. A taxation term for that part of overseas tax payable by a company which exceeds the relief for U.K. corporation tax to which it is entitled on the overseas profits.

overt. Open. *Cf.* MARKET OVERT.

overt act. An open act, one consisting of something more than mere words and evidencing a deliberate intention on the part of the person doing it, as in the law of treason or conspiracy.

overtime. Time worked and paid for at premium rates beyond the standard working week for which the basic wage is paid. Overtime earnings form an important part of total earnings for British workers.

ownership. The right to the exclusive enjoyment of a thing: the relation between a person and any right that is vested in him.

Absolute ownership involves the right of free as well as exclusive enjoyment, including the right of using, altering, disposing of or destroying the thing owned. It is of indeterminate duration. Land is in strictness not subject to absolute ownership because all land is ultimately held of the Crown.

Restricted ownership is ownership limited to some extent; as, for example, a life tenancy, or where the property is charged with the payment of a sum of money, or subject to an easement.

Beneficial ownership is the right to the enjoyment of a thing as contrasted with the legal or nominal ownership. Ownership is always subject to the rule that a man must so use his own property as not to injure his neighbour. See REPUTED OWNERSHIP.

P

P.P.I. [Policy proof of interest.] A wagering policy of insurance which may be expressly made " interest or no interest," " without further proof of interest than the policy itself " or " without benefit of salvage to the insurer." It is void.

paid-up capital. See CAPITAL.

paper profit. An unrealised capital or other profit; *i.e.*, the profit is on paper only.

paper tape. A tape in which data for a computer may be recorded by means of a pattern of holes.

par. Equality. (1) The par value of stocks and shares is the nominal value *i.e.*, when they are neither at a premium nor a discount. (2) The par of exchange is the recognised standard value of the coinage of a country in terms of the coinage of another.

par avion. [By air.]

parent company. A holding company (*q.v.*).

pari passu. [With equal step.] Equally, without preference, *e.g.*, a series of debentures may be issued subject to the condition that they are to rank *pari passu* as a first charge on the property charged by the debentures. If it were necessary to enforce the charge and the sum realised was insufficient to discharge the debentures, they would abate proportionately.

Parkinson's Laws. (1) Work expands so as to fill the time available for its completion; (2) Expenditure rises to meet income; (3) Expansion means complexity, and complexity decay. (Ironically promulgated by Prof. C. Northcote Parkinson.)

parol. Oral, as opposed to writing or under seal.
Parol evidence is not admissible to contradict or vary a written instrument.

part payment. Payment of part of a debt. It operates to revive a debt which would otherwise be barred by the statutes of limitation of actions; payment of part being evidence of a fresh promise to pay the whole debt.

part performance. The equitable doctrine that where a contract concerning an interest in land is not enforceable for want of a memorandum in writing under the Law of Property Act, 1925, s. 40, and it has been partly carried into effect by one of the parties, the other party cannot set up the informality as a defence; *e.g.*, where possession has been taken of the land and expense incurred.

participating preference shares. See CUMULATIVE PREFERENCE SHARES.

particular average. A partial accidental loss or damage to goods in transit caused by a peril insured against which falls exclusively on the owner of the thing damaged, he having no right to make others contribute. If goods are insured subject to particular average the underwriters bear the loss; if free of particular average, the underwriters are not liable. See GENERAL AVERAGE.

partition. The division of land owned by persons as co-owners among them as owners in severalty. Partition is either voluntary, by deed, or compulsory, by order of the court. Where a satisfactory partition cannot be made the court may order a sale.

partnership. The relation which subsists between persons carrying on business in common with a view to profit (Partnership Act, 1890), but excluding a company.

Every partner is entitled and bound to take part in the conduct of the business, unless it is otherwise agreed between them. Every partner is liable for the debts of the partnership to the whole extent of his property. As between the partners, each partner is bound to contribute to the debts in proportion to his share of the profits, unless otherwise agreed. As regards third persons, the act of every partner, within the ordinary scope of the business, binds his co-partners, whether they have sanctioned it or not. The relation between the partners being personal, no one of them can put a stranger in his place without the consent of the others. Where no time for the duration of the partnership is fixed, it is called a partnership at will, and may be dissolved at the pleasure of any partner.

The maximum number of persons who may constitute a partnership is limited to twenty, and, in the case of a banking partnership, to ten. If the number of members exceeds the maximum allowed, the association is illegal, and cannot sue in respect of any cause of action.

A partnership may be created by agreement, which may be either verbal, written or under seal, or it may be inferred from the course of dealing by the partners. The agreement is referred to as the partnership deed or agreement, or the articles of partnership, which may provide for the following:

(1) The names of the partners and the firm name; (2) the nature of the business; (3) the term of the partnership; (4) the capital to be introduced by each partner; (5) proper accounts and their audit; (6) the authority of partner; (7) the division of profits, partners drawings and salaries; (8) Interest on capital, advances or drawings; (9) death, bankruptcy and retirement of a partner, including the method of valuing goodwill.

See also LIMITED PARTNER; NOMINAL PARTNER; SLEEPING PARTNER.

party. A person who takes part in a transaction or legal proceedings.

party-wall. A wall used for the common benefit of the different owners of adjoining houses or land. Formerly, they were regarded as tenants in common in equal shares, but since the Law of Property Act, 1925, the wall is regarded as severed vertically, and the respective owners as having their former rights of user and support.

passage broker. A person who sells or lets steerage passages in any ship going from Britain to any place out of Europe but not within the Mediterranean. He requires a licence.

Passage, Court of. An ancient court of record for the trial of actions in Liverpool.

passim. Passages, opinions or statements occurring in various places in a book or document.

passing a dividend. Omitting to pay a dividend.

passing off. The " passing off " by one person of his goods, etc., as those of another: it is the wrong committed by a person who sells goods, or carries on business, etc., under such a name, mark, description or otherwise in such a manner as to mislead the public into believing that the goods or business, etc., is that of another person. The latter person has a right of action in damages, for an account, and for an injunction to restrain the defendant for the future.

passive trust. A trust which does not involve any active duties.

passport. Originally a permission to leave or enter a port, now a document issued by a government certifying that the holder is a subject or citizen of the issuing government and requesting all friendly governments to aid the holder in freely passing to and from, and in their territories.

patent. [Open.] (1) Letters patent from the Crown, as, *e.g.*, conferring a peerage. (2) A grant of the exclusive privilege of making, using, exercising and vending some new invention for a period of years. Grants are now made by the Comptroller-General of Patents, Designs and Trade Marks. The Patent Office is a branch of the Board of Trade. (Patents Acts, 1949, 1957.)

patent agent. A person carrying on for gain in the United Kingdom the business of acting as agent for other persons for the purpose of applying for and obtaining patents. He must be registered. See PATENT.

patentee. One who holds a patent, *i.e.*, is entered in the register of patents as grantee or proprietor of the patent.

pawn (or pledge). The deposit of goods or documents of title thereto with the lender of money as security for a loan. The legal ownership still remains with the pledger, pawner or borrower, who is handed a pawn-ticket in acknowledgment.

pawnbroker. A person who keeps a shop for taking goods or chattels by way of security for money advanced thereon, not exceeding £50, with the understanding that these goods may be afterwards redeemed.

Pawnbrokers must be licenced. If a pledge pawned for 40s. or more is not redeemed within 6 months and 7 days it may be sold by public auction. If less than 40s. is lent, the pledge becomes the pawnbroker's absolute property if not so redeemed. (Pawnbrokers Acts, 1872, 1922, 1960.)

pay-as-you-earn; P.A.Y.E. The system of collection of income tax, assessable under Schedule E, whereby the employer deducts tax from salaries or wages at the time of payment, and subsequently accounts to the Inland Revenue for that tax. Each employee is given a code number by the Inspector of Taxes, which is an index to his personal reliefs and allowances, and the employer deducts the appropriate tax by reference to tax tables with which he is supplied. (Income Tax Act, 1952, ss. 157, 158.)

payee. The person to whom money is, or is to be, paid or the person to whom a bill of exchange or cheque is made payable.

payer. The person by whom a sum of money is paid or payable.

paying-in slip. The document handed to a bank when money is paid into a customer's account. It gives particulars not only of the amount paid in, but specifies whether it be notes, silver, copper, cheques, money orders, or postal orders.

payment by results. A costing term concerning remuneration for increased effort, *e.g.*, by means of piecework, premium, bonus or similar system.

payment for honour. The payment of a bill for honour which has been accepted by the drawee and is later dishonoured by non-payment. It is first necessary to have the bill protested for non-payment, and then any person may intervene and pay it supra protest for the honour of any party liable thereon, or for the honour of the person for whose account the bill is drawn. See ACCEPTANCE SUPRA PROTEST.

payment in due course. Payment at or after the maturity of the bill to the holder thereof, in good faith, and without notice of any defect in his title.

payment into court. (1) The deposit of money with an official of a court for the purposes of proceedings pending in the court, *e.g.*, where the defendant in an action for debt or damages admits the plaintiff's claim to a certain amount he may pay that amount into court by way of satisfaction or amends. The plaintiff may accept the payment, or refuse it and continue the proceedings, at the risk of having to pay costs thereafter if the amount turns out to be adequate.

(2) The practice in the Chancery Division of trustees paying into court amounts due from them, but for which they are unable to get a good receipt and discharge.

pay roll. A book, sheet or list, showing names of employees, particulars of wages or salaries payable, appropriate deductions (*e.g.*, national insurance, income tax, etc.) the net wages or salaries payable and the employers' proportion of the national insurance contribution.

peace officer. A sheriff, coroner, constable, or justice of the peace.

Peers. Members of the House of Lords, whether hereditary peers or life peers. Hereditary peerages may be disclaimed (Peerage Act, 1963).

pegged market. Where the price of shares on the Stock Exchange is kept within defined limits by interested parties giving or withholding support.

penalty. (1) A punishment imposed by law for some offence. A fine is a pecuniary penalty.

(2) A sum of money recoverable by virtue of a penal statute, *e.g.*, for breach of duties of a public nature.

(3) The sums payable as prescribed by a statute for offences committed against its provisions, *e.g.*, the Income Tax Acts.

(4) An amount agreed to be paid in case of the breach of the condition of a bond, or of a term of a contract.

Where the parties to a contract agree that, in the event of a breach of its provisions, the one shall pay to the other a specified sum of money, and it appears that the sum so specified does not represent the amount of damage caused by a breach of the contract, but is merely an arbitrary sum, then the sum specified is a penalty and cannot be recovered. But if the amount named is a genuine pre-estimate of loss, it is termed "liquidated damages" and is recoverable.

pendente lite. While an action is pending but has not been decided.

pension. Regular income on retirement, which usually arises because of previous employment. There are many state and private pension schemes in operation. Pensions are earned income for tax purposes.

pension fund. The fund into which the receipts of a pension scheme are paid. Private pensions schemes either pay into an insurance company which handles the administration and guarantees certain benefits to participants or administration and investment is done within the employing company.

peppercorn rent. When land is let free of rent but the landlord wishes to be able to obtain an acknowledgment of the tenancy, a nominal rent may be reserved of one peppercorn a year to be paid when demanded.

per annum. By the year.

per capita; per stirpes. [by heads; by stocks.] When property is given to the descendants of a testator it is said to be divided *per capita* where it is shared between all the beneficiaries equally, and to be divided *per stirpes* where it is shared between surviving children and the descendants of a deceased child equally, that is the children of the deceased child take the share equally between them which their parent would have taken if still living.

per contra. [On the other side.]

per curiam. [By the court.]
per diem. [By the day.]

per incuriam. [through want of care.] A decision of the court *per incuriam* is not a precedent (*q.v.*).

per pro. [By procuration (*q.v.*).] The words indicate that the person signing has but a limited authority to sign, and signs in a representative capacity.

per se. [By itself; taken alone.]

per stirpes. See PER CAPITA.

per testes. [By witnesses.] As in proving a will in solemn form.

performance. (1) the carrying out of a contract according to its terms. A contract is discharged by such performance. The time for performance may be fixed in the contract, and if time is of the essence of the contract, the contract must be performed in that time: otherwise performance must be made within a reasonable time. Tender (*q.v.*) is an offer of performance, and if refused the party tendering is discharged from performance. Payment of the sum due also discharges the contract. See also PART PERFORMANCE.

(2) Performance of dramatic or musical works by actors, singers, musicians, dancers, etc., is governed by the Performers' Protection Act, 1963.

Performing Right Tribunal. The Tribunal established by the Copyright Act, 1956, to adjudicate in certain disputes as to licences for the public performance of literary, dramatic, or musical work, and broadcasts.

perils of the seas. All kinds of marine casualties such as foundering of a ship at sea (but not by scuttling (*q.v.*)), collisions, unintentional stranding, etc. Also damage done to the ship or goods at sea by the fortuitous action of the wind and waves.

perishable goods. Fruit, vegetables, fish, meat, etc. The unpaid seller may resell, and the court may order their sale in proceedings. Also a carrier of perishable goods, if unable to commmunicate with the owner, may sell. If the customs entry is taken to the officer at the quayside, they may be examined and cleared expeditiously.

perjury. The offence of making a sworn statement in a judicial proceeding which is material in that proceeding, which the person making it knows to be false or does not believe to be true. Perjury includes other false statements on oath, and certain false declarations, including statutory declarations (Perjury Act, 1911).

permit. A licence; written permission to remove dutiable goods, *e.g.*, spirits from warehouse.

perpetual inventory. A system of continuous accounting for usage and levels of materials and merchandise, by which receipts and issues of each type of material or merchandise are recorded and whereby the balances on hand at any time may be ascertained without a physical stocktaking. Also called continuous inventory.

perpetual succession. The attribute of a corporation or company of continuing to exist as a lawful entity irrespective of the death of its constituent members.

perpetuity. A disposition of property by which its absolute vesting is postponed for ever. Perpetuities are contrary to the policy of the law, because they " tie up " property and prevent its free alienation.

perpetuities, rule against. This rule forbids any disposition by which the absolute vesting of property is or may be postponed beyond the " perpetuity period." At common law, this period is the duration of any relevant life or lives of persons living at the time of the disposition and a further period of 21 years (with the possible addition of the period of gestation); the period is of 21 years if no life in being is applicable. Now, under the Perpetuities and Accumulations Act, 1964, a period not exceeding 80 years *may* be chosen instead of the common law period. See also ACCUMULATION.

person. In Acts of Parliament, " person," in general includes a body of persons, whether incorporated or not. A natural person is a human being, an artificial person is a legal conception such as a corporation or company.

personal accident insurance. A policy of insurance securing income during incapacity owing to accidental injury, or compensation therefor.

personal accounts. Accounts with persons being either debtors or creditors, in a system of bookkeeping.

personal covenant in mortgage. The personal promise or agreement, independent of the security, for payment of the moneys secured.

personal property (personalty). All property other than realty (*q.v.*); it includes, *e.g.*, leases, shares, rights of action, debts, stock, ships and money.

personal representative. An executor or administrator.

personnel officer. The management section which is responsible for personnel matters, *e.g.*, selection, training and welfare.

petition. A written statement addressed to a court or public officer setting forth facts on which the petitioner bases a prayer for remedy or relief, *e.g.*, as in bankruptcy proceedings. The subject may petition the Crown or Parliament for relief.

petitioning creditor. The creditor who files a bankruptcy petition against a debtor. The debt due to the creditor must be a liquidated sum of not less than fifty pounds, and the act of bankruptcy on which the petition is based must have occurred within three months before the presentation of the petition.

petty cash. An amount of cash advanced to the petty cashier to meet small disbursements, *e.g.*, fares, stamps, and other small items.

pidgin English. (" Business English.") The *lingua franca* or jargon of the East, especially as used between Chinese and Europeans; originally based, probably, on the language of English sailors.

piece work. Work done and paid for by the unit of production as distinct from work paid for by the hour or at a fixed wage or salary. It is a method of payment by results. (*q.v.*).

pilfering. Stealing goods surreptitiously in small quantities; as *e.g.*, from goods in transit, or at the place of work.

pillaging. The act of taking goods unlawfully, but openly, and wholesale, by force of arms; plunder.

pilot. A person taken on board a sea going ship for the purpose of taking it into or out of port. Pilots are appointed by the pilotage authority, for the particular district and receive a licence showing the territorial limits of their operations.

piracy. (1) The infringement of copyright (*q.v.*). (2) An unauthorised act of violence committed on the high seas by a private vessel against another with intent to plunder. It need not succeed in its purpose. Broadly, it includes all unauthorised acts of violence against persons or goods in a ship, whether by another private vessel, or by its own mutinous crew or passengers.

piracy jure gentium is piracy according to international law, and the pirates may be punished by any nation which is able to seize and try them.

161

placing. A method of introducing shares in a company to a stock exchange without the full expense and formality of a public offer for sale or prospectus offer.

plaintiff. One who brings an action at law. See DEFENDANT.

planning authority. Under the Town and Country Planning Acts, the local planning authority for each county or county borough is its council. It includes a joint planning board.

planning, economic. Direct intervention by the state to allocate resources by means of rationing, price, licensing, and other controls. In a completely planned economy, the distribution of factors of production and resources of all kinds is determined by the decisions of the central authority, in contrast to a " *laisser-faire* " economy in which decisions are made by private entrepreneurs, co-ordination being effected only through the functioning of a competitive price system.

planning permission. Under the Town and Country Planning Acts, the permission granted by a planning authority or the Minister of Town and Country Planning, authorising the development of land. See DEVELOPMENT.

plant. Whatever machinery or instruments are used by a firm in carrying on its business. It does not properly include stock-in-trade, premises or fixtures and similar fitments. Generally it applies to things subject to wear and tear, *e.g.*, the machinery and tools of a factory.

pleadings. Written or printed statements delivered alternately by the parties to proceedings to one another, setting forth their respective cases in preparation for the hearing. The objects of pleadings are to make known to each party the case to be made against him; to define the matters in dispute; to provide a short record of the case, and to ensure that questions in dispute are referred to the appropriate tribunal.

pledge. See PAWN.

plimsoll mark. The load line along a ship's side marking the depth to which her proper cargo causes her to sink. Overloading is punishable as an offence.

ploughed back profits. Net profit retentions.

pluvius policy. An insurance policy providing that if rain up to a given number of inches should fall during certain stated hours a specified sum will be paid.

point of order. A question raised at a meeting to call the attention of the chairman to some irregularity in the proceedings.

police court. See MAGISTRATE.

policy. The contract between the insurer and the insured providing for the insurer to pay money to the insured upon the happening of a given event, generally by way of indemnity.

poll. Taking a vote at an election, or on a motion. At a general meeting of members of a company, etc., questions are decided in the first place by a show of hands, but there is a right of members to demand a poll, unless expressly excluded. The poll is taken by counting the written votes of members present in person, or by proxy (*q.v.*).

pool. A common fund into which gains, or from which losses, are paid to the contributors, who are usually members of the same trade, or with a common interest.

pool betting. Betting other than betting at fixed odds. The only places which may be used for pool betting are approved horse racecourses, licensed dog tracks, and licensed betting offices; but in the last-mentioned case, only for pool betting on recognised horse races (Betting Duties Act, 1963; Betting, Gaming and Lotteries Act, 1963).

portfolio. A schedule giving details of the investments held by a particular person.

portion. The provision made for a child by a parent or one *in loco parentis* (*q.v.*). See SATISFACTION (*of portions*).

possession. Actual possession is the visible possibility of exercising physical control over a thing, coupled with the intention of doing so, either against all others, or against all except certain persons. Actual possession includes wrongful possession; *i.e.*, without right to possess. Possession is " nine points of the law " because a person in possession can only be ousted by one with a better right or title than himself.

possessory lien. See LIEN.

possibility. A future event, the happening of which is uncertain. Also an interest in land which depends on the happening of such an event.

post. (After) (referring to matter that follows in the text of a book), or in such terms as " post-nuptial " (after marriage).

Post Office Savings Bank. The savings bank (*q.v.*) run by the Post Office. Deposits and withdrawals may be made through branches of the Post Office, and interest, tax free within certain limits, is paid on depositors' balances.

post-date. To date a document or a cheque, etc., subsequent to the date on which it is actually signed. In general it will not be operative until the latter date.

post-war credits. That part of personal taxation paid during the Second World War which was regarded as a compulsory loan. Repayment of these credits was deferred until after the war and it is now made when holders attain a certain age.

post obit. [after death.] A bond payable on or after the death of a person other than the maker, in consideration of the prior loan or advance of money in expectation of benefits accruing to the maker on that event.

postal giro. A method of monetary transfer through the post office as an alternative to postal orders, etc. The maintenance and use of a postal giro account is akin to that of keeping a current account with a commercial bank.

postal order. A simple means of transmitting small sums of money. It is an imperfect instrument until it has been crossed for payment to a bank, or the name of the payee has been filled in.

postscript. An addition to a communication, after the signature.

pound. A place where straying or trespassing animals, etc., are kept until claimed or sold.

pound sterling. The British standard monetary unit equal to twenty shillings.

poundage. A tax or charge of so much in the £ on the value of the property concerned.

power. The ability conferred on a person by law to determine the legal relations of himself or others. A power is the converse of disability.

It differs from a right in that there are no accompanying duties. Powers are public when vested by the state in its agent or servant, or private when conferred by one person on another. General powers are those which are by law incident to an office, *e.g.*, of solicitor or trustee; special powers are those conferred specially, *e.g.*, by a power of attorney (*q.v.*). See POWER OF APPOINTMENT.

power of appointment. A power, given by deed or will, by which a nominated person, the donee, may direct certain estate or interests in property to devolve on a person or persons.

When the donee exercises the power and makes an appointment, he is called the appointor. The person in whose favour it can be exercised is the object of the power. A power is discretionary, not imperative, as is a trust. A general power of appointment is one where the donee may appoint to anyone, including himself; a special power is one where the donee can only appoint in favour of specified persons or objects.

power of attorney. A deed by which one person empowers another to represent him, or act in his stead either generally or for certain purposes. The donor of the power is called the principal, the donee is called the attorney. The attorney is not entitled to exercise his powers for his own benefit, *e.g.*, draw cheques on the principal's account to pay his own debts.

A power of attorney may be irrevocable if it is " coupled with an interest." Thus if a principal owes money to X and he executes a power of attorney authorising X to sell certain land and pay himself back, this authority is coupled with an interest and cannot be revoked. A power of attorney is revoked by the death of the grantor.

practice. (1) That which pertains to the actual conduct of legal proceedings. (2) The business or connection of professional men, *e.g.*, solicitor, accountant, etc. See GOODWILL.

pratique. A certificate granted to a vessel by the Waterguard officer when satisfied that there is no serious illness aboard ship.

preamble. The introductory part of an Act of Parliament containing the recitals showing the necessity for it.

precedent. (1) A judgment or decision of a court of law cited as an authority for deciding a similar set of facts; a case which serves as an authority for the legal principle embodied in its decision. An authoritative precedent is one which is binding and must be followed; a persuasive precedent is one which need not be followed but which is worthy of consideration; *e.g.*, decisions of Australian or American courts. Decisions of a superior court are authoritative precedents.

(2) In drafting legal documents, a precedent is a copy of an instrument used as a guide in preparing another similar instrument, *e.g.*, a conveyance.

precept. An order or direction given by one official to another requiring him to do some act: a mandate or command from one body to another; *e.g.*, to levy a rate.

pre-emption. The purchase of, or the right to purchase, a particular thing before any offer is made to others.

preference, fraudulent. The favouring of one creditor before another or others. All dealings by an insolvent debtor in favour of any creditor, having the effect of giving that creditor a preference, priority or an advantage over the other creditors, are, if the debtor becomes bankrupt on a petition presented within three months thereafter, void as against the trustee in bankruptcy.

preference shares. See SHARE.

preferential debts. The debts which are payable in preference to other debts in bankruptcy, administration of insolvent estates and winding up of companies; *e.g.*, one year's rates and taxes. They rank equally, unless the assets are insufficient when they abate in equal proportions.

preliminary contracts. Contracts made before a company is formed. They do not become binding on the company when formed nor can they be ratified by the company, but the company can make a new contract to carry the preliminary contract into effect.

preliminary expenses. The expenditure in connection with the promotion and formation of a company. It is usually capitalised and written off over a period of years—usually from three to five years. The amount not written off must be shown under a separate heading in the audited balance sheet.

pre-list. A pre-determined list of all items posted in machine accounting. Used to prove the accuracy of items posted.

premises. (1) That which has been before " premised " or before mentioned. Thus, after reciting preliminary facts, a deed normally provides that in consideration of the premises, *i.e.*, the facts recited, the parties have agreed to the transaction embodied in the deed. In a conveyance, when the property has been fully described, it is generally referred to in the subsequent parts of the deed as " premises hereinbefore described." From this, "premises" has acquired the popular sense of land or buildings.

(2) That part of a deed which precedes the habendum (*q.v.*).

premium. (1) A lump sum paid on the grant of a lease at a rent.
(2) The consideration for a contract of assurance.
(3) A bounty, bonus or reward.
(4) The excess over par value of shares and other securities.
(5) The fee charged for instructing a pupil in a particular trade or profession.

premium bonds. Bonds issued by the government to savers in denominations of £1 and upwards. Interest is calculated on the total fund and distributed in the form of monthly prizes which are drawn by number and are exempt from taxation.

prepayment. Payment in advance.

prerogative. Those exceptional powers and privileges of the Crown, *e.g.*, assembling and dissolving Parliament, sending and receiving ambassadors, pardoning convicted criminals. It may be said to be the residue of arbitrary authority which at any given time is legally left in the hands of the Crown.

prerogative writ. The writs of mandamus, prohibition and certiorari which were issued by the courts at their discretion, in special circumstances, on cause shown. They have been replaced by prerogative orders; *viz.* certiorari (*q.v.*), mandamus (*q.v.*), and prohibition (*q.v.*).

prescription. The acquisition of title by enjoyment of a right by long usage without interruption. Prescription applies mainly to rights and obligations connected with the use of land.

present value. The immediate value of a sum of money payable in the future.

presentment. The presentation of a bill of exchange for acceptance or payment.

presumption. A conclusion or inference as to the truth of some fact in question, drawn from other facts proved or admitted to be true.

Presumptions are either of law or of fact.

Irrebuttable or conclusive presumptions are absolute inferences established by law: evidence is not admissible to contradict them. They are more properly called rules of law.

Rebuttable presumptions of law are inferences which the law requires to be drawn from given facts, and which are conclusive until disproved by evidence to the contrary; thus a child born during the continuance of a marriage, or within a period of gestation thereafter, is presumed to be legitimate.

Presumptions of fact are inferences which a tribunal draws from the facts before it.

presumption of death. See ABSENCE FOR SEVEN YEARS

preventive detention. A sentence of detention in prison for from 5 to 14 years of a person aged at least 30, with three previous convictions for indictable offences. (Criminal Justice Act, 1948.)

previous question. The motion that the question be not now put which is moved in order to shelve a matter.

If the " previous question " is carried, the motion cannot be brought forward again at the same meeting. If it is not carried, the motion before the meeting must then be voted upon immediately. See also CLOSURE.

price. The sum of money for which a thing is bought or sold, or offered for purchase or sale. SEE MIDDLE PRICE. See also FUTURES.

price control. The fixing of prices in order to maintain economic stability; as, *e.g.*, in wartime.

price earnings ratio. The ratio of the earnings (profits less corporation tax) from an investment to the price of that investment.

price maintenance agreements. Agreements between manufacturers and retailers by which the retailers contract not to sell the manufacturers' products for less than a stated price. Such agreements are illegal under the Resale Prices Act, 1964 unless they have been before the Restrictive Practices Court and approved as being in the public interest.

prima facie. [At first sight; on the face of it.]

primage. A percentage addition to the freight paid to the owners or freighters of a vessel.

prime cost. Alternative term for direct, or variable, cost.

principal. First in importance; a capital sum invested at interest; the person employing an agent or attorney.

In criminal law, the actual perpetrator of a crime is a principal in the first degree, and those aiding or abetting are principals in the second degree.

principal debtor. See GUARANTEE.

prior charges. Claims on a company's assets which rank in front of the equity capital for principal and interest, *e.g.*, debenture and preference share capital. The aggregation of prior charges represents a company's fixed interest capital.

priority. Precedence or preference in establishing a right or claim. In general the first in time takes priority, but in some departments of the law, the first to give notice, *e.g.*, to trustees, has the prior claim. See also PREFERENTIAL DEBTS.

private company. See COMPANY.

private international law. That part of English Law which applies whenever a case before the court contains a foreign element. It prescribes the conditions under which the court can try such a case, and determines the particular foreign law which is applicable. It also specifies when a foreign judgment can be recognised as determining the question in dispute, and when the rights of a creditor under a foreign judgment can be enforced. See also INTERNATIONAL LAW, PUBLIC.

privilege. An exceptional right or advantage or an immunity or exemption from duties or liabilities as imposed generally by the law. In particular, it includes freedom of speech, as in Parliament, or in courts of law, freedom from arrest on civil process, and freedom from serving on juries. Privileges are enjoyed by holders of certain offices, so that their duties may be carried out without impediment; *e.g.*, Members of Parliament, judges, barristers and solicitors. See also DIPLOMATIC PRIVILEGE.

privity. The relationship between parties to a transaction, as opposed to strangers to it; participation in a matter by interest or knowledge.

Privity of contract is the relation which exists between the immediate parties to a contract, as distinct from possible beneficiaries under it. In general, only the parties to a contract can sue on it.

Privity of estate is the relationship which exists between the persons primarily interested in the ownership of it or their assignees; *e.g.*, lessor and lessee, tenant for life and remainderman, etc.

Privy Council. The pre-eminent and greatest Council of State, consisting of the Sovereign and her advisers nominated by her; who are designated " Right Honourable." The Cabinet, which is the chief executive body in the British Constitution, developed from the Privy Council, so that Cabinet Ministers must also be Privy Councillors.

The Judicial Committee of the Privy Council is a tribunal of Privy Councillors which was created in 1833 to hear appeals and petitions which previously could be brought before the King in Council. It acts as a final Court of Appeal from parts of the Commonwealth and in certain other matters arising in this country; *e.g.*, ecclesiastical appeals. It consists of the law lords, and certain other judges who are not peers. Only one judgment is given, in the form of advice to the Crown.

pro forma. As a matter of form.

pro forma invoice. One which is not an immediate charge in account; usually an invoice sent with goods to be sold on consignment or on approval. The invoice shows particulars of the goods sent out, such as quantity, description, marks, weight, packing, etc., including the price of the goods.

pro hac vice. [For this occasion.]

pro rata. [In proportion.]

pro tanto. [For so much; to that extent.]

pro tem. [For the time being.]

probate. The official grant of the court to an executor of the right to deal with the testator's property. In ordinary cases probate is granted in common form on proof by affidavit evidence, but where there is a dispute as to the validity of the will, persons interested may institute proceedings in the Probate, Divorce and Admiralty Division of the High Court. If the will is then held to be valid, it is said to be proved in solemn form.

probate value. For the purpose of obtaining probate, an Inland Revenue Affidavit, giving particulars and value of the deceased estate, has to be delivered for death duty purposes. Investments are valued so as to include dividends and interest which had accrued up to the date of the death of the deceased.

proceed to next business. A motion (*q.v.*) at a meeting, the object of which is to shelve for the time being the particular matter then being discussed. If it is carried, it terminates discussion on the matter and the meeting proceeds to the next business.

proclamation. (1) Royal proclamations are made and issued by the Crown by virtue of the royal prerogative, *e.g.*, proclamations to summon or dissolve Parliament.

(2) Statutory proclamations are issued by the Crown or a Minister under statutory powers.

Proclamations are published in the London Gazette. (*q.v.*).

procuration. Agency. An authority given by one person to another to sign bills of exchange, etc., as his agent. It is usual to sign thus—John Jones (the principal) per pro. or (p.p.) Adam Adams (the agent). The signature binds the principal only in so far as the agent signs within the limits of his authority, and does not make the agent personally liable.

productive wages. Those which are a direct part of the cost of manufacture.

productivity. The amount of production which can be achieved with a specified quantity of labour. Productivity may be improved through greater skill, organisation, investment or effort.

profit. Generally implies an increase in wealth; as applied to a business enterprise it indicates an increase in the wealth of the business resulting from the conduct of the business. When an enterprise speaks of its profits, it is difficult to know exactly what is intended, because the meaning of the term depends to a considerable degree on the methods of accounting adopted by that particular concern. In business and accounting the term has a variety of meanings, and without some qualifying term the word is indefinable. Some of the more common of these terms are—

GROSS PROFIT. The difference between the cost of goods or services which have been sold and the proceeds of their sale without any deductions in respect of the expenses of distribution or management.

NET PROFIT (OR LOSS). The result of the activities of an enterprise after taking into account revenue from all sources and expenses and losses of all kinds so long as they are properly attributable to the enterprise.

CAPITAL PROFIT. The profit made on the disposal of an asset not originally purchased with the idea of sale as distinguished from a profit made from trading operations.

TRADING PROFIT, OPERATING PROFIT (OR LOSS). The result of the operations of an enterprise in that field which forms the normal scope of its activities; the difference between operating revenue and operating expenses, the latter including, for trading and manufacturing concerns, the cost of goods sold and expenses of marketing, distribution, finance, etc.

SUPER PROFIT. The excess of the average profits of a business over the normal commercial profits of a business of the nature concerned.

TAXABLE PROFIT. That on which taxation is levied.

169

UNREALISED PROFIT. Profit not yet realised, *e.g.*, the profit on sales by instalments should be treated as unrealised in proportion to the instalments outstanding.

profit and loss account. An account designed to show the net profit earned or net loss incurred during the financial period covered by the account, also the various headings under which the profits have been earned and expenses incurred. The Companies Act, 1948 details the minimum contents of the published profit and loss account to be submitted, together with a balance sheet, to members in general meeting.

profit-sharing. A term given to instances where employees share in the profits of an enterprise, in the form usually of allocating part of the profits to be divided up among employees in relation to their wages and length of service.

profiteering. Making an undue profit by charging excessive prices.

profits a prendre. Rights of taking the produce, or part of the soil, from the land of another person; *e.g.*, a right to pasture one's cattle on another's land, or to dig turf.

profits prior to incorporation (of company). It often happens that the agreement between the vendor and the company provides that the company is to take over the business as from a date prior to that on which the company is registered. The profits earned between the date of taking over and the date of registration of the company may, by agreement, be payable to the vendors; otherwise they should be regarded as a capital item and be used to write down some intangible asset or credited to a reserve account.

profits tax. A direct tax of companies' profits which was the precursor of corporation tax (*q.v.*) in the U.K.

programme. A set of instructions, expressions and any other necessary data for controlling a computer run. Without instructions from a programme a computer will not operate.

prohibited imports. The importation of certain goods is prohibited (or restricted) under, *inter alia*, Customs and Excise Acts, and the Merchandise Marks Acts.

prohibition, order of. An order issuing out of a superior court to restrain an inferior court from exceeding its powers.

promise. The expression of an intention to do or forbear from some act. To have legal effect, a promise must either be under seal, when it forms a covenant, or must form part of a contract, that is, be made in consideration of something done or to be done.

promissory note. An unconditional promise in writing, made by one person to another, signed by the maker engaging to pay on demand, or at a fixed or determinable future time, a sum certain in money to, or to the order of, a specified person or to bearer.

By making the note, the maker engages that he will pay it according to its tenor, and he is precluded from denying to a holder in due course the existence of the payee and his then capacity to endorse

promoter. One who floats a company: any person who brings a company into existence by taking an active part in forming it or in procuring persons to join it as soon as it is formed, or by issuing a prospectus or procuring capital after the company is formed. However, a person merely acting as solicitor or in some other professional capacity in the formation of the company does not thereby become a promoter. Whether a person is a promoter or not, is a question of fact.

A promoter is not an agent or trustee for the company, but he stands in a fiduciary position towards it, and must disclose any profit he makes out of the promotion; otherwise he must account for it to the company.

proof. (1) A fact is said to be proved when the court is satisfied as to its truth, and the evidence by which that result is produced is called the proof. The general rule is that the burden or onus of proof lies on the party who asserts the affirmative of the issue or question in dispute. When that party adduces evidence sufficient to raise a presumption that what he asserts is true, he is said to shift the burden of proof: that is, it then lies upon his opponent.

(2) To prove a will is to obtain probate of it.

(3) An impression from type, taken for the purpose of checking and making corrections.

(4) Guns must be passed for proof at the Proof Houses in London or Birmingham before being dealt with. (Gun Barrel Proof Act, 1868.)

proof of debts. In the administration of an estate in bankruptcy the creditors must each formally establish their debts to the satisfaction of the trustee in bankruptcy, by lodging an affidavit of debt in the prescribed form, before being entitled to share in the distribution of the estate.

proof of posting (1) Proof that all documents have been correctly posted and that the new balances are correct. An integral part of machine accounting.

(2) Evidence that an item of mail has been despatched through the post office.

proof spirit. Spirit which at a temperature of 51°F. weighs 12/13 part of an equal measure of distilled water, and containing 49·28 per cent. of alcohol by weight, or 57·1 per cent. by volume at 60°F.

property. That which is capable of ownership; sometimes used as meaning a right of ownership, as in the phrase " the property in the goods." Property is either real property (*q.v.*) or personal property (*q.v.*).

General property is the right or interest of the absolute owner.

Special property may mean (1) the limited right of ownership in property which is incapable of absolute ownership; *e.g.*, wild animals while present on one's land, but which ceases on their escape; (2) the right of the lawful possessor of property belonging to another; *e.g.* that of a bailee.

proposal for insurance. As a general rule a contract of insurance is entered into by the person signing a form of proposal which contains particulars of the subject-matter to be insured and the class of insurance. The proposal is generally in the form of answers to a questionnaire, and a declaration by the proposer that the answers are true to the best of his knowledge and belief, which becomes the basis of the contract between the insurer and the insured. Any suppression, concealment, misrepresentation or mis-statement of a material fact will entitle the insurer to treat the policy as null and void.

proprietary rights. Those rights which an owner of property has by virtue of his ownership.

proprietorship. Excess of assets over external liabilities, representing the proprietor's interest in the business, *e.g.*, in the case of a sole trader, his capital; in the case of a company, the items comprised in shareholders' funds, *i.e.*, paid-up capital, reserves and undistributed profits. See also EQUITIES.

prospectus. Any notice, circular, advertisement or other invitation issued by the company itself offering to the public for subscription or purchase any shares or debentures of the company. The prospectus must give sufficient information to enable a would-be investor to decide whether or not to subscribe for the shares, etc. It must comply with the provisions of the Companies Act, 1948, and the rules of the Stock Exchange.

A public company which does not issue a prospectus on formation can file a statement in lieu with the Registrar.

protection. The restriction of trade by a country with other countries, usually with the purpose of assisting its own industries, by imposing duties on imports or granting subsidies on exports.

protective duties. There is a general protective tariff on imports charged by Orders made under the Import Duties Act, 1958.

protest. (1) An express declaration by a person doing an act that the act is not to give rise to an implication which it might otherwise do; *e.g.*, that payment of money is not to imply a pre-existing debt.

(2) A solemn declaration by a notary public stating that he has demanded acceptance or payment of a bill of exchange and that it has been refused by the drawee or acceptor. The object of a protest is to give satisfactory evidence of the dishonour to the drawer or other antecedent party; but it is not necessary except in the case of a foreign bill.

(3) A declaration by the master of a ship, made before a consul or notary public, of the circumstances in which injury or damage has been caused to the ship or cargo.

protocol. The minutes of the proceedings in the course of diplomacy or of an international conference, signed by the delegates or other responsible parties, also the rules of diplomatic ceremonial or etiquette.

provision. (1) An amount written off or retained to provide for depreciation, renewals or diminution in the value of assets, or to provide for a known liability the amount of which cannot be determined with substantive accuracy. See RESERVES.

(2) A clause in a legal or formal statement or document, *e.g.*, in a will.

proviso. A clause in a statute, deed or instrument beginning " provided that—." It operates as a condition, limitation, qualification or covenant.

provocation. Acts presenting the exercise of reason and self control, and so negativing malice (*q.v.*)

proxy. A person appointed to vote on behalf of another. A member entitled to attend and vote at a company meeting may appoint anyone to attend and vote as his proxy. A proxy is appointed by a written instrument in accordance with the articles. The two forms of proxy are (1) general, appointing a person to vote as he thinks fit; (2) special, to vote for or against a particular resolution. See also NOMINEE.

public. The aggregate of the members of the community. See also PUBLICATION.

public company. One in which the public can take an interest, which is done by buying and selling of the company's prior charge and equity capital through a stock market. Access to the public in this way enables the company to raise capital for use in its business.

public international law. See INTERNATIONAL LAW, PUBLIC.

public office. An office under the Crown or a joint-stock company or corporation.

public order. Offensive words and behaviour, and disorderly conduct, in public places or at public meetings, were dealt with by the Public Order Act, 1936. The penalties have been increased by the Public Order Act, 1963.

public ownership. Ownership by the state, of nationalised industries etc.

public policy. Certain acts are said to be against public policy, or against the policy of the law, on the ground that they tend to be injurious to the interests of the State or the community; *e.g.*, trading with the enemy, agreements contrary to good morals or in general restraint of trade. See also RESTRAINT OF TRADE.

public relations. Presentation and promotion of knowledge of the actions and policies of an individual or organisation on its behalf in its relations with the public.

Public Trustee. The Public Trustee was established as a corporation sole by the Public Trustee Act, 1906. He has perpetual succession and an official seal and may sue and be sued as a corporation.

He may act in administration of estates of small value; as custodian trustee, the management of the trust being left to the managing trustees, but the public trustee retaining custody of all securities, documents of title, etc.; as an ordinary trustee and also as judicial trustee, but not in the case of trusts exclusively for religious or charitable purposes.

public utility. Undertakings of public importance for which special powers are necessary; *e.g.*, for the supply of water, gas or electricity.

publication. Making publicly known; making known to another or others. A person seeking to obtain damages on grounds of libel or slander must show publication; that is, that the defamatory statement was made known to a person or persons other than the plaintiff.

puffing. To praise in an exaggerated manner for the purpose of advertisement; to bid up prices at an auction.

puisne. Junior or inferior; the judges of a court other than the chief judge.

punitive damages. Vindictive damages (*q.v.*).

purchase tax. A tax levied on certain goods which are called chargeable goods, whether imported or home produced. In general, persons whose sales of chargeable goods exceed £500 per annum are required to register with the Commissioners of Customs and Excise. The tax is charged on the wholesale value of chargeable goods which are purchased from registered persons, or which result from the application by such persons of chargeable processes. Liability to tax is on chargeable transactions; *i.e.*, when goods are sold to an unregistered person, or when they are transferred by a registered dealer to the retail side of his business. No tax is levied upon sales between registered persons.

Chargeable goods are divided into groups and the tax is charged at rates being a percentage of the value of the goods, as prescribed for each group. The tax is accounted for quarterly and a return made by accountable parties to the Commissioners of Customs and Excise. (Purchase Tax Act, 1963).

purchasing power. Money or claims to money or credit available to the public for the purpose of purchasing goods and services.

purchasing power parity theory. The theory that a change in the relative price levels of two countries will ultimately be followed by a similar change in the exchange rate between them, or *vice versa*.

pure economics. The principles of economic theory evolved from a general study of the subject rather than from consideration of particular economic problems. Contrast APPLIED ECONOMICS.

put option. Payment of a commission which secures the right to sell something at an agreed price within a given period. It is the opposite of a call option. Options are used as a means of hedging or speculating in shares or commodities.

pyramiding. A term used in connection with holding companies to describe a device whereby a group of persons can, with a minimum outlay of capital, control through successive tiers of subsidiary companies assets many times in excess of the original outlay. In this type of organisation a company which is subsidiary to a holding company is in turn a holding company for other (sub-subsidiary) companies. Persons outside the group of companies may own part of the share capital of subsidiaries.

Q

qua. [In the character of.]

qualified acceptance. One which in express terms varies the effect of the bill of exchange as drawn, and may be:

(1) Conditional; *i.e.*, one which makes payment by the acceptor dependent on the fulfilment of a condition, *e.g.*, " Accepted payable when goods are sold."

(2) Partial; *i.e.*, an acceptance to pay part of the amount only for which the bill is drawn.

(3) Local; *i.e.*, an acceptance to pay only at a particular or specified place, *e.g.*, " Payable only at Bank of England, Head Office."

(4) Qualified as to time; *i.e.*, a bill drawn for two months accepted payable in three months.

(5) Acceptance by some of the drawees only; *e.g.*, a bill drawn on A, B and C, accepted by A and B only.

The holder may refuse to take a qualified acceptance and if he does not obtain an unqualified acceptance he may treat the bill as dishonoured.

quality control. Examination of products to ensure that they comply with the required standard of quality.

quantum meruit. [As much as he has earned.] Where one person has expressly or impliedly requested another to render him a service without specifying any remuneration, but the circumstances of the request imply that the service is to be paid for, there is implied a promise to pay *quantum meruit*, *i.e.*, so much as the party doing the service deserves. Further, if a person by the terms of a contract is to do a certain piece of work for a lump sum, and he does only part of the work, or something different, he cannot claim under the contract, but he may be able to claim on a *quantum meruit* as, *e.g.*, if completion has been prevented by the act of the other party to the contract.

quantum valebat. [As much as they are worth.] An action analogous to *quantum meruit* (*q.v.*), but brought in respect of goods supplied.

quarantine. A period of 40 days. The period for the detention of a vessel arriving from a port where infectious disease is prevalent before persons on board are allowed to land. The term is also applied to regulations for landing and sale of cattle. Dogs and cats imported must be kept in quarantine for six months.

quarter days. Days of the year on which rent traditionally falls due every three months. In England they are March 25, June 24, September 29 and December 25.

quash. To discharge or set aside, *e.g.*, a wrongful conviction.

quasi. [As if, similar to.]

quasi-contract. When one person has benefited at the expense of another in circumstances calling for the repayment of the benefit, the obligation imposed on him to repay is by way of quasi-contract. The principal cases of quasi-contract are:—

(1) Where one person pays money for the use of another.

(2) Where money has been had and received by one party to the use of another.

(3) An account stated (I.O.U.) is an admission of indebtedness (and implies a promise to repay).

(4) Where money is paid on a consideration which has wholly failed.

(5) Where money has been paid under mistake of fact (but not of law).

Queen's Counsel. A barrister who has attained eminence in his profession and has been appointed Counsel to Her Majesty. Queen's Counsel have no active duties to the Crown to perform, but they wear a silk gown and sit within the bar. They are briefed to appear in court in important cases where they " lead " the junior barristers briefed with them.

Queen's evidence. An accused who, instead of being put upon trial, is permitted by the Crown to give evidence against those associated with him in crime, is said to turn Queen's evidence.

Queen's warehouse. A place for the deposit of goods forfeited to the Crown, or abandoned, because of non-payment of customs and excise duties. The goods are ultimately sold by auction or tender.

Qui facit per alium facit per se. [Who acts through another, acts himself.] A principal acts through an authorised agent.

quick asset ratio. See ACID TEST.

quick assets. Those which are already in the form of cash or readily convertible into cash without much risk of loss; *e.g.*, bank balance, government bonds, etc.

quid pro quo. (Something for something.) Consideration (*q.v.*).

quoad hoc. [As to that.]

quorum. (Of whom.) The minimum number of persons which constitutes a valid formal meeting, *e.g.*, of a board of directors, of a committee, or of a company.

quota, trade. The limited quantity of a commodity which may be imported, or be supplied to a trader within a stated period.

quotation. (1) The ruling price for money, stocks, shares, goods, and merchandise in their respective markets. (2) The result of being asked to quote (*q.v.*).

Quotations Committee. Formerly the Share and Loan Department of the Stock Exchange, it examines applications for quotation of stocks and shares and certain documents circulated to shareholders of quoted companies.

quote, to. To state the price at which goods can be supplied or work carried out.

R

rack rent. Rent which property let on yearly tenancy would command in the open market on the basis that the landlord is responsible for repairs, insurance and maintenance, while the tenant is responsible for rates.

railways. The railway network is a more or less vital part of a country's overall transport facilities, depending on the extent to which other methods have been developed and the distances involved.

rain insurance. See PLUVIUS POLICY.

rate; rateable. A rate is a sum assessed or made payable by a body (*e.g.*, a municipal or city council) having local jurisdiction over the district in which the person on whom the rate is assessed, resides or has property. There are also rates (*e.g.*, water rates) which are modes of charging for the sale of commodities. Rates are assessed in respect of the enjoyment or occupation of real property in proportion to its value (*pro rata*).

rateable value. The value of property on which rates are to be assessed. The Inland Revenue are responsible for the revaluation of property for rating.

ratification. Confirmation. The act of adopting a contract, or other transaction, by a person who was not bound by it originally; as where an unauthorised agent purports to act as agent for a principal: that principal may ratify the act. Ratification relates back to the time of the transaction concerned.

Treaties may require ratification before becoming operative.

ratio. The relation that one amount or quantity bears to another or others of the same kind, as may be expressed in the form of a proportion, *e.g.*, 3 : 5.

ratio decidendi. The reason or ground for a judicial decision. It is this which makes the decision a binding precedent (*q.v.*) for the future.

rationalisation. The re-organisation of an industry, or smaller economic unit, with the avowed intention of effecting extensive economies.

rationing. The fixing of a periodical allowance, *e.g.*, of food, clothing, etc. Under the unit system available supplies of goods are in effect divided equally among the population by reference to monetary values or physical quantities.

The point system of rationing involves fixing point values for each item and allowing each consumer to exercise selection among the items rationed up to a maximum total of points for a particular period.

raw materials. The material, in the state in which it is acquired, which is subjected to manufacturing processes in order to become part of a finished product.

re. [In the matter of; relating to.]

real income. Monetary income in terms of what it will buy rather than in terms of a depreciating currency.

real property. Land together with such other things as are annexed to or affixed to land; *e.g.*, fencing, houses. See PERSONAL PROPERTY.

real wages. Wages in terms of what they will buy.

real-time working. In computer parlance it denotes operation of a data-processing system which proceeds at the same speed as events being simulated and at sufficient speed to analyse or control external events happening concurrently.

realisation. Converting into cash; the act of selling a commodity or other property and obtaining cash therefor.

realisation account. An account prepared when a partnership or company is dissolved, showing the book value of the assets and the amount realised on their sale; also showing—usually—the net result of the winding-up.

realty. Real property (*q.v.*).

rebate. (1) An allowance or deduction from price, or a corresponding refund.
(2) The term is also used when retiring a bill before it is due. In a bank balance sheet, rebate is calculated on all bills discounted, but not matured; for the reason that the bank received the whole discount in advance, but up to the balancing date had only earned a portion of such discount.

receipt. A written acknowledgment of the receipt of goods or money paid in discharge of a debt. A receipt under hand alone is in general only prima facie evidence, but a receipt under seal amounts to an estoppel, and is conclusive. A paid cheque is acceptable as proof of payment under the Cheques Act, 1957.

receipts and payments account or statement. A statement, often prepared for non-trading enterprises, representing a summary of the cash transactions of an enterprise for a given period. See CASH BASIS OF ACCOUNTING.

receiver. (1) A person appointed to receive the rents and profits of property, to collect and get in personal property, to safeguard or preserve property, or to enforce the rights of those entitled to it. Thus an impartial and responsible person may be appointed a receiver by the court in an action for dissolution of partnership, or under the powers contained in a debenture or mortgage. If a business is to be carried on, the receiver may be appointed manager as well as receiver. A receiver appointed by the Court becomes an officer of the Court, and takes possession of the property in question. He is usually required to give security for the due performance of his duties. See also OFFICIAL RECEIVERS.
(2) A receiver of stolen property is one who receives or has in his possession, property knowing it to be stolen or obtained in unlawful circumstances. This is a criminal offence, except where the receiving is innocent of any wrong-doing.

recovery

receiving order. The order made by the court on a bankruptcy petition. Thereafter no proceedings for recovery of debts can be pursued, but debts are proveable in the bankruptcy. See also OFFICIAL RECEIVERS.

recession. A small slump. See TRADE CYCLE.

reciprocity. An arrangement between countries whereby goods are imported on specially advantageous terms as regards Customs duties.

recital. A statement of facts in a deed leading up and preliminary to the main purpose thereof. Such a clause usually begins " Whereas—."

recognisance. A bond of record, executed before a court or officer by a person who thereby acknowledges that he presently owes the Crown a sum certain, but containing a condition that if certain acts are done or certain events happen, the bond shall be void; otherwise that it shall stand in full force and effect; *e.g.*, recognisances of bail.

reconciliation. The bringing together again of husband and wife whose marriages have broken down. The Matrimonial Causes Act, 1963, is intended to facilitate such reconciliation. Cohabitation for one period of up to three months with a view to effecting a reconciliation is not a bar to ultimate relief. See also CONDONATION, COLLUSION.

reconciliation statement. A statement to bring into agreement accounts where there are outstanding items; or accounts between different parties where one or the other or both have not recorded all the transactions between them, *e.g.*, cash records of a trader and bank pass book or statement.

reconstruction and reorganisation (of companies). Reconstruction occurs when a company resolves to wind up, proposes the formation of a new company consisting of the old shareholders, and takes over the old undertaking with any alteration of objects deemed advisable, the old shareholders receiving shares in the new company. The old company ceases to exist in point of law, and there is in form a sale to the members of a new corporation. The term reorganisation is usually applied to a rearrangement of the rights of shareholders or creditors, or both, and therefore may, in some cases, require neither a liquidation nor a change of name of the company.

recorded delivery. The Recorded Delivery Service Act, 1962 authorises the sending by the recorded delivery service of certain documents and things required or authorised to be sent by registered post.

recoup. To pay back a person for any expense or damage made or incurred on behalf of the person recouping or of some third party. See also INDEMNITY.

recourse. The right of a holder of a bill of exchange to demand payment from some person other than the acceptor. Bills may be indorsed " without recourse," in which case the indorser does not become liable to any holder. (Bills of Exchange Act, 1882). See also SANS RECOURS.

recovery. The phase of the trade cycle (*q.v.*), following a depression, in which confidence revives and investment and employment increase.

rectification. The correction of an error in a register or instrument, *e.g.*, a conveyance or settlement, on the ground of mutual mistake, *i.e.*, a clerical error, or an error in draftsmanship.

redeemable preference shares. See SHARES.

redemption. The paying off of a mortgage, debt or charge upon property; the "buying back" of the property. See also EQUITY OF REDEMPTION.

redemption yield. The yield to maturity on a redeemable stock. That is to say, the flat yield from interest, plus the net capital gain on maturity, expressed as a composite annual yield.

re-discount. To discount again. At one time a common practice, when the discounter had need of funds.

reduction into possession. The obtaining of possession.

reduction of capital. A limited company having a share capital, may, if so authorised by its articles, by special resolution reduce its capital,which must be confirmed by an order of the court. The company may be required to add the words " and reduced " to its name. The three chief ways of effecting such a reduction are:
(1) The extinction of liability on shares not fully paid up;
(2) The cancellation of paid-up share capital which is lost or not represented by assets;
(3) The payment off of share capital which is in excess of the wants of the company.

redundancy. The cessation of a requirement for labour due to contraction of production or an improvement in methods, which renders part of the labour force surplus to requirements. Certain minimum payments must be made to those who become redundant, under the Redundancy Payments Act, 1965.

re-entry. The retaking of possession of land by the person entitled when the tenant's interest has come to an end by forfeiture or otherwise.

re-exchange. The loss resultant upon the dishonour of a foreign bill. It is ascertained by calculating the current rate of exchange at the place of dishonour upon a new sight draft, sufficient in the place of dishonour to meet the dishonoured bill, and all expenses consequent upon dishonour thereof.

re-exports. Imports which are subsequently exported, either in their original state or after alteration.

refer to drawer. Words which a banker puts on a cheque which he is returning to the payee as not paid, for technical reasons, *e.g.*, the cheque is drawn incorrectly, or because the drawer has insufficient funds.

referee. See OFFICIAL REFEREES.

reference. Disputes or differences may be referred to an arbitrator (or referee) by consent out of court or under an order of the court.
The proceedings before the arbitrator constitute the reference; these proceedings resemble those of an ordinary trial, except that they

are private; witnesses are examined, and the arbitrator is addressed on behalf of each of the parties, and he makes an award or report containing his decision. See also ARBITRATION.

referendum. A vote of electors on a particular matter or measure.

reflation. Inflation after deflation.

refresher. A fee paid to counsel on the trial of an action in addition to the brief fee. It is paid for every clear day which is occupied by the trial after the first five hours.

refreshing memory. A witness may refresh his memory while under examination, by referring to a document or note made by himself, although the document itself is not admissible as evidence.

register of charges. (1) A company must keep a register of mortgages and charges given by it at its registered office.

(2) The register kept at the Land Registry of mortgages and other charges on land.

register of directors and secretaries. A company must keep a register, containing particulars of its directors and secretaries, at its registered office. Particulars of the directors and secretaries, and of any changes, must be filed with the Registrar of Companies. The register is open to inspection by any member of the company free of charge and to any other person on payment.

register of directors' shareholdings. The register required to be maintained by all companies showing the holding of shares and debentures in that company and certain other companies by its directors. The register is open to inspection by members and debenture holders during 14 days preceding and three days succeeding the annual general meeting of the company.

register of members. The register required to be kept by companies, containing the prescribed particulars as to the members, their holdings of shares, amounts due and paid thereon, etc.

register of title. A register of title to land which is kept at the Land Registry. Freehold land may be registered with absolute, qualified or possessory title. Leaseholds of which more than 21 years are still unexpired may be registered with absolute qualified, good leasehold, or possessory title. See also LAND REGISTRY; REGISTERED LAND.

registered land. Land registered under the Land Registration Act, 1925, at the Land Registry (*q.v.*). In certain areas, which are constantly being extended by Orders in Council, registration is compulsory. See also REGISTER OF TITLE.

registered office. A company must have a registered office to which communications and notices may be addressed, notice of the situation of which, and of any change therein, must be given to the Registrar of Companies within fourteen days.

Service of a writ or process on a company is effected by leaving it at, or sending it by registered post to, the company's registered office.

181

The name of the company must be painted or affixed on the outside of the registered office of the company.

registered securities. Securities, fully paid, issued by a limited or chartered company, British Government and local authority securities, and units of a unit trust scheme, the holders of which are entered in a register. (Stock Transfer Act, 1963.) See STOCK TRANSFERS.

registers. The mechanism of an accounting machine which records the accumulated totals of items posted.

Registrar of Companies. All registered companies must make returns of certain information to the Registrar. Files of information are kept by the Registrar for each company, which are available for inspection by the public.

regulations, statutory. See STATUTORY INSTRUMENTS.

re-insurance. The act of an insurer in relieving himself of the whole or part of the liability he has undertaken by insuring the subject-matter himself in whole or in part with other insurers. Unless otherwise provided in the original policy, a settlement with the insured in the case of a loss is adjusted by the original insurers and not the re-insurers.

relation back. The doctrine by which an act is deemed to have occurred at an earlier time than in fact it did. Thus in bankruptcy to ensure a fair distribution of the bankrupt's property, the bankruptcy is deemed to have commenced at the time of the act of bankruptcy on which a receiving order is made (or, if more than one such act, then to the first within three months next preceding the presentation of the petition) instead of on the date of the receiving order itself.

For certain purposes, letters of administration (*q.v.*) relate back to the time of the death of the intestate, and not to the time when they were granted.

release. (1) The discharge, by a person entitled to a right or benefit, of the person or persons owing him the corresponding duty; also the deed or document embodying such release. Thus a party to a contract may waive his rights thereunder by granting a release to the other party.

(2) When trustees or executors have wound up an estate they usually require a release from the persons beneficially entitled before handing over or dividing it, in order to clear themselves of responsibility. A release may take the form of a covenant not to sue.

(3) The giving up by a person of his right in land to the owner; *e.g.*, release of a right-of-way to the owner of the land subject to it.

reliefs, income tax. For income tax purposes, an individual is entitled to reliefs according to his personal circumstances, as follows: earned income relief, personal allowance as a single or married person, age allowance, small incomes relief, child allowance, housekeeper or analogous allowances, dependent relative allowance, life assurance relief, wife's earned income allowance, and blind person's relief.

The total amount of the reliefs is deducted from assessable income and the balance is charged to tax at the standard rate, after allowing reduced rate relief.

remainder. When the owner of an estate in land grants more than one interest in it to different persons successively by the same document, the first is called a particular estate, and those following are termed remainders; *e.g.*, when X grants an estate to A, for life, and on his death to B., B has a remainder, and is called the remainderman. See also REVERSION.

remit. (1) To forgo; *e.g.*, a debt; (2) to send back; *e.g.*, a case by a higher court to a lower.

remittance. Money sent by one person to another.

remote parties. The parties to a bill of exchange who are not in direct relation to each other.

remoteness. A disposition of property which is not to take effect within the period allowed by the rule against perpetuities (*q.v.*) is said to be void for remoteness.

remoteness of damage. See DAMAGES.

rent. (1) A periodical payment due from a tenant of land, buildings, etc., to the owner for the right of occupancy or use of the property, and which can be enforced by distraint. It is usually payable in money but it may be payable in kind.

(2) In economics, rent refers to the surplus income over and above the economic return for a factor of production.

rent control. By the Rent Acts, tenants of dwelling houses are protected from excessive demands of landlords and safeguarded in their possession. See the Rent Act, 1965. See also TENANT, STATUTORY.

rentcharge. This exists where the owner of land charges his land with an annual payment to another. It is to be contrasted with a lease rent or rent service.

rentier. A person whose source of income derives from ownership of property, particularly stocks and shares.

renunciation. A disclaimer. (1) An executor who declines to take out probate of the will of his testator is said to renounce probate.

(2) A person entitled to the allotment of shares in a company may renounce that right and request the company to allot the shares to some other person.

repatriation. Returning a person to his own country. See also DEPORTATION; EXTRADITION.

repeal. The abrogation of a statute or part of a statute by a subsequent statute. It may be either express, *i.e.*, specially enacted, or it may be implied, *i.e.*, as the necessary result of the subsequent enactment.

representation. A statement or assertion of fact made by one party to a contract to the other, before or at the time of the contract, of some matter or circumstance relating to it. But a representation of belief, expectation or intention may be a representation of fact, for " the state of a man's mind is as much a matter of fact as the state of his digestion."

In making representations inducing a contract there is no duty to disclose all the material facts which might influence the other party in coming to a decision except in contracts *uberrimae fidei* (*q.v.*), but there is a duty to refrain from knowingly making a misrepresentation (*q.v.*).

A representation which is a term of the contract is either a warranty (*q.v.*) or a condition (*q.v.*). See also CAVEAT EMPTOR; PUFFING.

representation, grant of. A grant of representation of a will means the grant of probate or letters of administration.

representative. A person who takes the place of or acts on behalf of another. The personal representatives of a deceased are his executors or administrators.

representative action. One brought by a member of a class of persons on behalf of himself and all the other members of the class. Where there are numerous persons having the same interest, one may sue or be sued on behalf of the others.

repudiation. Denial or rejection. In relation to a contract repudiation is an anticipatory breach, whereby one party indicates an intention not to be bound by the contract, whereupon the other party is not bound to wait until the actual time for performance arrives, but may immediately sue for damages. If, however, the other party accepts the repudiation the contract is discharged.

repugnant. Contrary to or inconsistent with; as *e.g.*, where later provisions in a deed or will conflict with the earlier, or where a contract is against public policy.

reputed ownership. The doctrine that if goods are in the possession, order or disposition of a bankrupt at the commencement of the bankruptcy, with the consent and permission of the true owner, under such circumstances as to lead to a fair and reasonable interference amongst persons likely to have dealings with the bankrupt that the bankrupt is the owner, then those goods are included in the property of the bankrupt divisible amongst his creditors. The doctrine does not apply to goods subject to registered charges, etc.

requisitions on title. A list of questions which a purchaser or mortgagee of real or leasehold property, following an inspection of title deeds, puts in writing to the vendor, of mortgagor, for the purpose of ascertaining whether there is a clear title, and also to obtain information as to rates, rents, etc. In practice, the solicitors to the parties act for them.

res. [A thing.]

res derelicta. [An abandoned thing.]

res gestae. [The things done.] The facts surrounding or accompanying a transaction, or all facts so connected with a fact in issue as to introduce it, explain its nature, or form in connection with it one continuous transaction.

res ipsa loquitur. [The thing speaks for itself.] This maxim applies in actions for negligence where the circumstances of an accident are such that it is so improbable that it would have occurred without the negligence of the defendant, that it can be presumed that it was so caused; *e.g.*, where a moving motor car collides with a stationary vehicle. The onus is on the defendant to disprove the presumed negligence.

res judicata. A matter already settled by judicial decision.

res nullius. A thing which has no owner. See BONA VACANTIA.

resale price maintenance. See PRICE MAINTENANCE AGREEMENTS.

rescind. To abrogate, annul, or cancel a resolution, etc. on due notice being given.

rescission. Abrogation or revocation, particularly of a contract, as *e.g.* owing to a misrepresentation having been made. See REPRESENTATION

reserve liability. That portion of the share capital of a limited company which it has resolved shall not be capable of being called up, except in the event and for the purposes of the company being wound up.

reserved shares. Unsubscribed shares, *i.e.*, shares which the company is authorised to issue, but which have not been issued, but are reserved for future issue.

reserves. A company's reserves represent profits which have not been distributed to shareholders. They are an important source of finance for future expansion.

reside. To dwell permanently or for a considerable time; to have one's settled or usual abode.

residence. Ordinary residence is residence in the ordinary course of one's life. Actual residence means living or being physically present for a time. For income tax purposes a temporary resident is resident here if he spends six months or more here in a year.

residual value. The estimated return that may be obtained when the intended purpose or use of an asset has been fulfilled, or completed, *e.g.*, the scrap value of a machine.

residue. (1) The net residue is the surplus of a deceased person's estate after discharging all his liabilities; *i.e.*, debts, funeral expenses and the costs of the administration of his estate. (2) The residuary estate is that which remains of a deceased person's estate after paying or setting aside all sums and property specifically allocated by the deceased by his will.

A residuary bequest is a gift by will of residuary personal estate, and a residuary devise is such a gift of real property.

resolution. An expression of opinion or intention by a meeting. A motion before a meeting becomes, when passed by the meeting, a resolution.

Resolutions of the members of a company are either:

(1) An ordinary resolution: one passed by a simple majority in number at an ordinary meeting.

(2) An extraordinary resolution: one which has been passed by a majority of not less than three-fourths of such members as, being entitled so to do, vote in person or by proxy at a general meeting of which notice specifying the intention to propose the resolution as an extraordinary resolution has been duly given.

(3) A special resolution: one which has been passed by such a majority as is required for the passing of an extraordinary resolution (*i.e.*, three-fourths), and at a general meeting of which not less than 21 days' notice specifying the intention to propose the resolution as a special resolution, has been duly given. Special resolutions are required for, inter alia, the alteration of a company's objects, articles, name and for the reduction of its capital.

respondeat superior. [Let the principal answer.]

respondent. A person against whom a petition is presented, or an appeal brought. See also DEFENDANT.

respondentia. See HYPOTHECATION.

restitutio in integrum. [Restoration to the previous position.] Equitable relief which is given by rescission of contracts, etc. with a view to placing the parties in their original position, where that is possible.

restraint of princes. An expression in marine insurance policies. It covers any forcible interference with the voyage or adventure at the hands of the constituted government or ruling power of any country.

restraint of trade. A contract in restraint of trade is one which restricts a person from wholly or partially exercising his trade, profession or business and is prima facie void as being against public policy. It may, however, be enforced if its terms are reasonable. A contract; *e.g.*, on the sale of the goodwill of a business, to prevent undue competition by the vendor; or to prevent a former employee from revealing trade secrets, will be enforced if it is no wider than is reasonably necessary to protect the party in whose interest it is imposed; reasonable with reference to the party against whom it is made; and reasonable with reference to the public. See also PRICE MAINTENANCE AGREEMENTS.

restrictive indorsement. An indorsement on a bill of exchange which prohibits the further negotiation of the bill, or expresses that it is a mere authority to deal with the bill as thereby directed ,and not a transfer of the ownership thereof: *e.g.*, " Pay D only," or " Pay D or order, for collection."

restrictive trade practices. Restrictive trade agreements are agreements under which producers, suppliers or exporters restrict the manufacture, supply or distribution of goods; *e.g.*, by arranging minimum selling prices. Under the Restrictive Trade Practices Act, 1956, these agreements have to be registered with the Registrar. If they refer to exports they are filed with the Board of Trade. In general, such agreements are presumed to be invalid as contrary to the public interest, unless the parties can justify the restriction before the Restrictive Practices Court on any one of seven specified grounds; *e.g.*, that the removal of the restriction would be to the public disadvantage.

rests. The period for which accounts are balanced and interest is ascertained and charged and added to the principal sum, *e.g.*, half-yearly.

resulting trust. An implied trust where the beneficial interest in property, or in part of it, results, or comes back to the person (or his representatives) who created the trust, as where expressed trusts do not exhaust the whole beneficial interest, or the trust fails.

resumption. The retaking of possession of land; as by the landlord before the expiration of the tenancy.

retail. The sale of goods to the consumer, usually in small quantities in shops (*q.v.*), saloons, etc. See also WHOLESALE.

retail price maintenance. See PRICE MAINTENANCE AGREEMENTS.

retainer. The engagement of a barrister or solicitor to act for a client in legal proceedings, either generally, or limited to one particular matter.

retire a bill of exchange. To take up a bill, usually under rebate (*q.v.*) and thus withdraw (or retire) it from circulation. If a bill be retired by the acceptor, the bill is discharged in the same way as upon payment at maturity.

retirement pensions. State pensions are payable to individuals from age 65 for men and 60 for women. Many people make additional private provision for retirement pension.

returning officer. One appointed to count the votes at an election.

returns. (1) Reports by an officer of the court as to returns to writs; *e.g.*, of execution.

(2) Statements of facts, figures, etc., made as required by statute; *e.g.* the annual returns made by companies to the Registrar of Companies.

revaluation. Placing a revised value on something in order to reflect current opinion of its worth. It may be applied to capital assets and by a country to its currency.

revenue. The earnings derived from the activities of an enterprise.

revenue, public. The income of the Government which is mainly derived from taxation; *e.g.*, income tax, surtax, corporation tax, estate duty and stamp duties, customs and excise duties, import duties, purchase tax, and pool betting duty. Other important receipts include revenue derived from Crown lands, dividends and interest on investments in public companies, interest on advances made from the Consolidated Fund, and contributions payable by the Post Office.

revenue duties. Duties or taxes imposed for raising revenue for the Government, as contrasted with protective duties.

revenue expenditure. See CAPITAL EXPENDITURE.

reverse takeover. A colloquial financial term for the acquisition of one company by another, whereby the acquired (or sold) company comes to control the resulting group, either by arrangement or because of its relative size, instead of the more usual result of the acquiring (or buying) company controlling the subsequent group.

reverse yield gap. A description of the yield gap (*q.v.*) when the yield on fixed interest stocks is greater than that on equity stocks, a situation which arose as the risk on equity investment decreased and the rate of inflation increased.

reversion. Where land is granted by the owner for a less estate or interest than he himself has, his undisposed-of interest is termed the reversion; *e.g.*, where a tenant in fee simple grants the land to another person for a term of years or for life, the grantor has a reversion in fee simple. The estate created by the grant is called the particular estate, and tenure exists between the grantor (the reversioner) and the grantee (the tenant).

reversionary interest. Any right in property the enjoyment of which is deferred, *e.g.*, a reversion or remainder.

revocation. Recalling. Revocation is of the following kinds:

(1) Revocation by act of the party is an intentional or voluntary revocation, *e.g.*, of authorities and powers of attorney and wills.

(2) A revocation in law is produced by a rule of law, irrespectively of the intention of the parties. Thus, a power of attorney is in general revoked by the death of the principal.

(3) When a grant of probate or letters of administration has been improperly obtained, it may be revoked by the court at the instance of a person interested.

(4) In the law of contract, an offer may be revoked at any time before acceptance, but the revocation must be communicated to the offeree to be operative.

rider. (1) An additional clause " tacked on " to a document. (2) An expression of opinion or recommendation added to a jury's verdict.

rigging the market. Stock Exchange term signifying the artificial manipulation of prices in order to secure a profit.

right in personam. A right which imposes an obligation on a definite person as opposed to persons generally; *e.g.*, a right to payment by another of a debt owed.

right in rem. A real right, a general right; a right which can be enforced against the whole world; *i.e.*, one which imposes an obligation on persons generally, *e.g.*, the right to exclusive use of one's land.

right of action. The right to bring an action. Thus a person who is wrongfully dispossessed of land has a right of action to recover it.

right of reply. The right of the mover of a motion to speak after discussion has taken place thereon, and just before the motion is put to the meeting. The right of counsel for the plaintiff to speak in answer to counsel for the defendant.

right of way. The right to pass over the land of another. It may be public *e.g.*, a footpath or a highway; or private, *i.e.*, an easement (*q.v.*).

rights issue. The offer of additional shares or stock in a company by way of rights to its existing share or stock holders. Existing holders may pay for their entitlement or sell their rights to subscribe in the market.

ring. An association for the purpose of restricting the supply of goods or of fixing the price of goods.

riparian. That which relates to or is connected with the bank of a river. A riparian owner is a person who owns land through or past which a river runs; and riparian rights are the rights which a riparian owner has in respect of the water.

risk capital. The term demonstrates that equity capital (with which it is synonymous) is at risk, both in respect of income and principal.

road transport. That part of a country's transport system for goods and passengers which uses the road network. For long distances road transport is frequently in direct competition with the railways.

rolling stock. Locomotives, cars, trucks, etc., of railways.

Royal Commission. An order or authority by the Crown to do an act or exercise powers; *e.g.*, to give the Royal Assent to Bills which have passed through Parliament.

royalty. Literally, something due to the Crown; now used to express payment to landowners for minerals, etc., won from their property, or to inventors for the right to use patents or to authors for the right of publication, and so on.

rule. (1) A regulation made by a court of justice or a public office with reference to the conduct of business therein; *e.g.*, the Rules of the Supreme Court (R.S.C.).

(2) A rule made under the authority of an Act of Parliament; a statutory rule. See STATUTORY RULES AND ORDERS.

(3) An order or direction made by a court of justice in an action or other proceeding. A rule is either (i) absolute in the first instance, or (ii) nisi, *i.e.*, calling upon the opposite party to show cause why the rule should not be made absolute; if cause be shown, the rule is discharged.

(4) A principle of the law; *e.g.*, the rule in *Clayton's Case* as to appropriation of payments (*q.v.*).

rummaging. The searching of vessels by the Customs Waterguard to discover dutiable goods.

run. A single use of a computer to carry out a defined piece of work.

S

salary. A fixed periodical payment, usually a yearly sum payable in quarterly, monthly or weekly instalments, made to an employee, or the holder of an office, in respect of his services. Salaries are liable to income tax under Schedule E. See PAY AS YOU EARN.

sale. A transfer of the whole right of property in a thing in consideration of a sum of money.

sale of goods. A contract for the sale of goods is a contract whereby the seller transfers, or agrees to transfer, the property in goods to the buyer for a money consideration called the price. The property in the goods sold is transferred at the time when the parties intend it to pass, which is usually when the agreement is concluded. In the case of an agreement for the sale of unascertained goods, *e.g.*, 10 sheep to be selected from a flock, the property does not pass until the goods are ascertained and appropriated to the contract.

Where the transfer of the property in the goods is to take place at a future time, or subject to some condition thereafter to be fulfilled, the contract is called an agreement to sell.

Where there is a sale of goods by description, there is an implied condition that the goods correspond with the description, and where the seller deals in such goods, there is an implied condition that they are of a merchantable quality; provided that if the buyer has examined the goods there shall be no implied condition as regards defects which such examination ought to have revealed. The implied condition that the goods must correspond with the description applies in all cases where the purchaser has not seen the goods, but is relying on the description.

Where goods are sold by sample, it is implied that (1) the bulk shall correspond with the sample in quality; (2) the buyer shall have a reasonable opportunity of comparing the bulk with the sample; (3) the goods shall be free from any defect rendering them unmerchantable, which would not be apparent on reasonable examination of the sample.

The law was codified by the Sale of Goods Act, 1893. See also AUCTION, SALE BY.

sale or return. A contract whereby the buyer has the alternative of selling the goods and paying for them, or of returning the goods to the seller within a reasonable time.

salvage. (1) Compensation allowed to persons (salvors) by whose assistance a ship or cargo or the lives of persons belonging to her are saved from danger or loss at sea. The assistance must be voluntary and salvors have a retaining lien for their remuneration on the property rescued. The court will assess the amount payable as salvage. (2) The goods so saved.

sample. A small quantity of a commodity exhibited as a specimen. See SALE OF GOODS.

sanction, economic. The suspension of trade with a country with a view to influencing that country's policies.

sans recours. [Without recourse.] See RECOURSE.

satisfaction. (1) The extinguishment of an obligation by performance; *e.g.*, the payment of a debt, or some act equivalent to performance. A judgment may be satisfied by payment or execution. See ACCORD AND SATISFACTION; PERFORMANCE.

(2) The equitable doctrine of satisfaction relates to the doing of an act in substitution for the performance of an obligation. Thus, if A, after contracting a debt, makes a will giving B a pecuniary legacy

equal to or greater than the debt, the legacy is considered a satisfaction of the debt unless a contrary intention appears. Also when a father or a person *in loco parentis* has covenanted to provide a portion (*q.v.*) and subsequently by will provides a portion, or makes a gift in the nature of a portion, the second provision is presumed to be wholly or *pro tanto* in substitution for the first. Equity leans against satisfaction of debts but favours satisfaction of portions.

savings bank. Institutions for the safe custody and increase of small savings, which are regulated by statute; *e.g.*, Trustee Savings Banks; Post Office Savings Bank (*q.v.*).

schedule. A statement of detail appended to a statute or legal or financial document; also any tabulated or classified statement, *e.g.*, a bankrupt's statement of assets and liabilities.

Scheduled Territories. Those countries which make up the sterling area.

Shares or debentures cannot be issued or transferred to persons resident outside the Scheduled Territories; nor can be a policy of assurance. (Exchange Control Act, 1947.) See also EXCHANGE CONTROL.

scheme of arrangement. See ARRANGEMENT.

scienter. Knowingly; knowledge.

scrap. The residue or by-product of the article being manufactured; material which is useless for its original purpose.

scrip. [Subscription.] The provisional certificate of shares, debentures, etc. The letter of allotment (*q.v.*).

scrip dividend. A dividend otherwise than in cash. This may take the form of a dividend or bonus out of capitalised reserves, satisfied by the issue of fully paid shares, or by the discharge of uncalled liability on partly paid shares previously issued.

script. A writing; the original or principal document. In probate practice, it means a will, codicil, draft of will or codicil, or written instructions for the same. If the will is destroyed, a copy or any paper embodying its contents becomes a script.

scuttling. The intentional casting away of a ship for the sake of the insurance money, or to prevent its falling into enemy hands, etc.

seal. A solemn mode of expressing consent to a written instrument by attaching to it wax impressed with a device or a wafer with an impression; but any act done with the intention of sealing is sufficient. Such intention is generally expressed by the additional formality of delivery; *i.e.*, the handing over of the deed to the other party. See CONTRACT; DEED.

Every company has a seal on which the name of the company must be legibly engraved.

seal book. A book kept by the secretary of a large company in which is recorded each date on which the company's seal is used, the manner in which it is used, and by whose authority.

search warrant. An order under the hand of a justice of the peace authorising a named person to enter premises to look for and seize certain property, *e.g.*, stolen goods.

searches. Examination of any public register, record, etc., *e.g.*, Registers of Birth and Death, Land Registers.

seasonal trade. The demand for many products fluctuates with the season of the year, the main influences being weather and Christmas. Difficulties of production and distribution attend trades which are highly seasonal.

seaworthiness. The fitness of a vessel in design, structure, condition, equipment and crew to encounter the ordinary perils of the voyage contemplated. Seaworthiness of the ship is commonly one of the three conditions in regard to the conveyance of goods by sea. See also DEVIATION: DISPATCH.

Seaworthiness is an implied condition in contracts of marine insurance, but not if the policy is a time policy.

In contracts to which the Carriage of Goods by Sea Act, 1924, applies; *i.e.*, by outward bound ships, neither the carrier nor the shipowner is liable for loss resulting from unseaworthiness, unless due to want of diligence to make the ship seaworthy. The onus of proof of due diligence is upon the carrier.

second mortgage. A mortgage or charge ranking after a first mortgage.

secondary security. A security which is only to be resorted to after the principal security is exhausted, and not equally or *pro rata* with the principal security.

secret commission. A commission, rebate or profit taken by an agent without the knowledge of his principal. Where an agent has received a secret commission the principal may: (1) Repudiate the contract resulting from the secret commission; (2) Cancel the agency; (3) Refuse to pay the agent his commission or recover it if already paid to him; and (4) Recover from the agent the secret commission received by him.

secret reserve. A reserve which is not disclosed in the balance sheet. To create such a reserve either the assets must be understated or the liabilities must be overstated, to the extent of the reserve. The Companies Act, 1948 contains provisions the object of which is to prevent the creation of secret reserves, except in the case of banking, insurance and shipping companies.

secret trusts. Where a testator gives property to a person, on a verbal promise by the legatee or devisee that he will hold it in trust for another person, this is called a secret trust. The rule is that if the secret trust would have been valid, as an express trust, it will be enforced against the legatee or devisee while if it would have been invalid as an express trust, *e.g.*, if given for an illegal object, the gift fails altogether and neither devisee nor legatee, nor the object of the trust, takes any benefit by it.

secretary. Generally, one employed to conduct correspondence, to keep records, or transact business for another.

Every company must have a secretary. The secretary is an officer of the company and liable to penalties for non-compliance with statutory duties.

The secretary is appointed by the directors and is an agent of the company, but has not, as such, without authority, power to bind the company by contract, or borrow money on behalf of the company, nor issue a writ in the company's name.

The secretary can only register a transfer or strike a name off the register of shareholders, when authorised by the directors. He cannot summon a general meeting on his own authority. His name and address must be included in the register of directors and secretaries, and in the annual return.

His duties are to keep the registers and prepare and render the returns, as required by statute, and to take a prominent part in the internal management of the company.

sectional ledgers. Another name for self-balancing ledgers, the object being to divide the ledgers into suitable portions and to enable each ledger to be balanced separately.

secundum. According to.

secured creditor. A person who holds a security over the property of his debtor. For the purpose of the bankruptcy legislation secured creditor is defined as a person holding a mortgage, charge or lien on the property of his debtor, or any part thereof as security for a debt due to him from the debtor. In the bankruptcy of his debtor a secured creditor may
(1) rely on his security and not prove;
(2) realise his security and prove for the balance;
(3) surrender his security and prove for the whole debt;
(4) give credit for the security and prove for the balance.

Securities. For the purpose of the Stock Transfer Act, 1963 they are shares, stock, debentures, debenture stock, loan stock, bonds, units of a unit trust scheme, etc.

security. (1) Something which makes the enjoyment or enforcement of a right more secure and certain.

(a) *Nature.* A security is either

(1) a personal security, consisting of a promise or obligation by the debtor (*e.g.*, a promissory note), or by another (*e.g.*, a guarantee), in addition to the original liability or obligation intended to be secured, or

(2) a security on property by virtue of which the enforcement of a liability or promise is facilitated or made more certain (*e.g.*, a mortgage, a possessory lien), or

(3) a judicial security. This exists where a right is enforceable by means of the powers vested in a court of law. Thus a judgment is enforceable by execution against the property, and (in some cases) against the person of the defendant; and, therefore a judgment creditor who has

taken the proper steps to enforce his judgment is a secured creditor. A garnishee order is also an example of this type of security.

(b) *Origin.* A security is created either by agreement between the parties (*e.g.*, a mortgage), or by operation of law (*e.g.*, a retaining lien).

(c) *Purpose.* With reference to their purpose, securities may be divided into ordinary securities and securities given in legal proceedings. The latter may be given to secure a right in question in the litigation (*e.g.*, payment of money into court), or in relation to the proceedings themselves (*e.g.*, a plaintiff may be compelled to give to the defendant security for costs).

(2) In a secondary sense " security " denotes an instrument by which a security is created or evidenced, such as a bond, bill of exchange, debenture, scrip, etc.

secus. [Otherwise.]

sederunt. A meeting or sitting.

seisin. That feudal possession of land which only the owner of a freehold estate could have.

selective employment tax. A form of payroll tax payable by employers as an addition to the weekly national insurance contribution. For certain industries (broadly speaking, manufacturing industry) refunds are payable to employers in excess of their original contributions so that the incidence of the tax falls on employers in those industries (broadly speaking, service industries) to whom no refunds are payable. The tax was introduced by the Finance Act, 1966.

self-employed. Someone who does not pursue his employment for another (the employer) to whom he is responsible, but who works on his own behalf. Self-employed persons are in a special category for selective employment tax, national insurance and graduated pension contributions (*q.q.v.*).

selling costs. The expense incurred in selling a product, which would include the total expense of the sales force and advertising.

semble. [It seems.] A statement of the law which is not beyond doubt.

separation agreement. An agreement between husband and wife to live apart. To be enforceable, the agreement must either be by deed or be for valuable consideration. It usually contains provision for payment of certain moneys to the wife, for custody of children, etc. It is terminated by reconciliation and co-habitation but while in force it is a bar to a suit for restitution of conjugal rights.

sequitur. [It follows.]

seriatim. [Serially.]

service. In procedure, service is the bringing of the contents or effect of a document to the knowledge of the persons concerned. Direct service is effected by actually handing the document, or thing to be served, to the person (or it may be to his solicitor). Substituted service is ordered where the party to be served is keeping out of the way, or his whereabouts are not known, and is effected by serving the document on some person likely to bring it to the knowledge of the party (*e.g.*, his wife, agent, etc.) or by advertising it or by sending a copy by post to the party's address.

Service by post is effected by properly addressing, prepaying and posting the document as a letter, and, unless the contrary is proved, is deemed to have been effected at the time at which the letter would be delivered in the ordinary course of the post. See also ADDRESS FOR SERVICE.

service department. A department of an organisation which provides facilities ancillary to production and/or distribution.

servient tenement. The land over which an easement (*q.v.*) is exercised.

set. A bill may be drawn in a set, each part of the set being numbered, as first, second, etc., of exchange. The whole of the parts constitute one bill.

set-off. In an action to recover money, a set-off is a cross claim for a liquidated amount of money by the defendant, for which he might maintain an action against the plaintiff arising out of mutual debts, due in the same right, and which has the effect of extinguishing the plaintiff's claims *pro tanto*. The plaintiff can thus only recover against the defendant the balance of his claim. See also COUNTERCLAIM.

settled land. Primarily land limited to or in trust for persons by way of succession. Formerly settled land or estates could not be sold or leased except under the authority of the instrument by which they were settled; *i.e.*, the settlement (*q.v.*). By the Settled Land Act, 1925, settlements are effected by two deeds, namely: (1) a vesting deed, by which the legal estate is vested in the tenant for life, or statutory owner, and (2) a trust instrument, by which two trustees are appointed, and which provides for the persons who are successively to be entitled.

settlement. (1) A transfer of real or personal property to trustees for the benefit of a third party or parties or for the benefit of the settlor and/or third parties. Also the instrument by which property is settled. A compound settlement consists of a number of documents, *e.g.*, deeds and wills extending over a period, by means of which property is settled. A settlement does not include a trust for sale.

A marriage (or antenuptial) settlement is an instrument executed before a marriage, and wholly or partly in consideration of it, for the benefit of the spouses in respect of the property settled, and of the prospective issue of the marriage.

A voluntary settlement is one not made for valuable consideration.

(2) Settlement of an action means that some arrangement or compromise is arrived at instead of carrying on the action to its usual legal determination.

(3) The discharge of a debt or claim.

settling day. Last day of Stock Exchange settlement.

settlor. One who makes a settlement.

sever, severable. When some provisions of an agreement or instrument are valid, and some invalid, the valid provisions, if severable from the rest, may be enforceable, and the remainder abandoned.

several liability. A liability for which each of the parties concerned is separately liable for the full amount, as contrasted with joint liability (*q.v.*). See also JOINT AND SEVERAL LIABILITY.

severalty. Property is said to belong to persons in severalty when the share of each is ascertained (so that he can exclude the others from it) as opposed to joint ownership, or ownership in common.

share. A definite portion of the capital of a company. It is personal property. The holder of a share becomes a member of the company, and is entitled to receive a dividend paid out of the profits earned by the company. His rights are set out in the articles of association, which also regulate the mode in which shares can be transferred: see STOCK TRANSFERS.

Shares are divided into preference, ordinary, and deferred or founders' shares.

Preference shares are entitled to a fixed rate of dividend in priority to other classes of shares. Unless otherwise provided, preference shares have no priority in the return of capital on a winding up.

Preference shares are of the following kinds:

(1) Cumulative preference shares entitle the holder to receive a stated dividend yearly. Should there be any shortage in the payments in any year to these shareholders, any arrears are carried forward and paid as soon as possible

(2) Non-cumulative preference shares. If a dividend is not paid in any year, the member loses the right to any dividend for that year.

(3) Participating preference shares receive a stated preferential dividend yearly, but they also possess the right to participate in any further profits after the ordinary shareholders have received a stated percentage of dividend.

(4) Redeemable preference shares, if authorised by the articles of association, may be issued on the terms that they are to be redeemed by the company at a later date. Provided they are fully paid up, these shares may be redeemed out of profits or out of the proceeds of a fresh issue of shares.

Ordinary shares rank after the preference shares, and normally comprise the bulk of a company's capital. The owners of the ordinary shares are said to own the " equity " in the company. They are only entitled to dividends as declared.

Deferred or founders' shares are those shares in which the holders' rights are deferred until the claims of other classes of shares are satisfied, usually in the matter of dividends or return of capital. Sometimes this class of share is accepted by the vendors of a business as part consideration for the sale. (See NO-PAR VALUE.)

share and stock warrants. Documents issued under the common seal of a company, stating that the bearer thereof is entitled to the shares or stock specified therein. A company limited by shares, if authorised by its articles, may in respect of shares which are fully paid up, or with respect to stock, issue under its common seal a warrant stating that the bearer of the warrant is entitled to the shares or stock specified therein, and may provide by coupons or otherwise for the payment of future dividends on the shares or stock included in such warrant. These documents are termed share warrants, or if issued in relation to stock, stock warrants. They are negotiable instruments.

share certificate. An instrument under the seal of the company, certifying that the person therein named is entitled to a certain number of shares; it is not a negotiable instrument.

share hawking or sharepushing. Calling from house to house endeavouring to sell shares. The Prevention of Fraud (Investments) Act, 1958, pro hibits dealing in securities without obtaining a licence from the Board of Trade.

share premium account. The account to which must be transferred any premium (*q.v.*) derived from the issue by a company of shares, whether for cash or otherwise. The provisions of the Companies Act, 1948, relating to the reduction of share capital, shall, with certain defined exceptions, apply to this account.

shareholder. A person who has agreed to become a member of a company and whose name is entered in the company's register of members.

" shell " company. A company whose original business has ceased or is dormant and whose assets have largely been realised and distributed. The " shell " company retains its name, formal existence and possibly its Stock Exchange quotation, with the result that it may become a convenient corporate vehicle for a different business.

sheriff. The chief officer of the Crown in a county. He is the returning officer for Parliamentary elections and he summons jurors for assizes. His main duty is to attach and sell goods in execution of a writ. He is assisted by deputy sheriffs and bailiffs.

ship. Every description of vessel used in navigation not propelled by oars. A vessel cannot be registered as a British ship unless she belongs wholly to British subjects, or to a corporation formed under and subject to the laws of, and having its principal place of business in, the British Commonwealth. The property in a British ship is divided into 64 parts and no more than 64 persons can be registered at the same time as owners of a ship. But any number of persons not exceeding five may be registered as joint holders of a ship or share, such persons being regarded at law as one person (Merchant Shipping Act, 1894).

shipped bill of lading. One which states that the goods have been shipped on board. See BILL OF LADING.

shipping documents. Documents sometimes attached to bills of exchange. They consist of the invoice, policy of insurance, and bill of lading.

ship's husband. The agent of the owners in regard to the management of all affairs of the ship in the home port.

ship's papers. A ship's registry certificate, bills of lading, bill of health, charterparty and log, which show the character of the ship and cargo.

ship's report. The report to the customs made by the master within 24 hours of arrival at port, containing particulars of the crew, dutiable ship's stores, and cargo.

shop. A shop is a building used for the carrying on of any retail trade or business wherein the primary purpose is the selling of goods by retail and includes a building used for the purpose of a hairdresser, undertaker, ticket agency or dry cleaner's receipts of goods.

shop premises. (1) A shop, or building solely or principally used for retail trade or business; (2) a building, or part, occupied by a wholesaler, where goods are kept for sale wholesale (*q.v.*); (3) a building, or part, to which the public resort for delivering goods for repair or treatment, or themselves doing the repairs, etc. (Offices, Shops and Railway Premises Act, 1963). See also EMPLOYMENT.

shop steward. A trade union representative elected by members of one section of a works or " shop."

short. As to selling securities " short," see LONG OR SHORT.

short-term gains. Upon realisation of a capital gain (*q.v.*) residents of the United Kingdom become liable to tax. Realisation within one year of acquisition renders an individual liable to tax at his maximum personal rate for that year; after one year the standard rate of capital gains tax is payable. Companies are liable to the current rate of corporation tax on realised gains.

short-time. Working sub-standard hours per week in order to preserve the jobs, or retain the labour, of as many employees as possible in a time of restricted production.

short workings. The amount by which the royalties payable under a mining lease on actual output fall short of the minimum royalties payable under the lease. See DEAD RENT.

sic. In brackets after a word or expression in a quoted passage, it indicates that the quotation is exact.

sight bills. Bills of exchange payable at sight are treated as payable on demand. A bill may also be made payable at a fixed period after sight; it must then be presented for acceptance to the drawee (called " sighting a bill ") in order that the maturity be fixed.

signal. A physical entity in a computer representing data or exercising control.

signature. The name of a person, or his mark if unable to write, placed or made on a document by him or at his direction.

simple contract. An agreement which is oral or in writing but not under seal (*q.v.*). See CONTRACT.

simpliciter. Absolutely; without qualification.

simulation. Computer representation of physical phenomena to facilitate the study of such phenomena or systems or to train operators.

simultaneous computer. One which can perform different portions of the computation concurrently through the use of separate interconnected units. *Cf.* CONSECUTIVE COMPUTER.

sine anno. [Without date.]

sine die. [Without naming a day.] When a meeting or hearing is adjourned *sine die*, it is adjourned indefinitely.

sine qua non. [An indispensable condition.]

sinecure. An office without duties.

sinking fund. An account created by transferring an amount from profit and loss account or appropriation account by debiting that account and crediting sinking fund account in order to provide for the redemption of a known liability or for the renewal of a wasting asset. The amount that this account represents should be invested outside the business in gilt-edged securities and allowed to accumulate at compound interest, the investment being recorded in a sinking fund investment account.

skip. (1) The name given to the operation in machine accounting whereby particular columns in a tabulation are passed over by means of the manipulation of a key or lever.

(2) A cage, bucket or net in which men or materials are raised and lowered in mines or quarries or in which goods are placed in unloading a ship.

slander. Defamation (*q.v.*) by means of spoken words or gesture. It is a tort or civil wrong actionable only on proof of special damage, except in case of certain imputations of grave misconduct. See LIBEL.

slander of goods or title. False and malicious statements discrediting a person's goods, or title to the ownership of property.

sleeping partner. Someone who supports a partnership with money and name, but who does not actively engage himself in the management of the partnership business. Unlike a limited partner (*q.v.*), the sleeping partner is fully liable for partnership debts.

slip. A preliminary memorandum of agreement for a policy of marine insurance containing the terms, and binding the parties.

slump. A sharp fall in prices or demand. See TRADE CYCLE.

small bankruptcy. If the court is satisfied that the assets of the debtor are not likely to exceed £300, the estate is administered in a summary and simplified manner with the official receiver as trustee.

social security. Government-controlled assistance to individuals in case of need, *e.g.*, unemployment benefit.

society. An association (*q.v.*) of persons which is not incorporated as a company but which, if it is concerned with public financial or commercial dealings, is subject to statutory requirements. See BUILDING SOCIETY; CO-OPERATIVE SOCIETY; FRIENDLY SOCIETY.

soft goods. Textiles (*q.v.*).

sola bill. A single bill of exchange as distinguished from one in a set.

solatium. A sum paid to a person as compensation or consolation for injured feelings.

sole proprietor. A small, " one-man," business unit in which one individual provides the capital and the management and takes all the risk.

solicitor. A legal practitioner; a person employed to attend to and advise on legal matters and to conduct legal proceedings. A person is required to serve a term as an articled clerk (*q.v.*) and pass examinations before being admitted and enrolled as a solicitor. He is an officer of the court, and takes out a yearly certificate authorising him to practise. The governing body for the profession is the Law Society.

Solicitors are bound to use reasonable diligence and skill, and they occupy a fiduciary position towards their clients. They have no right of audience in the High Court, but may appear in County Courts and magistrates' courts.

solvent. In a position to pay one's debts as they fall due.

Sovereign. The person who is the head of the State: the King or Queen for the time being. See also, the CROWN.

special case. A statement of facts agreed between the parties to an action whereby the opinion of the court may be taken on questions of law arising thereon.

Special Commissioners of Income Tax. The Commissioners for the Special Purposes of the Income Tax Acts are civil servants appointed by the Treasury with mainly judicial functions in hearing appeals against assessments to tax. Appeals from their decisions are by case stated to the High Court.

special damage. Damage which is not presumed to result from the defendant's act, but must be claimed and proved to have been incurred. See also DAMAGES; NUISANCE.

special deposits. Amounts deposited by the commercial banks with the Bank of England at its request. Calling for special deposits is an instrument of monetary policy designed to reduce the liquidity of the commercial banks and therefore their ability to lend.

special indorsement. See INDORSEMENT.

special licence. A licence to marry at any time or place.

special property. A qualified or limited right of ownership in goods.

special resolution. See RESOLUTION.

specialty. A contract or debt due, under a deed.

specie. Gold and silver coin, or bullion.

specie point. A price in foreign currency at which it is more profitable to export gold than to purchase bills for the settlement of international debts.

specific bequest. A gift by will of a particular thing; *e.g.*, my Bentley car. See LEGACY.

specific devise. A gift by will of particular real property, *e.g.*, my dwelling-house at East Cheam.

specific goods. Goods which are ascertained and identified at the time the contract of sale is made.

specific performance. A decree made by the court to compel a party to fulfil his promise and carry out a contract where damages for the breach of it would not be an adequate remedy, *e.g.*, in a contract for the sale of land. Specific performance will not be decreed of contracts for personal service.

specification. A particular and detailed account; *e.g.*, a specification for a building contract; or a description of a patent.

speculation. A hazardous venture of buying or selling, with a view to making a profit. See SHORT-TERM GAINS.

splitting. A stock exchange term for the splitting of an allotment or holding of securities into more units or between more owners.

spot price. The price for delivery immediately, or on the spot.

spouse. A husband or wife.

spread. A financial term for the range of investments held by one person, investment and unit trusts, etc. The greater the spread the less the general risk of a major overall loss.

stag. An applicant for shares of a new issue, who applies with no intention of taking up the shares, but in the hope of selling any allotted to him at a premium.

stakeholder. A person with whom money is deposited pending the happening of an event, *e.g.*, the decision of a bet or wager. The stakeholder is the agent of each party, and either party may require the repayment of his stake before the money is paid away to the winner, but not afterwards. No action can be brought by the winner to recover the money deposited with the stakeholder by the loser.

Property as to which there is a dispute may be deposited with a stakeholder to abide the result of proceedings. Similarly the deposit on the purchase of property may be left with a stakeholder.

stale cheque. A cheque which appears on the face of it to have been in circulation for an unreasonable length of time; *e.g.*, six months or more. A person who takes such cheque does so subject to equities and at his own risk. A banker may refuse payment of a stale cheque if the drawer has not directed him to pay it.

stamp duties. Revenue raised by means of stamps affixed to, or impressed upon, written instruments such as receipts, agreements, conveyances, transfers of land or shares, leases, etc. Stamp duties are either fixed in amount or payable *ad valorem*, that is, proportionately to the value of the property passing. Stamp duties are managed by the Commissioners of Inland Revenue. Documents must be duly stamped before being put in evidence in civil proceedings. See RECEIPT.

standard coins. Coins whose stamped value equals the value of the metal in them.

standard costs. A system of cost accounting having the object of analysing the contributing causes of cost variations. Standards of performance and of costs are set up to provide a basis for selling prices and a means of control over manufacturing operations. Before manufacture is commenced a standard cost for each product is determined and, when production commences, records are kept to enable the deviations of actual cost from the standards set up to be assessed. By this means control is possible and attention is directed to keeping current costs down to the standard.

standard of living. The ability of a social unit to satisfy its economic requirements. The less of the basic requirements that can be satisfied the lower the standard of living.

standard rate of income tax. This is determined by the yearly Finance Act. Tax has to be deducted from dividends and annual payments at the standard rate, but the individual is entitled to allowances and reliefs (*q.v.*) so that his " effective rate " of tax is less than the standard rate.

standardisation. The manufacture of a standard product so as to enable mass production and the economies of scale to operate. Most consumer goods are standardised by the manufacturers.

standards. Primary standards of the yard, pound, metre and kilogramme are described in the Weights and Measures Act, 1963, Schedule 2. See also UNITS OF MEASUREMENT.

standing orders. Rules and forms regulating the procedure of each House of Parliament.

stannaries. Districts comprising the tin mines of Cornwall and Devon, formerly under Stannary Courts' jurisdiction.

staple. The paramount goods of medieval England: wool, leather, tin, lead. The seaports from which they were exported were the staple towns, and their merchants were the staplers. The mayors of the staple towns held a staple court, which applied the law merchant (*q.v.*).

State. (1) The organised community; the central government with sovereign powers.

(2) In international law a State is a people permanently occupying a fixed territory, bound together into one body politic by common subjection to some definite authority and exercising, through the medium of an organised government, a control over all persons and things within

its territory, capable of maintaining relations of peace and war, and free from external political control. See also FEDERAL STATE.

statement, consolidated. See CONSOLIDATED ACCOUNTS.

statement in lieu of prospectus. A public company having a share capital which does not issue a prospectus on or with reference to its formation (or has issued such a prospectus but does not proceed to allot any of the shares offered to the public for subscription) is required to file a statement in lieu of a prospectus before allotting any shares or debentures.

statement of affairs. A statement of the realisable value of assets and probable claims of creditors, showing a net surplus or deficiency of a concern or individual whose solvency is in question.

status. The legal position or condition of a person; *e.g.*, an infant, married woman or bankrupt. The status of a person is an index to his legal rights and duties, powers and disabilities, and is governed prima facie by the law of his domicile (*q.v.*).

status quo. That state in which things were.

statute. An Act of Parliament, particularly a public Act. Statutes are of the following kinds:—

(1) declaratory, when they do not profess to make any alteration in the existing law, but merely to declare or explain what it is;

(2) remedial, when they alter the common law;

(3) amending, when they alter the statute law;

(4) consolidating, when they amalgamate the provisions of existing statutes relating to the same subject-matter, with only such textual amendments as are necessary;

(5) codifying, when they reduce to one set of rules the existing statute and common law with respect to any subject.

statute barred. A claim which has become unenforceable under the Statutes of Limitation, which prescribe varying periods for prosecuting legal claims. The usual period for claims in contract, such as ordinary debts, is six years.

Statute of Frauds. See FRAUDS, STATUTE OF.

statutory books. Every company must maintain certain formal records, *e.g.*, minute book, under the Companies Act, 1948.

statutory declaration. A written statement of facts which the person making it (the declarant) signs and solemnly declares to be true before a commissioner or magisterial officer. It is used in extra-judicial matters in lieu of an affidavit. Making a false statutory declaration is a misdemeanour (Perjury Act, 1911).

statutory instruments. In general, where the power of subordinate legislation is conferred upon Her Majesty in Council, or on a Minister, any document by which that power is exercised is to be known as a statutory instrument (Statutory Instruments Act, 1946; Laying of Documents before Parliament (Interpretation) Act, 1948).

statutory meeting. The first general meeting of members which is compulsory for every public company limited by shares and for every company limited by guarantee and having a share capital. Its purpose is to afford shareholders an early opportunity of obtaining a report regarding the flotation of the company, a statement of its financial position made up for the period since incorporation, the amount of capital subscribed and generally whether the flotation of the company has been successful.

statutory rules and orders. Rules, regulations, ordinances, by-laws or orders made under the authority of an Act of Parliament between 1890 and 1947. See now STATUTORY INSTRUMENTS.

statutory undertakers. Persons authorised by an enactment or statutory instrument to construct or carry on any railway, canal, inland navigation, dock, harbour, tramway, gas, electricity, water or other public undertaking.

sterling. Coin of standard weight and fineness, normally the pound sterling.

sterling area. Those countries whose currencies are linked to sterling, both inside and outside the British Commonwealth. Sterling is a reserve currency and is used to finance a large proportion of world trade.

stet. [Let it stand.]

stipend. A salary or fixed periodical payment for services.

stipendiary magistrate. See MAGISTRATE.

stirpes. See PER CAPITA.

stock. (1) Originally, a common fund belonging to a partnership or trading company; the capital which enabled it to carry on business. The capital of a company was called its "joint stock," meaning the common or joint fund contributed by its members: hence the name joint stock company. Now: the mass or lump constituted by the conversion of fully paid-up shares of a company. Stock can be transferred in fractional amounts. It is never numbered.

(2) A fund or capital which is capable of being divided into and held in any irregular amount; e.g. British Government funds.

stock book. A book in which is kept a record of stock (goods) movements.

stock broker. A member of the stock exchange who, for a commission, sells and buys shares and stocks as the agent for others.

stock control. Control over the physical amount of stock in trade held by a business and therefore control of the amount of working capital tied up in stock in trade.

stock exchange. A market for the buying and selling of stocks and shares; also the association of stock brokers who operate there. The association has many rules which (unless they are recognised by the law) are binding upon its members only to such extent as they can be enforced by disciplinary action on the part of the committee, and upon persons who are not members so far as they are reasonable.

Recognised stock exchange for the purposes of the Companies Act, 1948, means the Stock Exchange, London, or a body of persons declared by an order of the Board of Trade for the time being in force to be a recognised stock exchange.

stock in trade. The goods in stock, manufactured or brought in the ordinary course of business with the intention of selling (or reselling) the same at a profit.

stock transfers. Registered securities (*q.v.*) may be transferred by means of an instrument under hand as scheduled to the Stock Transfer Act, 1963, executed by the transferor only, and specifying the consideration, the description and number or amount of the securities, the particulars of the transferor, and the full name and address of the transferee. The execution of the stock transfer need not be attested.

If the transfer has been executed for the purpose of a Stock Exchange transaction, a " broker's transfer " in the form scheduled to the Act may be used.

stock turnover. The number of times the average stock has been sold during a given period. It may be computed on a quantitative or monetary basis; in the latter case the cost of goods sold is divided by the average stock (valued at cost) carried during the period.

stocktaking. The process of counting (taking) and valuing stock in trade.

stoppage in transitu. An unpaid seller of goods has the right of stopping the goods *in transitu* when—

    (a) he has parted with possession of the goods, and

    (b) they are still in transit, and

    (c) the buyer becomes insolvent.

The unpaid seller may in these circumstances resume possession of the goods as long as they are in course of transit, and may retain them until payment or tender of the price. It will be noticed that this right applies when the ownership but not the possession of the goods has passed to the buyer, and the goods must be in the course of transit. The unpaid seller may exercise his right of stoppage *in transitu* either by taking actual possession of the goods or by giving notice of his claim to the carrier.

stoppage of payment. (1) An order given by a customer to his banker, directing him not to pay a certain cheque or bill.

(2) The ceasing by a bank or other financial institution to make payments that are due.

store. That part of a computer into which data is inserted for retention and whence it is extracted when required.

stores. Provisions taken on board a ship or aircraft, for maintenance of crew and passengers. See also DEPARTMENT STORE.

stranger. One not party or privy to an act or transaction.

strike. A concerted cessation of work by the employees in a trade, industry, or a particular concern; a " withdrawal of labour "; as contrasted with a " lock-out " by employers.

sub judice. [Under judicial consideration.]

sub rosa. Privately; secretly, in a clandestine manner.

sub voce. Under a word or heading—as in a dictionary.

sub-agent. A person employed by an agent to assist him in transacting the affairs of his principal. In general an agent is not entitled to delegate his duties to others, and if he does there will be no privity of contract between the sub-agent and the principal. But if the agent has express or implied authority to employ a sub-agent privity of contract does arise between the sub-agent and the principal.

subcontractor. One who enters into a contract with a principal contractor to carry out a part of the main contract, as in building construction. See also SUB-AGENT.

sub-lease. See LEASE.

sub-let. To underlet premises by a lessee, in whole or in part, by sub-lease or tenancy agreement.

subject to contract. A tentative offer made in negotiations; *e.g.*, for the sale of land or houses, which may be withdrawn before the final contract is executed.

subpoena. A writ issued in an action or suit requiring the person to whom it is directed to be present at a specified place and time, and for a specified purpose, under a penalty. The varieties most used are—

(1) The subpoena *ad testificandum*, used for the purpose of compelling a witness to attend and give evidence, either in court or before an examiner or referee; and

(2) the subpoena *duces tecum*, used to compel a witness to attend in court or before an examiner or referee, to bring with him certain documents in his possession specified in the subpoena, and also to give evidence, generally, concerning the documents.

subrogation. The substitution of one person or thing for another, so that the same rights and duties as attached to the original person or thing attach to the substituted one.

If one person is subrogated to another, he is said to " stand in that other's shoes "; *e.g.*, creditors are subrogated to the executor's right of indemnity against the estate where a business is carried on under the authority of the will; a person paying the premium on a policy of insurance belonging to another may be subrogated to that other; and an insurer is subrogated to the rights of the insured on paying his claim.

subscribe. To " write under "; to sign or attest; to give one's consent to; to apply for shares; to contribute towards, *e.g.*, a charity, etc.

subscribed capital. See CAPITAL.

subsidiary company. See HOLDING COMPANY. A company is a subsidiary of another, if that other (1) is a member of it and controls the composition of the board of directors, or (2) holds more than half of the nominal value of its equity share capital, or if the first-mentioned company is a subsidiary of any company which is that other company's subsidiary (Companies Act, 1948).

A company is not a subsidiary company merely because it is controlled by a foreign company.

subsidiary ledger. A ledger comprising accounts which contain the detail for reference purposes of transactions summarised in one account—the control account—in the general ledger. For example, a subsidiary debtors' ledger may contain the details of transactions relating to each debtor and posted from the appropriate books of original entry in an appropriate account, while a debtors' control account in the general ledger contains the same information in summary form, the posting being made from the books of original entry in totals only.

At any given date a schedule of balances of accounts in the subsidiary ledger should show a total identical in amount with the balance of the corresponding control account.

subsidy. Originally an aid or tax granted to the Crown: now financial assistance granted by the Crown; *e.g.*, to farmers, or to local authorities as for housing.

substantive motion. An original motion with amendments embodied therein.

substituted service. See SERVICE.

substitution. (1) In economics, substitution takes place between factors of production (*q.v.*) up to the point where the ratio of their marginal products (*q.v.*) is the same as the ratio of their costs. (2) In law, see SUBROGATION.

sue. To bring a civil action at law against another.

sui juris. A person who can validly contract and bind himself by legal obligation uncontrolled by any other person. Persons who are subject to any general disability; *e.g.*, infants or persons of unsound mind. are not *sui juris*.

suing and labouring clause. A clause in a marine insurance policy, to cover any loss or expenditure reasonably and prudently incurred by the insured in the course of his duty of protecting, preserving or recovering the property insured in the event of peril.

summary proceedings. Those which may be had and concluded before magistrates in respect of lesser offences, as opposed to trials of offences on indictment before judge and jury.

summing-up. A recapitulation by the judge of the evidence adduced in an action, including directions to the jury on the law applicable to the facts.

summons. A document issued from the office of a court calling upon the person to whom it is directed to attend before a judge or officer of the court for a certain purpose.

superannuation. An allowance or a pension, granted to a person on retiring from office or employment.

supermarket. A retail shop selling a large range of goods to customers who collect their own purchases and pay at a central point.

superesssion. The replacement of property which has outlived its usefulness.

supply. The amount of goods which will be offered at different prices. The supply of an item is one of the factors which govern its price, the other being demand. See also SUPPLY PRICE.

supply price. The price at which a certain quantity of goods or services will continue to be supplied, *i.e.*, the price necessary to " call forth " a certain rate of production.

supra. [Above.]

Supreme Court. The High Court of Justice and the Court of Appeal.

surety. A person who binds himself to satisfy the obligation of another person, the principal debtor, if the latter fails to do so; a guarantor. If a surety satisfies the obligation for which he has made himself liable, he is entitled to recover the amount from the principal debtor. If one of several sureties is compelled to pay the whole amount or more than his share, he is entitled to contribution from his co-sureties. A surety is entitled to the benefit of all the securities which the creditor has against the principal debtor. If the creditor releases the principal debtor this will discharge the surety from liability, unless the creditor reserves his rights against the surety. See GUARANTEE.

surplus. (1) Excess of revenue over expenditure for a period. (2) Excess of total assets over liabilities and contributed or paid-in capital.

surplus assets. What is left of a company's property after payment of debts and repayment of the whole of the share capital.

surrender. (1) The yielding up of an estate for life or for years in land, so that it merges in the reversion or remainder. Surrender must be by deed, or may be by operation of law, *e.g.*, if a lessee accepts a new lease incompatible with his existing lease, this operates as a surrender of the latter.

(2) The abandonment of an insurance policy by the party assured. The surrender value is the cash price which a life assurance company will pay to a policy holder, for the surrender of his policy and all claims thereunder.

surtax. In addition to income tax at standard rate, a further income tax at other rates known as surtax is charged upon the excess over a stated amount of the total income of the individual for any year of assessment, being regarded as a deferred instalment of income tax payable on January 1 in the following year. The tax is assessed by the Special Commissioners.

surtax direction. A direction by the Inland Revenue that all the earnings of a company shall be treated as the income of the shareholders for a particular period, with the result that the individual shareholders are liable to surtax (income tax being the liability of the company) on that income.

survivorship. The right of a person to property by reason of his having survived another person who had an interest in it, *e.g.*, on the death of one or two joint tenants the whole property passes to the survivor.

suspense account. A ledger account recording items in regard to which there is some uncertainty as to their proper destination at the time when the entry is made. A good illustration of this is a remittance through the post received from a customer who omits to state his name in the envelope containing the remittance. This amount may be credited to a suspense account pending further inquiries.

switching. Changing investments by switching money from one investment to another.

syndicate. An association or group of persons who combine to carry out on their own account a financial or industrial project—actually a special partnership for the venture. Also a combination, *e.g.*, of newspapers for the acquisition of matter and its simultaneous publication.

T

Table A. An appendix to the Companies Act, 1948, giving a model set of articles of association which a company may adopt with or without modifications. Where a company limited by shares does not prepare its own articles of association Table A automatically applies. See ASSOCIATION, ARTICLES OF.

take-over bids. An offer by one company to the shareholders in another company to buy their shares at a stated price, which may be higher than the market price of the shares. The consideration for the proposed purchase will be cash, or cash and securities of the company making the offer. The directors of the company to be taken over will support or oppose the offer. See AMALGAMATION.

tale. The number; an account of goods by number or quantity; *e.g.*, casks or tea chests.

tale quale. In contracts for the sale of produce, " tale quale " signifies that the goods were as sample when shipped, the risk of loss or damage in transit being borne by the buyer.

Tallymen. Those who sell clothing on credit from door to door; credit-drapers.

talon. A certificate attached to a bond, which enables the holder to get a fresh supply of coupons when those originally attached to the bond have been used.

tap. A stock exchange term for an open source of supply of a security. Securities which are on tap are available to the market in almost unlimited supply, from the issuing authority.

tare. An allowance for the weight of the container in which goods are packed which is deducted from the gross weight to ascertain the net weight of contents. Also the weight of a motor or railway truck to determine in a similar manner the weight of load after weighing on a weighbridge.

tariff. A table or catalogue of rates; *e.g.*, the Customs Tariff, which is the official list of customs and import duties. Most of the major insurance companies have agreed to a common schedule of rates applicable to the various types of fire and marine insurance risks, which are known as tariff rates.

tax avoidance. Legal minimisation by individuals or companies of the tax burden on their income.

tax evasion. Illegal failure to pay tax due by not declaring income and other means.

tax free. A dividend declared net without deduction of tax. It has to be grossed up for income tax purposes and the withholding tax paid.

tax reserve certificates. These may be purchased and held for surrender against subsequent tax assessments. Tax free interest is credited when certificates are used to make tax payment.

taxation. The levying or compulsory raising of money for the use of the government.

Direct taxes are those imposed directly on the individual, such as income tax.

Indirect taxes are imposed on persons other than those who will ultimately have to bear them, as where taxes are collected from importers, manufacturers or dealers, who add the tax to the cost of the goods; *e.g.*, customs and excise duties; purchase tax.

taxation of costs. The process of examining and, if necessary, disallowing or reducing a bill of costs of a solicitor by officers of the Court, the Taxing Masters.

The basis of taxation is that ordered by the Court, as follows:

(1) Party and party costs. The successful party to litigation is entitled to receive from the unsuccessful party the costs necessarily incurred by him in the proper conduct of the action.

(2) Common fund costs. This basis is more generous inasmuch as costs reasonably incurred are allowable.

(3) Solicitor and own client costs. Expenditure incurred by the solicitor on behalf of his client, within the scope of his instructions.

telegraphic transfers. A method used for the purpose of effecting speedy payments; in particular, from one country to another. A message is sent by telegram ordering the transfer of money from one account to another. It is, as a rule, a more costly method of discharging debts than by the purchase of bills.

television. The provision of television services by the Independent Television Authority is governed by the Television Act, 1963.

Telex. A Post Office service for making speedy communications by the use of teleprinters.

tellers. (1) Counters of votes; (2) bank cashiers.

tel-quel rate. An adjustment of the quoted rate for a bill to accord with the actual term of the bill.

tenancy at will. A tenancy not for any certain period which is constituted by entry and possession of the tenant under an agreement, or with the acquiescense of the owner, or by implication. It is terminable by either party at any time, or by death of the tenant.

tenancy in common. The mode of holding property where the tenants (or owners) all have possession in undivided shares. The share of each tenant need not be equal, but unlike joint tenancy (*q.v.*), there is no right of survivorship. The share of a tenant in common is his to dispose of in his lifetime, or on his death by will, as he wishes.

tenant. One who holds land by any kind of right or title, *e.g.*, in fee, in common or for life. Popularly a person in occupation under a lease or agreement of *e.g.*, a house or farm.

tenant at sufferance. One who has originally come into possession of land by a lawful title, and who subsequently continues to hold such possession after his title has determined.

tenant for life. One who is entitled to lands or tenements for the term of his own life.

tenant for years. One who holds lands or tenements for a term of an agreed number of years.

tenant from year to year. A tenant of land whose tenancy can only be determined by a notice to quit expiring at that period of the year at which it commenced. Ordinarily six months' notice to quit must be given but a tenancy of an agricultural holding can only be determined by a year's notice to quit.

Whenever one person holds land of another, and there is no express limitation or agreement as to the term for which it is to be held, then if the rent is a yearly rent (even though payable, *e.g.*, quarterly), the tenancy is deemed to be from year to year.

tenant, statutory. A person entitled to remain in possession of premises as his home by reason of the Rent Acts, notwithstanding that his tenancy of the premises has expired. It includes the widow of the tenant, and a member of his family living with him at his death.

tenant-right. The right of a tenant of agricultural land to claim a beneficial interest in the land on the expiration of his tenancy. The extent of tenant-right was a matter of local custom, but has now become statutory under the Agricultural Holdings Acts.

tender. (1) The offer of money by a debtor to his creditor in payment of his debt. The exact amount must be produced in legal tender (*q.v.*).

(2) An offer of goods or services in accordance with the terms of a contract. If refused the offeror is discharged from further performance and he may sue for breach of contract.

(3) An offer to make a contract of sale which, if accepted, results in the buyer undertaking to buy all the goods specified in the tender from the tenderer; or it may result in a standing offer to supply certain goods; *e.g.*, coal, as and when required by the buyer. See also AMENDS, TENDER OF.

tenement. That which may be held, or is the subject of tenure (*q.v.*), *i.e.*, land.

tenements. Houses let in flats; or separately rated parts of dwelling-houses.

tenor. (1) The tenor of a document is its purport and effect according to its terms. (2) The tenor of a bill of exchange is the period of time after which it is payable. (3) An executor according to the tenor is one whose appointment is implied from the words of the will.

tenure. The manner of holding an office or property. In principle, all land is held of the Sovereign, the subject merely having an estate. The only mode of tenure of land remaining since 1925 is in fee simple or for a term of years; *i.e.*, freehold or leasehold.

terminable annuities. Annuities granted in consideration of a lump sum paid down for a term of years, or for the life of the annuitant.

terminal costs. The costs of a definite specific job or contract, *e.g.*, the building of a ship.

term of a bill. The time for which a bill is drawn.

terms of reference. The terms of the appointment and powers of a person or body to inquire into certain matters, and which limit the scope of the inquiry.

terms of trade. An expression used to describe the volume of imports which can be secured in exchange for a given amount of the exports of a country. If the price level of imports is falling relatively to the price level of exports, the terms of trade are said to be moving in favour of the importing country; if the price level of imports is rising relatively to the price level of exports, the terms of trade are said to be moving against the importing country.

territorial waters. Such parts of the sea adjacent to the coast of a country as are deemed by international law to be within the territorial sovereignty of that country; generally they extend seawards for three miles from low water mark, but twelve miles are claimed by some countries. See also JURISDICTION.

testament. Formerly a disposition of a person's personal property, as opposed to his real property. Now used to mean a will (*q.v.*).

testamentary expenses. Expenses of and concerning the obtaining of probate (*q.v.*) of a will, in some cases including estate duty.

testate. Having made a will.

testator. One who makes a will.

textiles. Woven, knitted, felted or other materials manufactured from fibre; tops and yarns, cloth, etc.

third party. One who is a stranger to a transaction or proceeding. A " third party risk policy " is a policy of insurance against liability in respect of injury caused by the insured or his servants to the property or persons of others. Thus under the Road Traffic Acts, users of motor-vehicles are required to be insured against certain third party risks.

ticket. On the ticket or name day, the second day of the Stock Exchange settlement, the buying broker passes a ticket showing the amount of stock purchased, the price, name and description of purchaser, and name of broker. On receipt of this the selling broker prepares a transfer and delivers it direct to the buying broker.

tickler system. A system, usually on cards or in loose leaf books, kept to " tickle " or refresh the memory, *e.g.*, to indicate dates of obligations.

tied house. A public-house subject to a covenant, made with the freeholder or lessor of the premises, to obtain all supplies of alcoholic liquor from a particular brewer who usually owns the premises.

time charter. A charter for a period, as contrasted with a charter for a particular voyage.

time policy. One in which the risk undertaken is limited to a specified period of time.

time rate. Wages based on a rate per hour for a standard working week with overtime paid at higher hourly rates. The main alternative system is to base wage payments on results, the piece rate system.

tithe. Originally, the payment by inhabitants for the support of their church. Tithes generally were commuted for a rentcharge, replaced by redemption annuities payable to the Crown. They were compulsorily redeemable when the land was sold.

title. (1) The right to ownership of property. A title may be original, where the person entitled does not take from any predecessor, *e.g.*, a patent, copyright, etc.; or derivative, where the person entitled takes the place of a predecessor, by act of the parties or by operation of law. An absolute title is one free from encumbrances.

See REGISTER OF TITLE. See also POSSESSION.

(2) An appellation of honour or dignity.

(3) A heading.

title-deeds. The documents and instruments conferring or evidencing the title to land. They " savour of the realty " and pass with the land under a conveyance, except deeds relating to any part of the estate retained by the vendor. In such case the vendor must acknowledge the buyer's rights to production of such deeds, and undertake their safe custody.

token money. Notes, or coin of a metallic value less than its face value.

token payment. See EARNEST.

toll. A payment for passing over a highway, bridge, ferry, etc.

tonnage. The carrying capacity, weight, or displacement of a ship expressed in tons. There are different methods for calculating gross, displacement, deadweight, etc., tonnage.

top hat pensions. Pensions provided for senior executives by their companies; either under a company's normal pension scheme, or by a special individual arrangement, or both.

213

tort. A civil wrong. It is an act which gives rise to a right of action at common law for unliquidated damages and which is not exclusively a crime, breach of contract, trust or equitable obligation; *e.g.*, assault, trespass, negligence, nuisance, slander, deceit. The same act, however, may amount to a crime or breach of contract as well as a tort.

tortfeasor. One who commits a tort.

tortious. [Crooked] Wrongful. See TORT.

total loss. In marine insurance the total loss of the subject-matter insured may be either actual or constructive. Actual total loss arises where the ship or cargo is totally destroyed or so damaged that it can never arrive *in specie* at its destination. There is a constructive total loss where the subject-matter insured is reasonably abandoned on account of its actual total loss appearing to be unavoidable, or because it could not be preserved from actual total loss without an expenditure which would exceed its total value.

tourism. Recreational travel by visitors to countries outside their own. Tourist expenditure is an important invisible item in many countries' balance of payments.

towage. (1) The service rendered where a vessel, *e.g.*, a tug, is employed to accelerate the progress of another ship by hauling it along. (2) The remuneration for towage service. Compare SALVAGE.

trade. (1) The buying and selling, or barter (*q.v.*), of goods, usually with the intention of making a profit. Organised trading is called a business (*q.v.*). (2) A craft which normally has to be learned by apprenticeship.

trade association. An association for mutual benefit of businesses and concerns in a particular trade. The members must conform to its rules or incur penalties; or risk expulsion.

trade cycle. The alternation of periods of prosperity and depression, of good and bad trade. The principal phases of a trade cycle are:

Boom: Exceptional business activity accompanied by rising prices.

Recession: Confidence declines, prices begin to fall, unemployment increases.

Depression: Large and protracted decline in business activity.

Recovery: Confidence revives, investment and employment increase.

The depression stage of the trade cycle may be avoided by many countries if global trade conditions are favourable and internal policies stimulate recovery before depression sets in.

trade description. Any description, statement, figure, word, mark or other indication; (1) as to the number, quantity, measure, gauge, or weight of any goods; or (2) as to the standard of quality of any goods; or (3) as to the fitness for purpose, strength, performance or behaviour of any goods; or (4) as to the place or country in which the goods were made or produced; or (5) as to the mode of manufacturing or producing any goods; or (6) as to the material of which any goods are composed, or (7) as to any goods being the subject of an existing patent, privilege or copyright. (Merchandise Marks Acts, 1887 to 1953).

trade discount. A discount allowed to the trade, *e.g.*, by wholesaler to retailer. See CASH DISCOUNT.

trade dispute. Any dispute or difference between employers and workmen, or between workmen and workmen connected with the employment or non-employment, or the terms of the employment, or with the conditions of labour of any person.

trade gap. The margin between the value of visible imports and exports. Together with the margin on invisible trading it makes up the balance of trade.

trade investments. Investments held mainly to secure trade advantages. The term extends to stocks, shares and securities of a company associated in business, but not a subsidiary. See INVESTMENT.

trade marks. A mark used or proposed to be used in relation to goods, for the purpose of indicating a connection in the course of trade between the goods and some person having the right, either as proprietor or registered user, to use the mark whether with or without any indication of the identity of that person. Trade marks may be registered in the register of trade marks either under Part A or Part B. Under Part A the registered trade mark in itself becomes an exclusive and assignable property of the owner. Under Part B, registration affords prima facie evidence that the registered proprietor has the exclusive right to use the trade mark. (Trade Marks Act, 1938.)

trade name. A name which by repute indicates that a certain trade or business is carried on by a particular person.

trade protection society. An organisation formed for the protection and benefit of its members who carry on the trade in question. Members receive confidential reports as to the financial standing of individuals or firms who may be desiring credit, and information as to the deaths or bankruptcy of traders, dissolution of partnerships and winding up of companies, etc.

trade union. An organisation, owing its creation to modern industrial conditions, whose membership is made up of workers in a particular trade or industry or workers in a variety of trades and industries. The Trade Union Acts from 1871 onwards have provided for the formation and registration of trade unions. The object stated in the Act of 1871 is " for regulating the relations between workmen and master, or between workmen and workmen, or between masters and masters, or for improving restrictive conditions on the conduct of any trade or business." Unions are not subject to prohibitions against acts in restraint of trade. Members must contribute to union funds and adhere to the rules of the union, which in return works for the improvement of conditions of work.

trade usage. See USAGE.

trade, use for. As regards weights and measures, " use for trade " means weighing and measuring in Great Britain for the purpose of trading transactions. The weights and measures lawful for use in trade are laid down by the Weights and Measures Act, 1963, as follows:

Schedule 3: Linear, square, cubic, capacity and weights.
Schedule 4: Foods, including intoxicating liquors.
Schedule 5: Sand and other ballast.
Schedule 6: Solid fuel.
Schedule 7: Miscellaneous goods other than foods.
Schedule 8: Composite goods and collection of articles.

trader's credit. A method of settling a number of debts by making out instructions to a commercial bank to pay the amounts shown to the listed bank accounts of the listed traders. It is a convenient alternative to drawing individual cheques for each debt.

trading account. An account showing the sales of an enterprise for a given period and the cost of goods sold, the difference being gross profit, which is transferred to profit and loss account.

trading certificate. See CERTIFICATE, TRADING.

trading stamps. Inducement offered by retailers to consumers in the form of stamps in proportion to the value of purchases. The retailer pays the company which issues the stamps and the consumer collects the stamps and exchanges them for goods ("gifts") made available by the stamp company.

tramp steamers. Cargo carrying ships which " tramp " between the world's ports, their destinations depending on the cargoes they pick up, rather than sailing regularly between the same ports.

transcript. A written copy.

(1) A copy of certain proceedings in a court. When an appeal goes to the High Court the appellant must see that a " transcript " relating to proceedings in the court below and containing copy of judge's notes, notes of evidence if any, copy of pleadings and any other necessary documents is prepared and made available to the court as required by the High Court rules.

(2) The transcription of the shorthand notes of the proceedings at a hearing, *e.g.*, parties or their solicitors may obtain a transcript of the evidence taken.

transfer. The causing of a right to pass from one person to another so as to become vested in that other.

(1) by virtue of an act done by the transferor with that intention as in the case of a conveyance or assignment by way of sale or gift, etc. (transfer *inter partes*). Hence the name given to the document effecting the transfer, *e.g.*, share transfer, or

(2) by operation of law, as in the case of forfeiture, bankruptcy, descent, or intestacy. A transfer may be absolute or conditional, by way of security, etc.

transferee. The person to whom something is transferred.

transferor. The person by whom something is transferred.

transhipment. In common use this word is equivalent to loading and unloading goods on any vessel, train or lorry for transport. It may also
mean the transfer of goods from one ship to another, but not necessarily
implying that such goods are transferred direct from ship to ship. It is
not correctly used of goods which having been once entered for warehousing are subsequently sold and exported.

transmission. The passing of title to property otherwise than by transfer
inter partes, *e.g.*, transmission of shares on the death of the holder.

travellers' cheques. A facility offered by commercial banks to their customers
whereby payments may be made by means of prepaid travellers' cheques.
Alternatively they may be exchanged into foreign currency so that cash
may be paid. They are a convenient method of carrying widely acceptable
money without risk of loss.

treasure trove. Gold or silver in coin, plate or bullion, found concealed in a
house, or earth or private place, which had been intentionally hidden,
and not merely lost or abandoned. If the owner is unknown or unfound
treasure trove belongs to the Crown. The coroner holds an inquest to
determine whether it is treasure trove or not.

Treasury. The Government Department which, with the Department of
Economic Affairs, is entrusted with the supervision and control of the
national finances and economy. The Chancellor of the Exchequer is the
political head of the Treasury. The First Lord of the Treasury is
the Prime Minister, and there are five Junior Lords, a Finance Secretary,
and an Economic Secretary.

treasury bills. Issued at a discount by the Treasury through the Bank of
England and sold by tender. They are a form of Government borrowing
and part of the Floating Debt.

trespass. A transgression of the law less than treason or felony. Trespass
to land is the tort committed by entering upon the land of another
without lawful authority. Trespass to the person is the tort committed
by injuring the person of another; *e.g.*, assault or unlawful imprisonment.
Trespass to goods is the tort committed by taking away, detaining, or
damaging the goods of another.

trespasser ab initio. Where a person enters land of another with permission
but abuses his authority, he becomes a trespasser " from the beginning."

trial. The hearing of a civil or criminal cause by the appropriate tribunal;
the elucidation of the facts and truth of a matter and the decision by
the judge of questions of fact and law arising therefrom. But see JURY.

trial balance. A list of ledger account balances taken out at any time, but
especially at the end of an accounting period, for the purpose of testing the
arithmetical accuracy of the entries in the books of account by ascertaining whether the debit and credit balances of accounts agree in total. The
agreement of the trial balance is a necessary preliminary to the preparation of accounts.

troy weight. The standard system used in weighing precious metals, precious stones, gold, silver, etc. Each ounce is divided into 20 pennyweights, and each pennyweight into 24 grains; a pound (12 ounces), therefore, comprises 5,760 grains.

Truck Acts. The Acts of Parliament which prohibited the payment of wages to workmen in goods or otherwise than in money. Now the Payment of Wages Act, 1960, has legalised agreements that wages should be paid into an employee's bank account, or by postal or money order, or by cheque.

trust. A relation between two or more persons, by virtue of which one of them, the trustee, holds property for the benefit of the other, the beneficiary, or others, if there are more beneficiaries than one. As regards the rest of the world, the trustee is the legal owner.

The rights of the beneficiary are enforceable personally against only the trustee and those who have acquired the trust property with notice of the trust.

As between the trustee and beneficiary, and those claiming under them, the beneficiary is beneficial owner of the trust property, either absolutely or with the limitations imposed by the trust. As trusts were originally enforced only in equity (*q.v.*) the beneficiary is called the equitable owner. This equitable ownership is assignable.

No special form of words is necessary to create a trust, if that intention is shown or can be inferred, but "three certainties" are necessary; (1) the words used must be imperative; (2) the subject-matter of the trust must be certain; (3) the objects, or persons intended to have the benefit of the trust, must be certain. See ACTIVE TRUST, CONSTRUCTIVE TRUST.

trust corporation. The Public Trustee and any incorporated company with an issued capital of not less than £250,000, of which at least £100,000 has been paid up in cash; certain officials; *e.g.*, the Treasury Solicitor, and certain public corporations. Trust corporations may exercise any powers for the exercise of which two trustees would otherwise be required.

trustee. A person who holds property in trust for another. The prime duty of a trustee is to carry out the terms of the trust and preserve safely the trust property. In discharging the trust duties he must use as much diligence as a prudent man of business would exercise in dealing with his own affairs. In the exercise of his discretion, he must act honestly and impartially as between one beneficiary and another. Otherwise the trustee will be liable for breach of trust and will have to make good personally the loss thereby incurred by the trust estate. If necessary, the beneficiary may institute an action for the administration of the trust by the court. See also TRUST.

trustee in bankruptcy. The trustee in whom the debtors' property vests upon his adjudication as bankrupt. The trustee may be appointed by the creditors, otherwise the official receiver is the trustee.

It is the duty of the trustee to get in, administer and distribute the estate of the bankrupt in accordance with bankruptcy principles, and for that purpose to examine the bankrupt's accounts and affairs, and to investigate the proofs of debt of the creditors.

trustee investments. The mode in which a trustee can invest trust monies is primarily limited by the trust instrument. His statutory powers of investment are contained in the Trustee Investments Act, 1961. See NARROWER-RANGE INVESTMENTS; WIDER-RANGE INVESTMENTS.

turnover. (1) The amount in value or quantity of the sales during a given period. (2) The number of times certain assets, *e.g.*, stock, are " turned over " or replaced during a given period.

U

uberrimae fidei. [Of the utmost good faith.] A contract in which the promisee is bound to communicate to the promisor every fact and circumstance which may influence him in deciding to enter into the contract or not. Contracts of insurance of every kind are of this class. Contracts entered into between persons in particular relationships may necessitate the fullest confidence and good faith; *e.g.*, family arrangements and settlements. Contracts of suretyship and partnership, when once entered into, are also within this principle.

ubi supra. [In the place above (mentioned).]

ullage. The quantity required to fill a partly filled vessel, *e.g.*, a cask consequent upon leakage, or of its having been broached.

ultra vires. [Beyond the power.] An act in excess of the authority conferred by law, and therefore invalid. A company's powers are limited to the carrying out of its objects as set out in its memorandum of association, including anything incidental to or consequential upon those authorised objects, and any act or contract not within the scope of its objects is *ultra vires* and void.

Similarly, where powers are delegated by Parliament to other bodies, such as local authorities; *e.g.*, to make by-laws, any exercise of the power beyond the limits imposed is *ultra vires* and invalid.

umpire. A person appointed to make an award where there are two arbitrators appointed and these cannot agree. If necessary, the court will appoint an umpire.

unabsorbed expense. In costing, the excess of the total actual overhead over the amounts charged to orders, jobs or other cost units by pre-determined rates of absorption.

uncalled capital. Capital not called up on partly paid up shares. See CALL.

uncertainty. A gift by will or a trust may be void for uncertainty; a pleading may be struck out for the same reason.

under-lease. See LEASE.

undertaking. (1) A promise made in the course of legal proceedings by a party or his counsel, or solicitor. (2) The works, functions or concern of a public utility company (*q.v.*).

undervaluation. Valuation of a commodity or asset at less than its free market value. The effect of such undervaluation can be to distort the normal demand for the commodity or the effect of using the asset.

underwriter. (1) A person who underwrites a marine insurance policy; in particular, one who carries on the business of insuring marine risks. See LLOYD'S.

(2) Those persons (*e.g.*, insurance companies) who contract to take up all stocks and shares not allotted to the public on a public issue, in consideration of an underwriting commission.

undischarged bankrupt. A bankrupt in respect of whom an order of discharge has not been made. If he obtains credit of £10 or upwards without disclosing that he is an undischarged bankrupt, he commits an offence.

undisclosed reserve. See SECRET RESERVE.

undue influence. The equitable doctrine that where a person enters into an agreement or makes a disposition of property in such circumstances that he has not been allowed to exercise a free and independent judgment on the matter, the Court will set it aside. Undue influence may be expressly proved, or it may be presumed where the parties stand in a fiduciary relationship to each other which implies mutual confidence; *e.g.*, parent and child, guardian and ward, spiritual advisers and penitents, solicitor and client.

The presumption may be rebutted by showing, *e.g.*, that the transaction was made in good faith with independent advice. In gifts by will the onus of proof shifts to the person alleging undue influence.

unearned income. For tax purposes income is unearned when it derives from investment, either in the form of interest or capital profit. It is not subject to as many tax allowances as earned income.

unemployment. That part of the total labour force which is willing to work but is unable to find employment. Many factors affect the level of unemployment, including the level of demand, technological innovation in the form of labour saving machinery and the mobility of labour. Some unemployment is inevitable, but most countries aim to keep it as low as possible by stimulating demand as it appears necessary and by insisting on retraining facilities for workers who are displaced from old skills.

unenforceable. That which cannot be proceeded for, or sued on, in the courts. A contract may be good, but incapable of proof owing to want of form; *e.g.*, writing. But the contract exists for certain purposes, *e.g.*, a deposit paid under an unenforceable contract by a person who subsequently failed to carry out the agreement, could not be recovered by that person.

unit cost. In cost accounting, the cost of a unit of product or service.

unit trusts. A method of investing in shares through the medium of a unit trust investment. The essential principle of a unit trust is the purchase by a management company of a diversified block of stock exchange securities: the " unit," and the transfer of it to a trustee, *e.g.*, a bank, to be held on the trusts of a trust deed which divides the unit into sub-units. The management company then offers sub-units (or " units ") to the public at a price which covers the manager's expenses and also a service charge to provide a profit or remuneration for the managers.

Unit trusts may take two forms: " fixed " and " flexible." In a fixed trust, the investments are stated in advance and generally may not be changed; they are fixed or rigid. The managers of a flexible or managed trust are, however, free to select the investments from a wider field and to change them when advisable.

Units of Measurement. The yard or the metre is the unit of measurement of length, and the pound or the kilogramme is the unit of measurement of mass. The yard = 0·9144 metre and the pound = 0·453 592 37 kilogramme. (Weights and Measures Act, 1963). The definitions of units of measurement are contained in the first schedule to that Act as follows: Part I: length; Part II: area; Part III: volume; Part IV: capacity; Part V: mass or weight; Part VI: electricity.

A Commission on units and standards of measurement was also established by the Weights and Measures Act, 1963.

unlimited company. A company not having any limit on the liability of its members. Its name does not include the word " limited." See LIMITED LIABILITY.

unliquidated. Unascertained; *e.g.*, damages left to a jury to determine. See DAMAGES.

unlisted shares. Shares which do not appear on the Stock Exchange official list, either for non-compliance with regulations, or because due application has not been made.

unofficial strike. A withdrawal of labour which is not supported by the union(s) of the striking workers.

unsecured creditor. A creditor who has no charge over specific assets of his debtor, but who relies on the general fund of the debtor's assets remaining after meeting secured creditors' claims.

unsound mind, person of. An idiot, lunatic, or mentally deficient person. Such a person is subject to certain legal disabilities; *e.g.*, with respect to capacity to contract, bringing actions, etc.

The term " person of unsound mind " is now superseded by " persons mentally disordered " (Mental Health Act, 1959). See MENTAL DISORDER.

upset price. The lowest price at which the vendor is willing to sell by auction. See AUCTION, SALE BY

usage. Uniformity of conduct of persons with regard to the same act or matter. A usage may harden into custom (*q.v.*).

A usage of a particular trade, market or occupation, in order to be enforced as part of a contract must be (1) notorious; *i.e.*, generally known among persons in the particular trade or profession concerned; (2) certain; (3) reasonable; (4) legal; *i.e.*, not contrary to law.

use and occupancy insurance. An insurance providing an indemnity to traders against losses by interruption of business after fires, etc.

use and occupation. A claim which arises where a person has used and occupied the land of another with his permission, but without any actual lease or agreement.

usury. Originally the reward taken for the use of money; it came to mean the taking of an exorbitant amount of interest, or greater than the rate allowed by law. See MONEYLENDER.

utility. Usefulness, the capacity to satisfy a human want.

utility, marginal. The additional utility (*q.v.*) which a person enjoys through acquiring one additional unit of any article or service, or according to some economists the utility or importance to the buyer of the least important or marginal part of his current consumption of any commodity.

utter. To pass off, or to attempt to pass off as genuine a document, die, seal, etc., or counterfeit coin, when it is known to be forged.

V

vade mecum. (Go with me; constant companion.)

value; valuation. The utility of some particular object, its purchasing power; the one may be called value in use, the other value in exchange. Value is often used as an abbreviation for " valuable consideration " as in " purchaser for value."

The assessment of value is the process of valuation, which involves proceeding upon the proper basis. Thus market value is the price which a thing will fetch in the open market as between a willing buyer and seller. If there is no general demand or market the cost of replacement may be taken. Break-up value is the price to be obtained on the sale piecemeal of the assets of a business, as opposed to valuation as a going concern. See also ANNUAL VALUE.

value received. Words used on a bill of exchange to indicate that the drawee (who becomes the acceptor) has received consideration from the drawer. These words are still used from force of custom, though they are unnecessary, since consideration in the case of bills of exchange is always presumed.

valued policy. One in which the value of the subject-matter is agreed upon and stated in the policy.

valuer. One whose business or profession is to appraise or set a price or value on property. It is part of the profession of a surveyor to value land and buildings. The District Valuer is a member of the Valuation Office of the Inland Revenue, and his valuations of property are required for official purposes.

variable costs. Expenditure which is assumed in cost accounting (*q.v.*) to vary directly with the quantity of production. Contrast FIXED COSTS.

variance. A costing term for the difference between standard cost (*q.v.*) and actual cost. The main variances are due to differences between standard price and actual price or differences between standard and actual quantity or time. Price and use or time variances are shown for materials, labour and overhead.

velocity of circulation of money. The frequency with which money and credit are transferred from the ownership of one party to another.

vendee. A purchaser of property; one to whom a thing is sold.

vendor. The seller of any property. Where the vendor of land has not received the purchase money, he will have a lien (*q.v.*) as against the purchaser.

vendor's shares. Shares taken by the vendors of an undertaking, upon the incorporation of a trading or other concern as a limited company. The shares are accepted instead of cash, in payment for the goodwill, stock, fixtures, etc.

venue. The place where an action is to be tried.

verbatim et literatim. [Word for word and letter for letter.]

verification. Proving a statement to be true, *e.g.*, the verification of cash on hand involves counting it.

versus. [Against.] Abbreviated to *v*.

vertical integration. Of an industry or a group of companies it means that specialisation is undertaken at successive stages of production. *Cf.* HORIZONTAL INTEGRATION.

vest; vested. When a person becomes entitled to a right, or an estate, etc., it is said to vest in him.

An interest is vested in possession when it gives a present right to the immediate possession of property; while a present right to the future possession of property is said to be vested in interest.

vesting instrument. The deed, order of court, or assent whereby settled land is conveyed to or vested in a tenant for life, or statutory owner, as the estate owner. See also ASSENT.

vesting order. An order of a court under which property passes as effectually as it would under a conveyance, *e.g.*, one vesting property in trustees.

vexatious action. A proceeding by which the party bringing it merely wishes to annoy or embarrass his opponent. See ABUSE OF PROCESS.

vicarious liability. Liability incurred without fault on behalf of another.

vice versa. [The order being reversed.]

vide. [See; refer to.]

videlicet. [Namely; that is to say.] Abbreviated to *viz*.

vindictive damages. Damages given to punish the defendant.

vintner. A wine dealer. A " free vintner " is a freeman of the Vintners Company and may sell foreign wines without licence.

visa. An indorsement on a passport to indicate that it has been authenticated by a representative of a foreign country so as to permit the bearer to enter that country.

vis-à-vis. The relationship of one of two persons or things to the other, when facing or situated opposite each other.

vis major. Irresistible force; *e.g.*, a storm, earthquake, or armed forces. One of the " excepted perils " in a policy of marine insurance.

viva voce. [By word of mouth.]

void. Of no legal effect; a nullity, *e.g.*, an agreement for an immoral consideration. A contract may be void on the face of it, or evidence may be required to show that it is void. But when an unlawful contract has been executed, money paid either in consideration or performance of the contract cannot be recovered.

voidable. An agreement or other act which one of the parties to it is entitled to rescind, and which, until that happens, has full legal effect, *e.g.*, in case of fraud in a contract. If the party entitled to rescind the contract chooses to affirm the contract, or if he fails to exercise his right of recission within a reasonable time, so that the position of the parties becomes altered, or if he takes a benefit under the contract, or if third parties acquire rights under it, he will be bound by it.

voluntary. Without valuable consideration. A voluntary gift, conveyance or contract is valid if under seal. A voluntary conveyance may be avoided if the owner becomes bankrupt within a specified period.

voluntary liquidation. When a company is being wound up by resolution of its shareholders it is said to be in voluntary liquidation.

vote. To express or signify the will or preference regarding any proposition.

voucher. A written document or note, or other material evidence, serving to attest the correctness of accounts or monetary transactions, to prove the delivery of goods or valuables, etc.

voyage policy. One in which the risk undertaken is limited to a specified voyage or voyages.

W

wager. A promise to give money or money's worth upon the determination or ascertainment of an uncertain event; the consideration of such a promise is either something given by the other party to abide the event, or a promise to give upon the event determining in a particular way.

The essence of gaming and wagering is that one party is to win and the other to lose upon a future event; that is to say, if an event turns out one way A will lose, but if it turns out the other way A will win. See also BETTING ; GAMING ; STAKEHOLDER.

wages. Money payable by a master to his servant in respect of services. See also SALARY; TRUCK ACTS.

waive; waiver. To waive a benefit, right, or remedy, is to renounce or disclaim it. A waiver may be either express or by implication. Thus where an act is both a tort and a breach of contract, to sue in contract will be to waive the tort.

Wales was annexed to the British Crown on its conquest by Edward I. In 1536 Wales was by statute incorporated with England, and Monmouth was established as an English county. English law prevails in Wales and in 1961 only one per cent. of the population could not speak English.

ward. An infant or minor under the care of a guardian (*q.v.*). A ward of court is an infant so made by order of the court, and cannot be taken out of the jurisdiction, or, if female, married without leave of the court, under pain of commital to prison for contempt of court.

warden. A keeper or guardian on behalf of the Crown.

warehouse receipt. A document of title to goods lying in a warehouse, signed or certified by or on behalf of the warehouse keeper.

warehousing. The deposit of goods in a warehouse pending delivery to retailers or consumers.

warrant. In judicial process, a warrant is a document issued by a competent person or authority, to some person or officer empowering and directing him to do the acts specified in it, *e.g.*, the enforcement of judgments and orders.

warranty. (1) A representation which is a term of a contract, but which is not vital to it, being subsidiary to or collateral with the main purposes of the contract. A breach of warranty gives merely a right to sue for damages and gives no right to rescind the contract. It may be made verbally or in writing. Whether a term is a warranty or condition (*q.v.*) is a question of the true intention of the parties, irrespective of the terms used by them.

(2) In marine insurance a warranty is in fact a condition (*q.v.*); *e.g.*, that the ship is seaworthy.

(3) An action for breach of warranty of authority may be brought against an agent who acts in excess of the authority granted him by his principal.

waste. (1) Uncultivated land.

(2) Whatever does lasting damage to the freehold or inheritance of land, or anything which alters the nature of the property. It is either voluntary or permissive; the former an offence of commission, such as pulling down a house, converting arable land into pasture, opening new mines or quarries, etc.; the latter one of omission, such as allowing a house to fall down for want of necessary repairs. A tenant for life is not held liable for permissive waste, but he must not commit voluntary waste.

(3) In cost accounting, waste may be dissected under two headings
   (a) that which is unavoidable, being part of the process of manu-facture, and which may result in a by-product either having a sale value or not (see SCRAP) and

(b) that which is avoidable, being due to faulty methods of manufacture or of records kept. The latter may be subdivided under
(1) *material wastes;* due to wrong buying, excess issues of raw material,
lack of supervision of manufacture, or spoilage due to bad workmanship;
(2) *labour wastes;* due to inefficient workers taking longer on the work
than the time allowed, training of workmen (this may sometimes be
unavoidable), and
(3) *expense wastes;* due to lack of proper control over expense incurred,
or increase in expenses which cannot be passed on in the sale of the
product.

wasting assets. Assets whose value wastes away with use rather than depreciating with time and use. Wasting assets cannot be replaced, *e.g.,*
mines and oil wells, and have a useful life limited to the period over
which it is economically feasible to extract the substance on which the
value of the wasting asset depends.

water resources. Water for the time being contained in any " source of
supply " in that area, as defined in the Water Resources Act, 1963, s. 2.

watering stock. Overcapitalisation of a company's share capital due to
issuing shares to such an extent that the company is unable to earn
profits sufficient to represent a fair commercial return for the shareholders on their capital.

way-bill. A document giving particulars of goods in course of transit.

way, right of. See RIGHT OF WAY.

wealth. The aggregate economic resources of an individual, group or
country.

wear and tear. That part of the depreciation of a capital asset which arises
from use rather than obsolescence or the passage of time.

weighbridge docket. A slip issued by a weighbridge owner stating the gross
weight—tare (*q.v.*)—and net weight of anything weighed on his " bridge."

weights and measures. These are dealt with comprehensively by the Weights
and Measures Act, 1963 as follows: Part I: Units and standards of
measurement; Part II: Weighing and measuring for trade; Part III:
Public weighing or measuring equipment; Part IV: Regulation of certain
transactions in goods; Part V: Local administration; Part VI: Miscellaneous and General. See also STANDARDS; UNITS OF MEASUREMENT.

wharfage. Charges payable for the use of a wharf when loading or discharging the cargo of a vessel.

White Paper. A Government publication in which the considerations
bearing upon a particular matter are set out.

Whitley Councils. Joint industrial councils formed to further co-operation
between employers and workmen.

wholesale. The selling of articles or goods in large quantities to be sold
retail (*q.v.*). A wholesale shop is one occupied by a wholesaler where goods
are kept for sale wholesale to customers resorting to the premises. (Shops
Act, 1950.)

wider-range investments. In general, trustees may invest up to one-half of the trust fund in wider-range investments which consist of company securities, unit trust units, etc., but not without proper advice. See also NARROWER-RANGE INVESTMENTS.

will. A disposition or declaration by which the person making it (the testator) provides for the distribution or administration of property after his death. It is always revocable by the testator and does not take effect until after his death. No particular form of words is required to make a valid will so long as the testator's intention can be ascertained; otherwise its provisions will fail from uncertainty.

A will must be in writing, and signed at the foot or end by the testator, or by someone in his presence and by his direction, and the signature must be made or acknowledged by the testator in the presence of two or more witnesses, who must be present together at the same time, and must attest and subscribe the will in the presence of the testator.

A devise or bequest to an attesting witness, or to his or her wife or husband, does not affect the validity of the will, but the gift is void.

A nuncupative will is a declaration by the testator without any writing before a sufficient number of witnesses. Nuncupative wills are invalid except those made by members of the services on active service or by mariners or seamen at sea.

A holograph will is a will entirely in the handwriting of the testator.

winding up. The operation of stopping the business of a company or partnership, realising the assets and discharging the liabilities of the concern, settling any questions of account or contribution between the members, and dividing the surplus assets (if any) among the members.

The winding up of a partnership is either voluntary (*i.e.,* by agreement between the partners), or by order of a court made in an action for the dissolution of the partnership.

The winding up of companies may be as follows: Compulsory winding up by the court; voluntary winding up without the intervention of the court, being either a member's or a creditor's voluntary winding up, and voluntary winding up under the supervision of the court.

window-dressing. The practice of so arranging the disposition of assets and liabilities as to present a financial picture in a subsequent balance sheet which is not representative of the normal financial position of the business.

with profits. If an insurance policy is taken out " with profits," bonuses from the company's profits are allocated to it and consequently increase its value. Premiums are, of course, higher than for " without profits " policies.

withholding tax. Tax withheld when payment of dividends and interest is being made and accounted for to the Inland Revenue by the payer.

without prejudice. Communications made " without prejudice " for the purpose of negotiating a compromise are not admissible in evidence unless they result in a concluded agreement.

without recourse to me. One who so indorses a bill of exchange protects himself from liability. See SANS RECOURS.

without reserve. Goods put up for sale at auction (*q.v.*) " without reserve ", are for sale to the highest bidder without any minimum price being reached.

witness. A person who gives testimony in court; one who sees an act done, or a document executed and signs his name thereto. See EXPERT.

wool exchange. A market where wool is offered for sale by and to members of the exchange, called wool brokers.

work to rule. Alternative action in labour disputes to a strike, overtime ban etc., it involves rigid adherence to the rule book governing the work being done, which will involve a slowing down of output per man hour.

working capital. See CAPITAL, WORKING.

working conditions. The general environment, amenities and benefits which people receive at work. As standards of living rise there is pressure for improvement of working conditions, which embrace such things as safety, comfort and terms of employment.

workman. A person employed by way of manual labour in the course of his employer's trade or business, other than an outworker, person in H.M. forces, or the police.

workmen's compensation. The statutory right of a workman (*q.v.*) to compensation from his employer in respect of an accident arising out of, and in the course of, his employment, causing personal injury to him. The Workmen's Compensation Acts, were superseded by the National Insurance (Industrial Injuries) Act, 1946.

writ. A legal instrument, being a document in the Queen's name and under the seal of the Crown, a court or an officer of the Crown, commanding the person to whom it is addressed to do or forbear from doing some act.
Judicial writs are writs issued by a court under its own seal, as follows:
(a) writs originating actions and other proceedings, *e.g.*, writ of summons (*q.v.*);
(b) interlocutory writs, issued during the course of an action before final judgment;
(c) writs of execution for the purpose of carrying a judgment into effect, *e.g.*, a writ of *fieri facias*. See also FI. FA; PREROGATIVE WRIT.

writ of summons. Usually the first step in a High Court action. It is a process issued at the instance of the plaintiff for the purpose of giving the defendant notice of the claim made against him and of compelling him to appear and answer it if he does not admit it.

write down. An accounting term for reductions and provisions made to the value of assets. Depreciation and bad debts are examples of assets being written down to lower values.

write up. In accounting, the recording of an increase in book values without realisation or transfer, presumably to reflect in the accounts an actual or presumed increase in the value of an asset or assets.

writing. A document, whether manuscript or printed, as opposed to mere spoken words. Writing includes printing, lithography, typewriting, photographic reproductions, etc.

wrong. A violation or infringement of a right. A civil wrong or tort (*q.v.*) is an offence against an individual; a public wrong or crime (*q.v.*) is an offence against the community.

Y

year. (1) A year consists of 365 days (or 366 days in a leap year), 52 weeks, or twelve calendar months (*q.v.*).

(2) The civil, ecclesiastical and legal year began at Christmas until the end of the thirteenth century. In and after the fourteenth century, it commenced on March 25, and so continued until 1752. Thereafter the first day of the year was January 1 (Calendar (New Style) Act, 1750).

(3) The regnal year commences on the Sovereign's accession.

(4) The financial year ends on March 31. The fiscal or income tax year runs from April 6 to the following April 5.

year to year. See TENANT FROM YEAR TO YEAR.

yield. (1) (Mining). The quantity of metal recovered from the ore treated.

(2) (Stock Exchange.) The relationship of the annual amount of dividend or earnings to the market price, expressed as a percentage.

yield gap. The difference between the income yield from fixed interest and equity securities. The gap represents the general market assessment of the relative effect of such factors as potential future income growth, inflation and risk on holding the different types of security.

York-Antwerp Rules. The rules for adjustment of general average drawn up at conferences of the International Law Association at York (1864), Antwerp (1877), Liverpool (1890), and revised at Stockholm (1924). The application of the York-Antwerp Rules, if desired, must be stipulated in the contract.

Z

zone. A region or area within limits as may be defined for any particular purpose.

Part II

DICTIONARY OF ABBREVIATIONS

A

@., at; *i.e.,* at the rate of.

A.1., of the first quality.

A.A.C.C.A., Associate of the Association of Certified and Corporate Accountants.

a.a.r., against all risks.

A/c, account.

A/C, account current.

A.C.A., Associate of the Institute of Chartered Accountants in England and Wales.

A.C.C.S., Associate of the Corporation of Certified Secretaries.

A.C.I.S., Associate of the Chartered Institute of Secretaries.

A.C.W.A., Associate of the Institute of Cost and Works Accountants.

a/d, after date.

A.D., *Anno Domini.* [In the year of our Lord.]

a.f., advance freight.

A.F.A., Associate of the Faculty of Actuaries.

A.-G., Attorney-General.

A.G.M., Annual General Meeting. See GENERAL MEETING.

A.I.A., Associate of the Institute of Actuaries.

A.I.B., Associate of the Institute of Bankers.

A.I.C.E., Associate of the Institute of Civil Engineers.

A.I.C.S., Associate of the Institute of Chartered Shipbrokers.

A.I.M.T.A., Associate of the Institute of Municipal Treasurers and Accountants.

A.L.A., Associate of the Library Association.

a.m., *ante meridiem.* [Before noon.]

a.o., account of.

A.O.B., any other business. An abbreviation which may appear on the agenda for a meeting.

a/or, and or.

A.R., advice of receipt; account rendered; annual return.

A/R, all risks.

A.R.I.B.A., Associate of the Royal Institute of British Architects.

A.R.I.C.S., Associate of the Royal Institution of Chartered Surveyors.

A.S., after sight.

A/s, account sales.

a/v or ad val., *ad valorem.* [According to the value.]

ad. or advert., advertisement.

ad lib., *ad libitum.* [At pleasure.]
admin., administration.
admor., administrator.
adv., advice.
afft., affidavit.
agt., agent.
amt., amount.
anon., anonymous.
ans., answer.
appro., approval.
approx., approximate.
art., article.
assn., association.
ats., at the suit of.
Att.-Gen., Attorney-General.
av., average.
avoir., avoirdupois.

B

b., born.
B.B., bill book.
B.B.C., British Broadcasting Corporation.
B.C., Before Christ.
b/d., brought down.
B/D, bank draft.
B/E, Bill of Exchange; Bank of England.
B.E.A., British Electricity Authority; British European Airways.
b/f, brought forward.
B.I.M., British Institute of Management.
B.I.S., Bank for International Settlements.
B/L, bill of lading.
B.N., bank note.
b/o, buyer's option.
B.O.A.C., British Overseas Airways Corporation.
B/P., bill payable.
B.P.B., bank post bill.
B.R., British Rail; Bank rate.
B/R, bill receivable.
B.R.S., British Road Services.
B.S., Balance sheet.
B/S, bill of sale.
B/s, bales.
B.Th.U., British thermal unit.
B.T.U., Board of Trade Unit.
B.U.P., British United Press.
back., backwardation.

bal., balance.
bar. or brl., barrel.
Bart., Baronet.
Benelux, Belgium, Netherlands and Luxembourg Economic Union.
bk., book.
bkg., banking.
bkpt., bankrupt.
bot., bottle.
bt., bought.

C

C., 100.
c., cents; century; circa (about).
C.A., Chartered Accountant (Scottish).
C/A, capital account.
c. & f., cost and freight.
C.B., cash book.
C.B.I., Confederation of British Industries.
c.c., continuation clause.
C.D., cash against documents; *Corps Diplomatique.* [Diplomatic Corps.]
c/d, carried down.
c.d., cum dividend.
C.E., Civil Engineer.
c/f, carried forward.
C.G.T., Capital Gains Tax (see CAPITAL GAIN).
C.H., Custom House.
C.I., Channel Islands.
C.I.C., Capital Issues Committee.
C.I.F., Cost, insurance and freight.
C/N, credit note.
C/O, cash order.
c/o, care of.
C.O.D., cash on delivery.
C. of E., Church of England.
C/P, charterparty.
C.R., at company's risk.
C.S., Civil service.
c/s., cases; cash sale.
C.T., Corporation Tax (*q.v.*).
C.T.L., constructive total loss.
C.W.O., cash with order.
Cantab., Cambridge.
cap., capital; chapter.
car., carat; carriage.
cent., *centum.* (100); centigrade.
Cento, Council of the Central Treaty Organisation.

cert., certificate.
Cf., *conferatur*. [Compare.]
Ch., chapter.
Cie., *compagnie*. [French company.]
ck., cask.
cm., centimetre.
Cmd., or Cmnd., Command Papers.
Co., Company.
com., commission.
comecon., East European Council for Mutual Economic Aid.
con., *contra*. [Against.]
Cons., Conservative.
Consols, Consolidated stock (Government).
cont., continued; contrast.
cp., compare.
Cq., or Chq., cheque.
csk., cask.
cts., crates.
cum div., with dividend.
Cum Pref., Cumulative Preference (shares).
cwt., hundredweight.

D

d., *denarii*. [Pence.]
D/A, documents on acceptance; deed of arrangement; deposit account.
D.B., day book.
D.C., documents against cash; deviation clause.
D.C.F., Discounted cash flow (*q.v.*).
D.D., demand draft.
D.d., days' date; days after date.
D.L.O., Dead Letter Office.
D/N., debit note.
D.O., delivery order.
D.P., deposited plan.
D/P., duty paid; deferred payment; delivery against payment.
d.r., dead reckoning.
D/R, deposit receipt.
d.s., day's sight.
D.T.R., Double Taxation Relief (See DOUBLE TAXATION).
D.V., *Deo volente*. [God being willing]; development value (of land).
D.W., Dock warrant; dead weight.
dbk., drawback.
dd., delivered.
deb., debenture; debutante.
dec., declaration.
def., deferred.

deft., defendant.
deg., degree.
deld., delivered.
dely., delivery.
dept., department.
dft., draft.
diam., diameter.
diff., difference.
dis., discount.
div., dividend.
do., ditto. [The same.]
dols., dollars.
doz., dozen.
dr., debtor.

E

E, east.
E.C., east-central.
E.C.G.D., Export-Credits Guarantee Department.
E.C.S.C., European Coal and Steel Community.
E.D.C., European Defence Community.
E.E., errors excepted.
E.E.C., European Economic Community. (The Common Market.)
E.F.T.A., European Free Trade Association.
e.g., *exempli gratia.* [For example].
E.I., East Indies.
E.I.D., East India Dock.
E. & O.E., errors and omissions excepted.
E.P.U., European Payments Union.
ed.; edn., edition.
Edith, Estate Duties Investment Trust Ltd.
Efta, European Free Trade Association.
encl., enclosure.
ency., encyclopedia.
Eng., England; engineering.
entd., entered.
eq., equal.
equiv., equivalent.
etc., *et cetéra.* [And other things.]
et seq., *et sequentia.* [And the following.]
Euratom, European Atomic Energy Community.
Eurofinas, European Finance Houses Association.
ex., out of; without.
ex cp., without coupon.
ex div., without dividend.
ex int., without interest.
ex new; ex rights, without the right to new shares about to be issued.

234

exch., exchange.
Exch., Exchequer.
exd., examined.
exors., executors.
exs; exes, expenses.

F

F.A.A., free of all average.
F.A.C.C.A., Fellow of the Association of Certified and Corporate Accountants.
F.A.Q., fair average quality.
F.A.S., free alongside ship.
F.B.I., Federation of British Industries which was merged into the Confederation of British Industries (C.B.I.).
F.C.A., Fellow of the Institute of Chartered Accountants in England and Wales.
F.C.C.S., Fellow of the Corporation of Certified Secretaries.
F.C. & S., free of capture and seizure.
F.C.I.S., Fellow of the Chartered Institute of Secretaries.
F.C.W.A., Fellow of the Institute of Cost and Works Accountants.
F.D., free delivered at dock.
F.F.A., Fellow of the Faculty of Actuaries in Scotland.
F.G.A., free of general average.
F.H.A., Finance Houses Association.
F.I.A., Fellow of the Institute of Actuaries.
F.I.C.S., Fellow of the Institute of Chartered Shipbrokers.
F.I.F.O., first in, first out (stock valuation).
F.I.M.T.A., Fellow of the Institute of Municipal Treasurers and Accountants.
F.L.A., Fellow of the Library Association.
F.O., Foreign Office.
F.O.B., free on board.
F.O.C., free of charge.
F.O.R., free on rail.
F.O.S., free on steamer (or ship).
F.O.T., free of income tax.
F.P., fire policy; floating policy; fully paid.
F.P.A., free of particular average.
F.R.I.B.A., Fellow of the Royal Institute of British Architects.
F.R.I.C.S., Fellow of the Royal Institution of Chartered Surveyors.
fac., facsimile (exact copy).
fahr., fahrenheit.
fcp., foolscap.
ff., folios.
fig., figure.
fl., florin.
fo.; fol., folio.
Fr., franc.

frt., freight.
ft., feet.
fur., furlong.
fut., future.
fwd., forward.

G

G.A., general average.
G.A.T.T., General Agreement on Tariffs and Trade.
G.B., Great Britain.
G.C.E., General Certificate of Education.
G.L.C., Greater London Council.
g.m., good merchantable.
G.M.T., Greenwich Mean Time.
G.N.P., Gross National Product.
G.P., general medical practitioner.
G.P.O., General Post Office.
gal., gallon.
Gaz., Gazette.
gm.; grm., gram; gramme.
Gov., Government.
gr., gross.
gr. wt., gross weight.
grs., grains.
gs.; gns; guas., guineas.

H

h., hour.
H.B.M., Her Britannic Majesty.
H.C., House of Commons.
H.I.F.O., highest in, first out (stock valuation).
H.L., House of Lords.
H.M., Her Majesty the Queen.
H.M.C., Her Majesty's Customs; Hospital Management Committee.
H.M.I., Her Majesty's Inspector.
H.M.S., Her Majesty's Ship.
H.M.S.O., Her Majesty's Stationery Office.
H.O., Head office.
h.p., horse power.
H.P., Hire purchase.
H.R.H., Her Royal Highness.
h.t., high tension.
hm., hectometre.
hon., honorary; Hon. Sec., Honorary Secretary; Hon. Treas., Honorary Treasurer.
Hon., The Honourable.
hr.; hrs., hour; hours.

I

I.A.T.A., International Air Transport Association
I.B., invoice book.
I.B.A., Industrial Bankers Association.
I.B.R.D., International Bank for Reconstruction and Development (World Bank).
i/c, in charge.
I.C.A.O., International Civil Aviation Organisation.
I.C.J., International Court of Justice.
i.e., *id est.* [That is].
I.L.O., International Labour Organisation (United Nations).
I.M.F., International Monetary Fund (United Nations).
I.O., Inspecting Officer.
I.O.M., Isle of Man.
I.O.U., I owe you.
I.O.W., Isle of Wight.
I.R., Inland Revenue.
I.R.C., (1) Commissioners of Inland Revenue. (2) Industrial Reorganisation Corporation.
I.T., Income Tax.
I.T.A., Independent Television Authority.
I.T.O., International Trade Organisation (United Nations).
I.T.U., International Telecommunications Union (United Nations).
ib., ibid., *ibidem.* [The same].
imp., imperial
in., inch.
in trans., in transit.
inc., including; increase.
Inc., Incorporated. (Limited company, U.S.A.).
incog., incognito.
ins; insce, insurance.
inst., instant (the present month).
Inst., Institution.
instns, instructions.
int., interest.
inv., invoice.
ital., italics.

J

J, Justice; a judge of the High Court.
J.A., joint account.
J.P., Justice of the Peace.
JJ., Justices.

K

K.B., King's Bench.
K.B.D., King's Bench Division.
K.C., King's Counsel.
kg.; kilo., kilogram.
km., kilometre.
Kt., Knight.
kw., kilowatt.

L

£, pound sterling.
L, Latin; 50.
L.C., Lord Chancellor.
L/C, letter of credit.
l.c., lower case (printing).
L.C.C., London County Council (succeeded by G.L.C. (*q.v.*)); London
   Chamber of Commerce.
L.C.J., Lord Chief Justice.
l.c.m., lowest common multiple.
L.I.F.O., Last in, first out (stock valuation).
L.I.P., life insurance policy.
L.J., Lord Justice; Law Journal.
L.M.T., local mean time.
L.O.B., Location of Offices Bureau.
L.S., *locus sigilli*. [The place of the seal].
£.s.d., *librae* [pounds], *solidi* [shillings], *denarii* [pence].
L.S.E., London School of Economics.
L.T.B., London Transport Board.
L.V., Licensed Victualler; Luncheon Voucher.
LL.B., (*Legum Baccalaureus*.) Bachelor of Laws.
LL.J., Lords Justices.
Lab., Labour.
lat., latitude.
lb., pound weight.
Lib., Liberal.
loc. cit., *loco citato*. [In the place in the book just referred to].
loco., locomotive.
loco price., the price of goods ex warehouse.
long., longitude.
ltd., or **Ltd.**, limited.

M

M., Monsieur; thousand.
m., metre; mile.
M.A., Master of Arts.

238

M/C, marginal credit.
M/D, months after date.
M.D., Doctor of Medicine; memorandum of deposit.
M.I.C.E., Member of the Institution of Civil Engineers.
M.I.P., marine insurance policy.
M.M., Mercantile Marine.
mm., millimetre.
M.O., money order; Medical Officer.
M.P., Member of Parliament.
m.p.g., miles per gallon.
m.p.h., miles per hour.
M.R., mate's receipt; Master of the Rolls.
m/s, months' sight.
MS., manuscript.
MSS., manuscripts.
M.V., motor vessel.
max., maximum.
memo., memorandum.
Messrs., Messieurs.
mfg., manufacturing.
mgee., mortgagee.
mgor., mortgagor.
misc., miscellaneous.
Mlle., Mademoiselle.
MM., Messieurs.
Mme., Madam.
mo.; mos., month, months.
Mon., Monsieur; Monmouth.
Mr., Mister.
Mrs., Missis (Mistress).

N

N., north.
N.A, not applicable.
N/A, no advice; non-acceptance; no account; New Account.
N.A.T.O., North Atlantic Treaty Organisation.
N.B., *nota bene*. [Mark well.]
N.C.B., National Coal Board.
N.D., no date.
N.E., no effects; not entitled.
N.E.D.C., National Economic Development Council (" Neddy ").
N.E.I., not elsewhere included.
N.E.S., not elsewhere specified.
N.F., no funds.
N.I.C., National Incomes Commission ("Nicky").
N.O.E., not otherwise enumerated.

N.P., Notary Public.
n/p, net proceeds.
N.P.F., not provided for.
N.R., no risk.
N.S., New Series.
n.s., not specified.
N.S.F., not sufficient funds.
n.t., net terms.
nem. con., *nemine contradicente.* [No one contradicting.]
nem. dis., *nemine dissentiente.* [No one dissenting.]
No.; Nos., number; numbers.
nom., nominal.
nr., near.
nt.wt., net weight.

O

o/a, on account of.
O.C., Officer Commanding.
o/c, overcharge.
o/d, on demand.
O.D., overdraft; overdue.
O.E.C.D., Organisation for Economic Co-operation and Development.
O.E.E.C., Organisation for European Economic Co-operation.
  (superseded in 1961 by O.E.C.D.).
O.H.M.S., On Her Majesty's Service.
O.M., Order of Merit.
%, per cent.; by the hundred.
%₀, by the thousand.
o.p., out of print.
O.P., open policy.
O.R., owner's risk; Official Receiver.
O.S., old style.
o/s, outstanding.
O.T.C., Overseas Trading Corporation (*q.v.*).
op. cit., *opere citato.* [In the work just referred to.]
Oxon, Oxford.
oz., ounce.

P

p.; pp., page; pages.
p.a., per annum.
P.A., particular average; public authority; private address.
P.A.Y.E., Pay As You Earn.
P.C., Privy Councillor; postcard; Police Constable.
P/C, petty cash; price current.

P.C.B. Petty Cash Book.
P/E ratio., Price earnings ratio (*q.v.*).
P.E.P., Political and Economic Planning.
P.L., partial loss; Private Ledger.
P.L.A., Port of London Authority.
P. & L. A/C, profit and loss account.
P.M., Prime Minister.
p.m., *post meridiem.* [Afternoon.]
P.M.G., Postmaster General.
P.N., promissory note.
P.O., postal order; Post Office; Press Officer.
P.O.B., Post Office Box.
P.O.D., Pay on Delivery.
P.O.O., Post Office Order.
P.O.S.B., Post Office Savings Bank (*q.v.*).
p.p.; per pro., *per procurationem.* [On behalf of.]
P.P.I., policy proof of interest.
P.P.S., Parliamentary Private Secretary.
P.R., personal representative.
P.R.O., Public Relations Officer.
P.S., Private Secretary.
P.T.O., please turn over.
pc.; pcs., piece; pieces.
pd., paid.
per an., *per annum.* [By the year.]
per cent., *per centum.* [By the hundred.]
pkg., package.
pref., preferred; preference.
prm., premium.
pro., for.
pro tem., *pro tempore.* [For the time being.]
Prof., Professor.
" pros and cons.," the " for and against."
prox., *proximo.* [Next month.]
PS., postscript.
ptg., printing.

Q

Q.B., Queen's Bench.
Q.C., Queen's Counsel.
Q.E.D., *quod erat demonstrandum.* [Which has been demonstrated.]
Q.E.F., *quod erat faciendum.* [Which was to be done.]
q.v., *quod vide.* [Which see.]
qr. quarter; quire.
qt., quart.
qua., as; in the character of.

R

R., Regina. [The Queen]; Rex. [The King.]
r., rule.
R.A., refer to acceptor.
R/D, refer to drawer (dishonouring a cheque).
R.D.C., running down clause; Rural District Council.
R.I., reinsurance.
R.M.S., Royal Mail Steamer (or ship).
R.O., receiving order.
R.P., reply paid.
R.P.M., Resale Price Maintenance.
R.S.C., Rules of the Supreme Court.
R.S.V.P., *Répondez s'il vous plaît.* [Kindly reply.]
re., in the matter of; with reference to.
recd., received.
ref., reference.
reg., regulation.
regd., registered.
res., things.
retd, returned.
rev., revenue.
rly., railway.
rom., Roman: ordinary type.

S

S., south.
s.; sect., section.
s., *solidi* [shillings].
$, dollars.
S.A., *Société Anonyme.* [Fr. limited company.]; South Africa.
S.C., Supreme Court; Special Commissioners.
s.c., *son compte.* [Fr. his account.]; small capitals.
S.C.I.T., Special Commissioners of Income Tax (*q.v.*).
s.d., *sine die.* [Without a day; indefinitely.]
S.E., Stock Exchange; south-east.
S.G., Solicitor General; *Salutis Gratia.* [For the sake of safety—as appearing in a Lloyd's policy.]
S.I., Statutory Instrument.
S.M., ship's manifest.
S.N., shipping note.
s.o., seller's option.
S.O.S., " save our souls "—the signal of distress.
S.P., supra protest; under protest.
S.R., shipping receipt.
S/R; s.o.r., sale or return.

S.R. & O., Statutory Rules and Orders.
S.S., steamship; special settlement.
s.v., *sub voce.* [Under the word, heading, title.]
S.W., south-west.
Sc., *scilicet.* [Namely.]
sec., *secundum.* [According to.]
seq., *sequelae.* [The following.]
sic., so; an exact quotation.
sig., signature.
sing., singular.
solr., solicitor.
stet, let it stand.
stg., sterling.
stk, stock.

T

t., tons; tare.
T.B., trial balance; Treasury Bill; tuberculosis.
T.C., till countermanded.
T.E., trade expenses.
t.l., total loss.
T.L.O., total loss only.
T.M.O., Telegraphic Money Order.
T.O., turn over; telegraph office.
t.q.; tal. qual. *talis qualis.* [Just as they come; average quantity.]
T.R., tons registered.
T.S.S., twin-screw steamer.
T.T., telegraphic transfers.
T.U.C., Trade Union Congress.
trees, trustees.
trs., transpose.

U

u.a., underwriting account.
U.D.C., Urban District Council.
U.K., United Kingdom.
U.N., United Nations.
U.N.E.S.C.O.; Unesco, United Nations Educational, Scientific and Cultural Organisation.
U.N.O., United Nations Organisation.
U.P.U., Universal Postal Union.
U.S.A., United States of America.
U.S.I., United States of Indonesia.
U.S.S.R., Union of Soviet Socialist Republics (Russia).

u.w., Underwriter.
ult., *ultimo.* [Last month.]
univ., University.

V

v., *versus.* [Against.]
v.v., *vice versa.* [The order being reversed.]
viz., *videlicet.* [Namely.]
vol., volume.

W

W., west.
W.A., with average.
w.b., water ballast.
W.B., way-bill.
W.C., West-Central.
w.f., wrong fount (of type in printing).
W.H.O., World Health Organisation (United Nations).
W.I., West Indies.
W.P., weather permitting; without prejudice.
W.P.A., with particular average.
W.S., Writer to the Signet (Scotland).
w.t., watertight; wireless telegraphy.
w.w., warehouse warrant.
whf., wharf.
wt., weight.

X

X, (Used as a short form of Ex.); 10.

Y

Y.A.; Y.A.R., York-Antwerp Rules (as to general average (*q.v.*)).
yd., yard.
yr., year; your.

Z

Zn., Zinc.